Lords of Parliament

MANCHESTER
1824

Manchester University Press

To Cleo and the Cross-benchers

Lords of Parliament

Manners, rituals and politics

Emma Crewe

Manchester University Press
Manchester and New York

published exclusively in the USA by Palgrave

Published by
Manchester University Press
Oxford Road, Manchester M13 9NR, UK
and Room 400, 175 Fifth Avenue, New York, NY 10010, USA
www.manchesteruniversitypress.co.uk

Distributed exclusively in the USA by
Palgrave, 175 Fifth Avenue, New York,
NY 10010, USA

Distributed exclusively in Canada by
UBC Press, University of British Columbia, 2029 West Mall
Vancouver, BC, Canada V6T 1Z2

British Library Cataloguing-in-Publication Data
A catalogue record for this book is available from the British Library

Library of Congress Cataloging-in-Publication Data applied for

ISBN 0 7190 7206 9 *hardback*
EAN 978 0 7190 7206 2
ISBN 0 7190 7207 7 *paperback*
EAN 978 0 7190 7207 9

First published 2005

14 13 12 11 10 09 08 07 06 05   10 9 8 7 6 5 4 3 2 1

Typeset by Helen Skelton, Brighton, UK
Printed in Great Britain
by Biddles Limited, King's Lynn

Contents

List of tables

List of figures

Preface

The House of Lords has such self-confidence it seems sometimes to be in a parallel universe. When, nervously, I first called on the Clerk of the Parliaments in his office in the Palace of Westminster, I found it distinctly lordly: panelled in dark polished wood, lit by a huge mullioned and fretted bay window. I was given a glass of white wine and the time to explain why I felt the House deserved anthropological study. He listened, and promised to put it to the "usual channels". "What the hell are they?" I wondered.

The usual channels, after a hiccup or two, said yes, although actually very few peers understood what anthropology was. Most were mystified by why I was there, and some seemed displeased that I had done research in East Africa and South Asia, as though ceremonial robes of ermine (the winter coat of the stoat) should not be considered in the same light as those of fish skins, or feathers, or cowry shells, and they were puzzled when I lingered on aspects that appeared to them to have little to do with politics.

This is the only attempt to date to examine the House of Lords as a whole and show the indivisibility of relationships and rituals from politics there. During two years of fieldwork I interviewed peers and staff and between engagements passed the time of day with them, sat in the Chamber, fed the Queen's horses at the State Opening of Parliament, accompanied the yeoman guard on their tour of the cellars on 5 November, sat in on committees and meetings, picnicked in Black Rod's garden, sold pictures to peers, registered hereditary peers for their elections, attended parties and the wake for hereditary peers, drank from the Lord Chancellor's 'Loving Cup', held the Mace and examined the Great Seal, among other things. The Cross-benchers generously lent me a desk and allowed me into their weekly meetings, and in time the political parties, the staff and even the usual channels let me attend sensitive deliberations. Within a year I was, according to the doorkeepers, part of the fixtures and fittings: the ideal status for studying 'natives'. But when I told Sir General Edward Jones (Black Rod) that I had two years to get to know the Lords, he told me I needed ten. I laughed: but he was right. Almost anything you say about the House is true only for a particular group or for a short time: it is a complicated, dynamic institution only to be understood by endless watching, and asking; and it is electric in its changeableness. It is so peculiar it is easy either to romanticise or to mock. I have tried to avoid both.

This book aims to convey an anthropological interpretation of the Lords: one reached by squeezing meaning from a reality that often seems chaotic: by comparing the differences between how people say they behave and how they are observed to behave; examining the differences between individual interpretations; and by unravelling layer upon layer of assumption. It captures an institution in transition, offers a unique historical record of it before (as well as after) the exclusion of the hereditary peerage, and suggests how a better understanding of power, rituals and manners in the present House should be the first step to further reform.

It was tempting to call this book, 'The End of the Peer Show', but like Mark Twain, reports of its death have been much exaggerated. It may be heading towards a revival. Presently, government legislation is being more vigorously opposed in the Lords than in the Commons. Lords in Parliament deserve credit for their conscientiousness, courtesy and wit, but might think again about their aloofness. For the British to love their lords again, they probably need to get closer to them.

Acknowledgements

I would like to thank the Economic and Social Research Council for funding this part-time research project between 1998–2001, the Department of Anthropology at University College London for administering the grant, and the International Forum for Rural Transport and Development, and others, for employing me since 2002 so that I could afford to complete this book.

Thanks to the usual channels – Leaders of the House, Lords Richard, Cranborne and Rodgers of Quarry Bank, the Cross-bench Convenor Lord Weatherill – the Administration and Works Sub-Committee and, in particular, to the former Clerk of the Parliaments, Sir Michael Davies, for giving it their approval. The project would not have happened, nor been such fun, if it was not for Michael. He could not have been more generous with his time, advice and trust both during the research and when commenting on draft chapters and I owe him a huge debt of thanks.

I am grateful to the hundreds of peers and staff who spoke to me and gave assistance in many ways: Lord Acton for introducing me to countless peers and commenting on the draft manuscript; Viscount Allenby and my office-mates for letting me use a desk in the Cross-bench smoking room; both Lord Carter and Lord Strathclyde for talking to me often and with honesty, for allowing me to observe party meetings and for commenting on drafts; Lord Cope of Berkeley for my first lunch at the House of Lords and for valuable advice; Julian Dee (Personal Assistant to the Cross-bench Convenor), Celia Thomas (head of the Liberal Democrats' Whips Office) and Nicholas True (director of the Opposition's Whips Office) for valuable information; Lord Graham (chair of the Labour back-benchers), and various Liberal Democrats, who allowed me into many party meetings; Lord and Lady Stanley of Alderley for their hospitality and access to thirty years of archive; Lord Wallace of Saltaire for regular guidance during the project and comments on drafts;

Lord Wakeham for comments on drafts; Lord Weatherill for persuading the Cross-benchers to open their doors on every occasion and for his comments on a draft; and I am grateful to Earl Ferrers, Earl Russell and the late Lord Williams of Mostyn, for entertaining me with their star performances in the chamber.

Derek Dunn, staff adviser, explained more to me than anyone about the Lords' staff. Paul Hayter gave me the chance to do real participant observation (assisting in the hereditary peers' elections). My research was also greatly assisted by many other House of Lords staff, especially David Beamish, Stephen Ellison, Geoff Embleton, Paul Goldstein, David Jones, General Sir Edward Jones (former Black Rod), Peta Jones, Brendan Keith and Elizabeth Murray.

I greatly appreciate comments on seminar papers made by my colleagues at University College London as well as historians at the History of Parliament, particularly Sir John Sainty, former Clerk of the Parliaments, the anthropology subject group at Edinburgh University, and Professor Jonathan Spencer (who gave the analysis on political ritual a push). Thanks to Dr Marion Müller for useful discussions while we co-organised a conference on 'rituals in parliaments' and co-authored a book with the same title, and to Julia Kruger for her valiant work on the database of peers' expertise. I am grateful to Deryc Sands for his photograph of the final sitting of the hereditary peers for the front cover. I would also like to thank my step-father for encouraging me to undertake this project, my mother for lending me posh outfits, and my family, Nicholas, Joe, Cleo and Scarlett Vester, for ceaseless support. Without Nicholas this endeavour would have sunk. I discussed it with him incessantly throughout and any elegance or clarity in this book are due to his suggestions, questions, editing, rearranging and writing huge chunks. The mistakes are, of course my responsibility. It is dedicated to Cleo for putting up with my absences and to the Cross-benchers for putting up with my presence.

A note on the text

When informants have expressed a view in speech, it is related with double quotation marks, without a reference. Their written statements have single quotation marks. If the name is mentioned, permission has been given. A painful number of names and stories have been left out.

1 Background: an outline of composition, powers and culture in the House of Lords

To enter the House of Lords is to be translated from the gritty urban pavement to a serene and comfortable palace where there is time for laughter, letters are often handwritten and a drink at eleven o'clock in the morning does not necessarily mean tea. The world of abruptness remains outside. Lords who want to make a go of it, and have it in them, learn to be courteous and amusing just to fit in. But it is not frozen in time. Until the mid-nineteenth century it was a focus of authority where the aristocracy called the shots for the nation, and until 1958 all its members were male and nearly all had acquired their right to a place in Parliament by birth. Now it is a mere revising chamber and most hereditary peers have been excluded. Though the legislators in the 'upper House' are still lords and ladies, appointment is now only for the life of the recipient, and a sixth of peers are women.[1] Besides sharp discontinuities, evolution has been constant as old peers die, new ones are ennobled and change seeps in from outside. The House of Lords may, however, have evolved in a different direction from any other political institution.

The building itself is a royal palace, the Palace of Westminster, lent by the monarch for use by parliamentarians. Beside Big Ben at the northern end is the House of Commons, whose members are elected. At the other end, next to the bigger but less famous Victoria Tower, is the infinitely grander House of Lords, with its spacious, comfortable and ornate debating Chamber. Although they are under the same roof and similar in function, the Houses contrast in their cultures. Inevitably, there is earnestness about the people's representatives in the Commons. The weight of their constituencies does not rest easily on all and many aspire to high office. Peers are less ambitious and the House of Lords is more relaxed. Though those who regularly attend are serious about their work, they do not, on the whole, take themselves too seriously. Wit is greatly appreciated, and courtesy even more so, not necessarily to win arguments, but to help to keep the noble audience's attention.

Both because it is a political institution and because of the heavy freight it carries from the past, Lords procedures are numerous, complex and often arcane. Its business is often mediated through layers of symbols, rules and conventions, and through the interaction of people with peculiar and sometimes ancient titles such as the Keeper of the Great Seal and the Lord Great Chamberlain and, of course, dukes (there are still two in the House), earls, baronesses and so on. Such has been the state's historic largesse with titles that a single individual can combine a considerable number at the same time (such as the Government Chief Whip who is, of course, a lord, and who is also Captain of the Honourable Corps of Gentlemen at Arms; or the Lord Chancellor who has at least eight titles including Lord Keeper of the Queen's Conscience). Within the House are numerous other institutions, like the political parties and the formidable college of clerks, some of which need to be understood to make sense of it. The glossary may be useful in reading the following broad-brush outline (see Appendix 3).

There are several categories of peer who can sit in the House. At the time of writing, besides 92 remaining hereditary peers who hold their right to participate primarily by birth, there are 551 appointed, or life peers, including the law lords, and 26 bishops of the Church of England. By a paradox typical of the House, only the hereditary peers are elected.[2] As none is elected by popular franchise, democratic legitimacy is absent from the House of Lords. Power consequently resides in the Commons, and the Lords has been under threat of abolition, or at least radical reform, for a century or more. Without constituents to whom to feel responsible, many peers feel little or no obligation to attend the House. Some only drop in occasionally and others not at all (not surprisingly, with an average age of sixty-eight, some are too infirm to attend). Attendance at debates is about 300 to 400 on a typical day.

About half of peers belong to one of the two main political parties, the Labour party (the party in government at the time of writing) or the Conservatives. Of the remainder, a minority belong to the Liberal Democrat party but the majority have no party affiliation. These are known as Cross-benchers and form a loose group with no common policy except not to have one.

Because they have no electoral mandate (apart from the hereditaries, in an extremely limited sense) the ties that bind peers to party are voluntary, and consequently difficult to enforce. Though most party regulars believe in party loyalty as the essential moving force in politics, many others are semi-detached from the parties of which they are nominally members.

The business of the House entails, principally, the passage of bills by means of debate in the Chamber. Each bill has to go through at least five separate stages. Perhaps as much work again is done by peers outside the Chamber, in the form of preparing amendments, lobbying for votes and strategising.

A 'whip' is the name given to the announcement by each party of the importance of items of parliamentary business. A piece of business about which the party issues a three-line whip is considered critical, and peers who are party members are expected to vote at whatever cost to themselves, whereas two- and one-line whips are less grave. The most junior front-benchers are also called 'whips';[3] their unenviable job is to try to persuade other peers to vote for the party. Although not always popular, they are indispensable to the party system.

Chief whips are altogether grander and are critical to the functioning of the House. Each party has one, and the Government Chief Whip is the supreme political fixer for the whole House. It is his or her primary job to ensure that the legislation the government wants will be passed with the fewest changes that the other parties can be persuaded to tolerate. The chief whips of the three main parties confer frequently, and the business of the House is thus achieved, on the whole, smoothly. The chief whips, together with a handful of co-conspirators, are known as the usual channels. They operate in secrecy, surrounded in ambivalence. They control the timetable of the House, and much else besides, but the range of their co-operation is not perceived by most peers; and while they are appreciated by peers for competently arranging the infinite complexities of the business agenda, they also receive opprobrium for monopolising the power to do so.

The most visible part of their work is in arranging the timetable for each bill through its stages in the Chamber. A less celebrated part is horse-trading between the parties on the outcome of some debates: a couple of hours of debate on a certain issue here for an amendment there; mutual support for each others' amendments; agreeing when a vote should be held or giving a warning about the strength of their whip.[4] Back-benchers are not often aware of the extent of this.

One of the Lords' most peculiar and prized characteristics is self-regulation in debate. The Lord Chancellor, currently Lord Falconer of Thoroton, who sits at one end of the Chamber on an unusual piece of furniture known as the Woolsack, is the presiding officer of the House; but neither he, nor his deputies (deputy speakers or chairmen) intervene during debate. In a debate where there is no list of speakers ('speakers' list'), peers decide as a body who will be heard, by means of murmurs and shouts, and they enforce the rules and conventions in the same way. New peers often find this chaotic at first, but most learn to appreciate its advantages: it intimidates unruly or verbose peers, demands courtesy, brevity and restraint, and ensures that back-benchers are heard.

Peers are assisted in their legislative work by a team of officials of sacerdotal appearance, whose job it is to know the procedures and conventions, and to be on hand always to emolliate the business of the House. These are the clerks. Also close to the peers during their work in the Chamber are the doorkeepers, a body mostly of retired non-commissioned officers (NCOs) of astounding dignity, humour and aplomb, whose duties include guarding the doors of the Chamber, keeping order among visitors and carrying messages to, or between, peers while in the Chamber.

Power lies with the House of Commons, which now has the primary control in money matters, most aspects of law-making and the administration of public services. The House of Lords is left with five main functions:

- *Revising laws.* Lords have more formal power in this than they use in practice. In theory, peers could reject all bills introduced in the Lords, and delay most of those from the Commons, but by convention they seldom flex their muscles. Were the lords to use their powers more, the Commons might curtail them further. Instead they edit the texts. This is done by introducing and discussing amendments to bills. In the 2002–03 session, 9782 amendments were introduced in the Lords. 2996 were approved, of which 83 were defeats for the government. Of these, 35 were reversed when the bills returned to the Commons.[5]
- *Holding the government to account.* The Prime Minister and nearly all principal members of governments are now, by convention, MPs. But the Lord Chancellor, the Leader of the House, and ministers for each department are in the Lords, and through them governments can be challenged in debate, or in writing, or by enquiries through the committee system.
- *Influencing policy.* Peers who are members of the party in government have some access to the top ministers in the Commons, and are invited to briefings at which their views are sought (and then often ignored); the rest can lobby the ministers in the Lords. Peers also hold policy debates every Wednesday on important issues.
- *Protecting the constitution.* Britain's constitution is an untabulated collection of laws, rules and conventions. Among them are that the House of Lords can veto the dismissal of key office holders, such as judges, and can stop a government attempting to extend its term beyond five years. In practice, when Oliver Cromwell abolished the House, lords did not demur.[6]

- *Constituting the highest court of appeal.* Peers once acted, as a body, as the highest court of appeal. This function has been delegated to twelve senior judges who are ennobled (i.e. made peers) and sit as Lords of Appeal in Ordinary. They also take part in debate on legislation in the Chamber.

Despite these significant functions the Lords is considered by many – particularly MPs and especially members of the government – a political backwater, and it is neglected by political journalists. MPs will do anything for publicity, while peers are seldom interested in the press. In relation to government, the House of Lords presents the paradox that while there can be no democracy without opposition, when the government has a hefty majority in the Commons the only effective opposition in Parliament comes from the unelected Chamber. There have been no government defeats in the Commons since 1997 (for government defeats in the Lords, see Table 4.1).

Like all institutions of governance, it exists, in part, to mediate power between groups and individuals, and many of the curious forms of behaviour described in this book are, to some extent, caused by the unseen workings of both formal and informal power. Like electricity, power is invisible, energising and dangerous. It charges the relationships in Parliament. And, like money, it is prized by many, so that whoever obtains a position of power in relation to another is likely to be resisted and puts themselves at risk of dispossession, sometimes by inventive means. The House of Commons has, in the last two centuries, dispossessed lords of most of their power by means of the ballot box, from which all legitimate authority in Parliament is now derived, but peers still influence debate and have the "power to embarrass" the government.[7]

Appointed peers are chosen from among the most prominent members of certain sections of British society, and are often accustomed to power and influence in their own fields. They tend to have less as peers. Their influence in the House depends on their position in it. Most of the government's political decisions are made in Downing Street and in the Commons, leaving the government back-bench peers with little clout but some access to ministers. The opposition parties, on the other hand, defeat the government regularly in the Lords; while it is presently not defeated at all in the Commons. With the departure of most hereditaries, and the near parity created between the two main parties, the Liberal Democrat peers, in particular, have the satisfaction of being the 'swing party': it is they who decide who will win when Labour and Conservative are on opposing sides.

Power inheres in relationships between offices or positions and groups and can be expressed in symbolic, as well as concrete, forms.

Symbols can help to reveal who is powerful and who is weak. They can be manipulated to reinforce or challenge the *status quo* and they allow people to make sense of what would otherwise be a chaotic world.[8] Symbolism and ritual – the context within which symbolism is often communicated – pervade politics the world over. Peers often recognise the weight of the symbols among which they work. Lord Goodhart expressed it thus: 'titles are symbolic, but that does not mean that the issue is unimportant. Symbols have potency.'[9] Yet academic observers of politics often assume that they are unimportant. Monographs on the composition, organisation and functions of the Lords appear every twenty years or so,[10] but from an anthropological perspective, they fail to address some very interesting questions, about ideas, for instance, or relationships, symbols or rituals. Culture tends to be seen as subjective and tangential to 'real' politics.[11] But the idea of politics being peopled by rational actors who calculate their self-interest before making each move leaves out much that makes us human. Although we like to see ourselves as goal-oriented, Thurman Arnold observed that 'society is generally more interested in standing on the side lines and watching itself go by in a whole series of different uniforms than it is in practical objectives'.[12] Those, like parliamentarians, using symbols to make sense of complex situations may disregard or even be nearly oblivious to their practical significance because their meanings are taken for granted. But we cannot manage without them.

Rituals, rules, symbols and hierarchies are an integral part of the political process and important in all political institutions. They are the principle subjects of this book.[13] Chapters 2 to 5 offer an introduction to the Lords: how peers are socialised (Chapter 2), the ways in which they establish their reputation (Chapter 3), the exclusion of most hereditary peers from the House (Chapter 4), and who is part of the micro-society of the House of Lords (Chapter 5). Chapters 6 to 9 describe various relationships within the Lords – social hierarchies, political factions and power structures. The last three chapters delve into the rules and rituals of the House and how they interact with its power structures, providing an illustration of how symbolism pervades politics.

Notes

1 In 1958 the Life Peerages Act introduced the appointment of peerages for life that could not be inherited and which allowed the ennoblement of women.

2 See Chapter 4.

3 Ministers and whips sit on the lowest or 'front-benches', nearest to the 'Table', while other peers sit on the 'back-benches', see Figure 2.1. 'Whip' derives from the 'whipper-in' at a fox-hunt, whose job it is to keep the hounds hunting as a pack, whipping in those that stray.

4 See Chapter 9. The extent of co-operation varies. For example, currently the Liberal Democrats frequently discuss the strength of their whip with the Conservatives, but only warn the government about it rarely. Tories and Labour almost never reveal their whip to each other.

5 The remainder were either not reversed or reversed but with amendments in lieu, House of Lords Public Bill Sessional Statistics for 2002–2003, House of Lords Public Bill Office, December 2003.

6 As Walter Bagehot put it in his seminal *The English Constitution*, 'the House of Lords, as a House, is not a bulwark that will keep out revolution, but an index that revolution is unlikely' (1867, Chapman and Hall, London).

7 This is Lord Wallace of Saltaire's phrase.

8 D. Kertzer, 1988, *Ritual, Politics and Power*, Yale University Press, New Haven and London, pp. 2–8.

9 Lord Goodhart, HL Deb., 13 July 2004, col. 1149.

10 Notably P. A. Bromhead, 1958, *The House of Lords and Contemporary Politics 1911–1957*, Routledge and Kegan Paul, London; J. P. Morgan, 1975, *The House of Lords and the Labour Government 1964–1970*, Oxford University Press, Oxford; and D. Shell, 1992, *The House of Lords*, Harvester Wheatsheaf, New York and London. An edited volume by D. Shell and D. Beamish (1993, *The House of Lords at Work: A Study Based on the 1988–89 Session*, Clarendon Press, London) offers similar material, as do various papers and articles by N. Baldwin, e.g., 1990, *The House of Lords*, Wroxton Papers in Politics, Wroxton College.

11 Exceptions include contributions to a forthcoming book edited by E. Crewe and M. Müller, 2005, *Rituals in Parliaments: Political, Anthropological and Historical Perspectives on Europe and the United States*, Peter Lang, Frankfurt am Main, as well as Aronoff and Laitin, as cited by Kertzer, *ibid.*, p. 186, n. 22, and feminist scholars such as S. Rai, 2000, *International Perspectives on Gender and Democratisation*, Palgrave, Basingstoke.

12 As cited by Kertzer, *ibid.*, p. 3. See also p. 12.

13 See Appendix 2 for information on anthropological research methodology and theory.

2 Kind words and coronets

I met one peer who had waited over a decade before making his first speech to the House; some hereditaries never addressed it at all. New peers were expected to wait until they understood the Chamber before claiming its attention. It is still frightening – even those already hardened to speaking in public find their first speech to the House of Lords awesome. One was warned: 'Do you realise you are about to address the most terrifying audience in the world?' Speakers have to face leading specialists in almost every field, from the judiciary, the media, academe, the military and multinationals. Some years ago, when one quoted the *Financial Times* in debate, the owner, a Conservative peer, stood up and said crossly: 'That is not the policy of my newspaper.' Politicians 'parachuted in' as ministers make their maiden speeches from the despatch box. One, coming straight onto the front-bench, had to speak about defence, about which he knew little, in front of five former chiefs of the defence staff. Close to the opposition, front-benchers can see every unnerving change of expression.

The Chamber is a minefield of rules and conventions that can seem arbitrary. New peers are expected to know the form. Transgressions meet subdued but terrifying disapproval: the threatening murmur of a disapproving crowd: "No one showed the way through this place, they just howled when I did something wrong." Rules that have an obvious purpose, such as those forbidding peers to cast aspersions on other peers (let alone insult them) or obliging them to address the whole House, never an individual, are mixed with more obscure prohibitions, such as the interdiction on walking between the Woolsack and the speaker, or getting up when the Lord Chancellor or his deputy is on his feet.[1] Obscure or not, these solecisms provoke roars of 'Order, order' from other peers.

A new Labour minister entered the Chamber for the first time and found himself a convenient empty bench. At once, a lord interrupted debate by rising to his feet to say that it had come to his notice that someone was sitting in the archbishop's seat. Embarrassed and humiliated under the eyes of scores of peers ranged in banked seats, the minister found a bench at the opposite end, only to be told that he had taken a privy counsellor's place. After he had lost half a stone because he had no idea where to eat, he one day followed someone from his own party and found himself in a splendid grill. He took a table by himself and some "harum-scarum" man promptly asked if he could join him; he did not know what to say because he was uncertain whether he was allowed to lunch with the opposition.

Why, one wonders, should prodigiously successful people endure these ordeals or take the time to learn such an abundance of procedural niceties in order to occupy positions with relatively little political power?

The fairy palace

For some new peers the House of Lords is instantly seductive; to others it is absurd. Ex-public schoolboys, Oxbridge graduates and gentlemen who frequent the august London clubs near Pall Mall tend to feel at home there. They recognise the long tables in the dining rooms, the leather armchairs in the library, spotted dick on the menu, arcane regulations, hierarchical organisation, prefectorial front-benchers and headmastery clerks. It is a grander version of Eton or Harrow. The past is everywhere: soaring arches, the luxuriance of sculpted dead kings sprouting from the mouldings, painted historical tableaux on the walls, marble statues of deceased parliamentarians. The ceremonies seem of another era, binding the everyday to ancient splendour; and the names, titles and families of some hereditary peers are a roll call of national history. The present and the past are even linked in individual peers. In one debate Earl Russell quoted what his great-grandfather said to Lord Cranborne's[2] great-grandfather (both prime ministers). In another Earl Ferrers interrupted to say: 'I see that the noble Lord takes great pride in his name. He really should not do so because the only reason that his predecessor was made Lord Henley was to ensure that my predecessor was executed.'[3] Henley responded dryly that at least his ancestor had ensured that Ferrers' was hanged by a silken rope, the privilege of peerage.

The Lords presents a seductive version of the nation's history, apparently unfolding in perfect continuity from the place in which one stands. For its devotees, the House is a shrine to this beloved, majestic, patriotic saga, conjuring endless genial associations, while still being thoroughly alive in the present. For others, exactly the same qualities – the public-school atmosphere, elaborate architecture and the historical associations – jar on the nerves. The Palace of Westminster is too small, they say, and inappropriate for a parliament, and encourages backward-looking attitudes.

Peers who like it least tend to stay away. Nothing obliges noble lords to attend the House, except their consciences, and some peculiarities of the House arise from the consequent thinness on the ground of malcontents. More oddities still are due to the fact that peers can attend for life, should they so choose. The clerks, who run the show, tend to arrive straight from university and spend their whole careers there. Nearly everyone rubs along with all the others in this closed voluntary village, obliged by their permanence to learn respect and avoid confrontation, till death or retirement take them away. The consequences of this reach every aspect of the Lords community.

Like any village, there is a turnover of population. Old peers die and new ones arrive. Between ten and twenty-five in a year used to be typical until 1997, and the absorption of this small number was remarkably effective. I was told again and again that iconoclasts who arrived determined to reform, or abolish, the upper House often became its greatest defenders, and that within six months any peer would "go native" and become "one of us". The large influx of new peers since 1997 has put this process under strain. This chapter describes the influences that made seditionists into conformists, and why they no longer work so well.

Initiation rites

On hearing they are to be ennobled, most people feel overwhelmed and unworthy; a very few think it is overdue. One modestly replied to the Downing Street phone call:[4] 'Don't be bloody stupid.' Partners often advise 'Say yes, you might regret saying no', but some do bitterly regret it. One told me that vanity had got the better of his judgment, and that although his daughter had commented, 'That's sad Dad. Is it a job for grown-ups?', he had accepted.

Quite a few of the older peers inherited their titles unexpectedly through the carnage of World War II, but most hereditaries knew their destiny from an early age. Even so, some who succeeded fathers (or a few mothers) were taken aback to find themselves in the Lords. The idea that they were groomed for the role is exaggerated and to many heirs the House seemed alien and associated with the death of someone close. Like the lifers, the more modest hereditary peers often felt undeserving – 'Why do I deserve this privilege or honour?', or something like survivors' guilt. Many were reluctant to take their seats. Lord Stanley of Alderley was persuaded with difficulty and, because snow had made farming impossible, decided he would visit London to 'kill two birds with one stone by taking the great uncle's sword to be repaired and take my seat in the House'.[5] He related that in 1971:

> [The Chief Whip] taught me my first lesson ... that however much you dislike the job, or person, aristocratic good manners are essential, and, rising from his chair he opened an impressive cabinet revealing, not state papers but an array of alcoholic beverages, and immediately welcomed me on taking the Conservative Whip, which in fact I had not decided to do until that moment as I had assumed that my political views might be asked before being invited to join the Party.[6]

It's no longer that relaxed. The hours have lengthened, the business grown, and, in recent years, Labour and Liberal Democrats have demanded that prospective peers attend the House regularly or decline the peerage. New peers have little comprehension of what they are letting themselves in for, nor how demanding they will find the whips – pleading, cajoling and emotionally blackmailing them to stay late or come in at short notice.

Having accepted, a new peer has to have a title in order to sit in the House, and a visit to Garter King of Arms to acquire one is mandatory. Peers tend to find the interview irritating, amusing or absurd: a "unicorns in the forest" experience. The conventions that govern Garter's arcane craft are found in a document entitled *1965 Rules, College of Arms. Submitted by Harold Wilson*, though Garter maintains a degree of control by keeping this strictly secret. The intricacies of titles are complicated and dull in contrast to the magical effect the title has, once acquired. Earls or above may choose a British county, city or London borough. Barons should pick somewhere smaller than a city but larger than a farmhouse or street, as the latter would be "beneath the dignity of the peerage". Foreign places have been allowed in some circumstances, such as Lords Allenby of Megiddo and Montgomery of Alamein, and ex-colonies now and again.

Garter points out to peers that they may buy coats of arms. He has allowed some surprising images, including one for a judge of two naked men and eight fishnet-stockinged ladies' legs with the motto 'I persevere'. Equal numbers of Labour and Conservative peers have purchased arms – over eighty since 1996. Scottish peers go to the equivalent – Lyon King of Arms – as the late Lord Annan described:

> ... he said to me, 'What do you intend to call yourself?' I said that I hoped to be able to call myself Lord Annan, as to the best of my belief there was no other Lord Annan. He said, 'Who's the head of your family?' I said that I did not know. He said, 'You can't call yourself Lord Annan unless you are Annan of that Ilk'. At this point I became terrified. He said, 'You must change your

name at once'. So I consulted and looked at the map of Annandale and I found a small tributary called the River Ae, which flows into the River Annan. I asked Lord Lyon whether I could then become Lord Annan of Aeside and would have to sign my name in that way. He said, 'That would be so'. At this point my family intervened. My 13 year-old daughter said, 'Do you realise that pop records on the gramophone have an A side and a B side and that I shall call you Lord Annan of B side if you accept this?'.[7]

Hereditaries, already endowed with titles and armorial bearings, do not need Garter, but contact the Crown Office to establish their eligibility. The procedure for them is more of a family affair: to prove their right to sit, birth certificates, parents' marriage certificates, affidavits from their fathers' sister (if extant) and other documents have to be produced. Claims are not usually made until after the memorial service of the late peer. Sometimes, through grief or respect, it may be months, or years, before the successor establishes his claim, although a few are impatient: one telephoned the Crown Office while his father was dying in the next room.

The public rite of passage for peers into their new status is the Introduction Ceremony, during which he or she is escorted into the Chamber by Garter King of Arms (in Jack of Hearts costume), Black Rod and two enrobed 'sponsors' chosen from among the same rank of peers. It is usually preceded by a celebratory lunch with family, close friends, and sponsors (to which Garter expects to be invited), and ends with the new peer bowing and shaking hands with the Lord Chancellor. At this point those present in the Chamber call out 'hear, hear' in welcome. (Singularly, this cry was very muted when the former Tory party Treasurer Lord Ashcroft took his seat.) The new peer is now of higher status than he was before lunch, and so too are his family; his wife is a 'Lady', and the children are all 'Honourable' (to the delight of some Labour offspring, who, according to rumour within the party, immediately put it in their passports).[8]

This initiation ceremony is experienced by some as a solemn ritual signifying great honour and by others as a Gilbert and Sullivan-style absurdity. For most, it is a proud, or even their proudest moment: they feel appreciated and welcomed. For those whose parents have never known wealth or privilege it can have particular poignancy; it is felt as recognition of arduous personal achievement. The robes, the procession, the seventeenth-century language, and the hushed Chamber combine to give the event immense dignity. On the other hand, Lord Dubs' description of his Introduction Ceremony[9] emphasised the comic:

> Then came this terrible ordeal which is the introduction. You have to wear
> this sort of red thing with ermine, and some of the animal rights people

immediately lobbied me before my introduction ... I asked the Chief Whip if anybody refused to wear the gear and he told me that if they did they wouldn't be able to take their seats ... I felt such a blithering idiot because I was wearing this thing with a funny hat and the Labour peers apparently mark you out of ten as to how well you do ... At one point you are on the backbenches and have to sit down, stand up, bow, and again the Garter King of Arms with that air of Dostoevskyian gloom kept saying, 'Sit down. Bow. Take your hat off.' I knew my daughter in the public gallery was giggling and I could not keep a straight face, it was excruciatingly embarrassing, complete nonsense.[10]

Hereditaries' introductions, by contrast, are low key:[11] they have only to take the Oath of Allegiance or Solemn Affirmation, and quite often even this is ignored in the murmuring and movement before the start of business. It is not an event – no peerage is being created; the newcomer is merely the latest incumbent. Lord Stanley related:

I made a rush to the Table, presented my Writ to the Clerk and swore that I would be loyal to the Queen and her heirs and successors. Needless to say I had difficulty in remembering my name, which was not on the dirty crib sheet for me to read, but as there was plenty of background noise of peers taking their seats it did not matter and, having surmounted that hurdle, I approached the Woolsack to shake the Lord Chancellor's hand to be greeted with the remark 'I knew your predecessor Edward quite well, do you intend to take a part in the proceedings of the House?' Bearing in mind Edward's characteristics, of womanising, gambling and drinking and the flicker in the Lord Chancellor's eye, I replied that I wasn't sure but, if I did, it would be on agriculture.[12]

Although now initiated into membership of the House, and able to vote, peers are not allowed to participate fully until they have made their maiden speech – the ordeal that effects the final transition from attender to participant. It should be short and uncontroversial, and it cannot be interrupted, nor should peers walk about during it, or the congratulations that follow. Very few get away with more than ten minutes. Harold Macmillan's was over twenty and was rapturously received. Baroness Thatcher spoke for the same length but in the wrong style, as though she were still in the House of Commons – an impropriety that has never been forgotten, even by her own party. Like many of the rules, those about maiden speeches are said to be losing effect, and I was told of one New Labour peer who, having finished his, tried to bolt to the bar without waiting for the next peer's congratulations. This was seen as outrageous; though usually it is other peers who walk out during congratulations, and even that is widely and bitterly resented. The socialisation of peers into this unusual institution relies on unfailing courtesy. If it is breached the whole seductive process becomes less effective, and of all the areas in which adherence to the rules is seen to be slipping, this is the one that causes old hands most grief.

Maiden speakers are generally nervous, not to say frightened.[13] This is a result of the close, near-silent attention of unusually well-informed listeners; the high standards of debate; the anxiety of the speaker about the unknown, unpredictable and ferociously policed rules; the knowledge that their acceptance depends on whether they speak well; and, most of all, the fact that they are all there for the rest of their lives. They assume that a humiliation will be remembered to the grave (though in fact, most first speeches are forgiven however bad they are – even Baroness Thatcher might have recovered her reputation in the Lords if she had attended and spoken regularly.) There is also a curious and unnerving combination of grandeur and intimacy about the actual Chamber, like a stately drawing room, so there is not even the psychological prop of an impersonal environment.

Learning to be a peer

After introduction, peers find out where in the Chamber to sit (see Figure 2.1). Bishops join their fellow clergy on the two benches near the throne on the spiritual side of the Chamber. Also on this side are the government and some overflow Cross-benchers, while opposition parties face them on the temporal side. Most working peers go straight to the benches of the party they already support. Law lords, former civil servants, and others who are expected, or wish, to appear, or are politically neutral, and those who are unable to decide which party to join, go to the cross-benches, facing the throne.

Ennoblement can create huge practical difficulties. The upper House still operates on the assumption that members do not have full-time jobs elsewhere but are either wealthy enough to work part-time or retired. New peers who want to attend regularly often have to rearrange their lives to fit the Lords' timetable: they may have to leave lucrative jobs, give up socialising outside the House, and move to, or closer to, London. Others work elsewhere in the mornings but manage to get to the start of Lords' business at 2.30 p.m. on most days. It is not an easy place to conduct outside affairs: meetings usually have to be held in the coffee room, as although nearly all peers now get a desk (before 1999 they could wait years before they were allocated even a locker), most share an office.

The geography of the Palace is complicated (see Figure 2.2) and for security reasons few get their hands on a detailed map of the whole building. Lord Haden-Guest said:

PRINCE'S CHAMBER

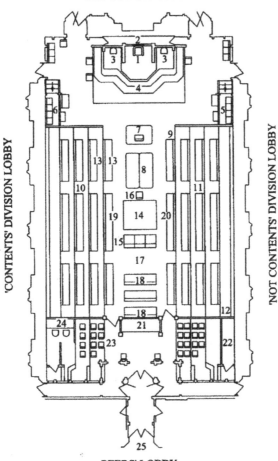

'CONTENTS' DIVISION LOBBY

'NOT CONTENTS' DIVISION LOBBY

PEERS' LOBBY

Key

1	Throne	14	Table of the House
2	Cloth of Estate	15	Clerks at the Table
3	Chairs of State	16	Chairman of Committee's Chair at the Table
4	Steps of the Throne	17	Wheelchairs
5	Clerk's box	18	Cross-benches
6	Official's box	19	Government front-bench
7	Woolsack	20	Opposition front-bench
8	Judges' woolsacks	21	Bar of the House
9	Upper end of Earls' bench	22	Black Rod's box
10	Spiritual side of House	23	Seats for members' spouses
11	Temporal side of House	24	Hansard reporters
12	Lower end of Barons' bench	25	Brass gates
13	Bishops' benches		

Figure 2.1   Seating within the Chamber.

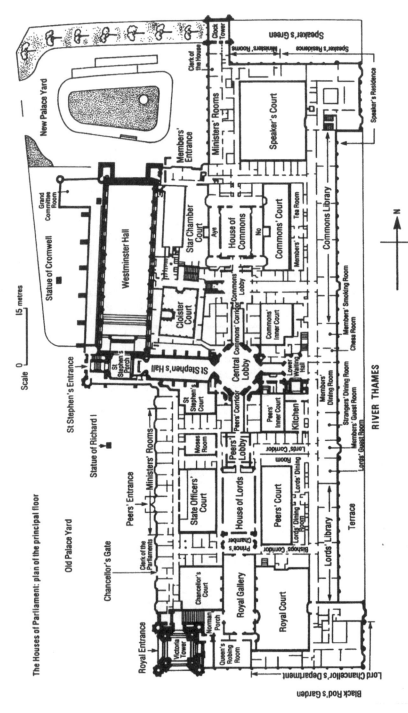

The Houses of Parliament: plan of the principal floor

Scale 0 _____ 15 metres

RIVER THAMES

N

Figure 2.2 Map of the Palace of Westminster.

On my first day, I walked in and got lost immediately. It goes around in a circle and you find yourself in these hallways and they all look the same as the one you were in five minutes ago. One of the gentlemen that worked there saw me coming around the third time and, as I passed by, he said, 'Perhaps my Lord would like a compass?' I turned and looked and he had a smile on his face. There were some wonderful senses of humour in that place.[14]

One peer reported that she knew it well only after seven years. If peers leave the red carpet of the Lords for the green of the Commons they are in forbidden territory unless they were once MPs or are attending a meeting. They are gently but firmly guided by staff as to which areas are taboo, or, for other misdemeanours, told off like anyone else. On one occasion a doorkeeper admonished the distinguished Lord Weatherill: 'Excuse me My Lord, you may have been Speaker down there but the doorkeepers keep order up here.'

It can still take years to feel at home in the Lords and know the procedures inside out, but it is easier for some than others. Lord Stanley, with appropriate public school and army experience, found the problems it presented familiar: 'I was greeted by a "Red Coat"[15] and entered the building, memories of the Coldstream [Guards] and Public School life came flowing back ... I became increasingly aware as time wore on that, as in holding a Coldstream Commission, there was little more to it than knowing how to behave.'[16] The tendency of new arrivals to be treated as though they already knew the form was even more pronounced in the past. Seeking advice was felt to be inappropriate, if not vulgar, and newcomers mostly learnt the rules by breaking them.

Advice is now far more freely given, but it remains the case that there is too much information to be assimilated all at once. With a few exceptions, new peers are already prominent people, but at the moment of first arriving in the House as peers, their confidence often leaks away. They start by visiting the Clerk of the Parliaments. Some speak to him in that meeting with the diffidence of a parent meeting the headteacher at their child's prospective private school. He tells them how to find their way around, and about the facilities such as the library and restaurants, and how clerks can help their parliamentary business. Clerks avoid patronising them by tactfully disguising instruction as conversational generalisations on the behaviour of other peers. Information such as a club secretary might give to new members, regarding desks, lockers, visitors and so on, is given at a similar interview by Black Rod.

Peers would understand procedure if they retained all the information in the three indigestible books[17] given them on arrival, but it takes time to remember who sits where, the names of officials, the various ceremonies and symbols, the array of documents, rules of debate, what happens during a vote and, most complicated of all, the regulations governing legislation. It is years before the *Companion* becomes a well-thumbed and familiar reference book, and then only for the regulars.

Some advice is always dispensed by other peers. One was impressed by the admonition: 'Sit quietly, soak up the atmosphere by osmosis, and then speak.' Another, fairly typically, was told by a senior to keep his nose clean and to avoid drawing attention to himself for at least five years. Although a novice was warned in 1996 that he would be seen as 'new' for six or seven years, the flow of new peers after 1997 greatly accelerated his novitiate, so that he, and his intake, were considered old hands within a few years.

The former Prime Minister Clement Attlee used to advise peers to 'specialise and stay out of the bars',[18] and to specialise is still the most common advice. The composition of the House encourages it: unelected, with no democratic legitimacy, if peers did not specialise they would have less *raison d'être*. The point is also made that since MPs are now nearly all generalists, it makes sense for the revising chamber to comprise specialists, and those who are not risk never establishing enough authority in any area to be listened to with respect.

The Chamber, where the main work of the House takes place, is where rules and conventions are concentrated and is consequently the most hazardous place for newcomers. 'Self-regulation', whereby the peers act collectively as chair in debate (rather than having a Speaker, as in the Commons) is the Chamber's most challenging, and cherished, peculiarity. One explained how it works:

> what struck me most was the emphasis on good manners and the fact that the house disciplined itself for although the Lord Chancellor sits on the Woolsack, he is not chairman or responsible in any way for the disciplining any peer – this is done by other peers, usually like school, by those who have been there longest.[19]

Time is a parliament's critical resource, and greed with it makes speakers particularly unpopular. Peers frequently beg each other to keep contributions short. After a speech that might have been shorter, one Liberal Democrat was delighted to receive a note saying: 'Really good speech, don't do it again.' She was flattered to be complimented at all, in the circumstances. Some debates are timed, and if peers speak for longer than allocated, the government Leader (*primus inter pares* during debate), Government Chief Whip or other whip may intervene.

Misuse of time not only endangers the miscreants' reputations, but endangers the principle of self-regulation. It is therefore an issue that brings together all peers to act as collective police, and the 'howling' that takes place when rules are infringed is self-regulation in action. The reasons it is so valued are cogent: first, that self-regulation makes debate less lawless, antagonistic and unrestrained because the collective is a deal more intimidating than a lone Speaker (i.e., chair); and Speakers, standing alone against the mob, need the protection of yet more rules, which are usually manipulated by government. Secondly, that a Speaker has little choice but to favour prominent party members over back-benchers, which tends severely to restrict independent-minded and thoughtful debate, and again, works to the advantage of government. Self-regulation, on the other hand, (at least in theory), is controlled by back-benchers. It is valued by them accordingly.

Question Time, forty minutes for five questions at the start of business, puts self-regulation under most strain. Each topic is given up to seven or eight minutes and, because the number of peers wanting to speak can be tremendous, pressure is sometimes intense: when many rise to speak, all but one must give way. At the slightest breach of etiquette, shouts of 'Order' are deafening. Neophytes often have no idea of their crime: on hearing the shouting new peers can guiltily break off from their speech and sit down, only to find that the misdemeanour was someone else's. Old hands seem almost to be waiting for solecisms on which to jump.

Procedure, however, is less than half the battle: unwritten conventions governing behaviour and language in the Chamber are an even greater hurdle. One said "the flowery language is like a quadrille, an elegant dance". The most important quality by far is courtesy, and speakers should show respect to the House, and each other, listening carefully to others and avoiding repetition of points already made. They should remember contributions of importance, or expressions of particular felicity, and compliment those who made them; and they should express disagreement gently and kindly, always refraining from low party politics or personal attacks. Breaches can cause terrifying collective intervention in the form of cries of 'Shame' or 'Order'. Pompous or aggressive speakers risk being ignored or provoking exodus from the Chamber; arrogance is seldom respected; modesty is esteemed; complacency loathed. Some find the politesse hypocritical and suffocating; some relish its courtly elegance; the majority recognise that the courtesy is beneficial in many ways to the business of the House, and even those who find it excessive go along with it so as not to jeopardise their own future support.

Pressures to conform

The House assimilates and socialises most newcomers, however tricky, with awesome smoothness. It helps that those who really dislike it have the option to stay away, and do; but those who love it are proud that its critics, once they understand it, can become its staunchest defenders. Lord Windlesham admitted: 'more than most assemblies it has a seductive quality, and after twelve years in the House I must accept that I have ceased to look at it as critically as an outside observer.'[20]

Conversion from critic to defender is seen by most insiders as a rational process: participating, it is felt, removes the scales from the eyes of unbelievers who, perceiving the House does an important job most effectively, come to appreciate and even enjoy its peculiar make-up and quaint customs. There is considerable truth in this view, but not all newcomers are swept off their feet by its charm; there is a remarkable range of social forces at work ensuring that peers do not step out of line, and many quietly harbour reservations but are powerless to withstand the pressures to conform.

Ennoblement is irrevocable. Lifers can decline, and a hereditary peer can renounce a peerage if he has not claimed it, but once accepted neither lifers nor hereditaries can shed their titles. They have not only joined an organisation, their identities are drastically changed in all the spheres in which they operate, like taking vows as a priest or nun. They can stay away but they remain peers. They have adopted a new name and rank and will never be treated the same again. Those who attend regularly tend to find that their social life becomes dominated by the House – peers replace older friends outside, and more than just work becomes wrapped up in their new identities as lords. The all-encompassing, complete and permanent nature of the change puts most new peers on the threshold of something that is subjectively big. Impressionability is heightened, some political baggage can be judiciously discarded and old prejudices may more easily take second or third place to new experience.

Since peers receive no salary, the pressure to conform is not financial. There are other incentives. Many enjoy the satisfaction of knowing that the House is doing an important job, and as a revising chamber it is often considered – especially those who know Parliament well – to be incomparable. Lords' committees earn respect and prestige and many of their reports (especially those produced by the European Union and Science and Technology Committees) have had considerable influence on policy debates.[21] Scrutiny of the government – through questions, debates or informal meetings – all help to hold the executive to account.

At the same time, the seduction of social power cannot be easily dismissed. The majority of peers use their titles not only in the House but outside as well, where they help them to gain access to exclusive perks – seats in popular restaurants, upgrades on aeroplane flights, invitations to gatherings of VIPs. Wives, but not husbands, of peers gain a title as well, so a few peers may have gained wives by it. The French anthropologist Bourdieu has observed that titles are a form of property in symbolic form.[22] This symbolic property confers increased status and the impression of power, which are helpful in accruing real power, wealth or influence through, for instance, the acquisition of directorships of companies, trusteeships of charities and space in the media.

The process of socialisation starts with the palace itself. It was an architect who worked there who famously said, 'we shape our buildings and afterwards our buildings shape us'.[23] Its restrained gigantism, statues of parliamentarians mingling with paintings of *Events*, sculptures of monarchs, mosaics of saints, frescoes of *Courtesy* and *Justice*, and King Arthur in carved oak, all quietly but powerfully suggest a moral consensus from the past. In a most British way, without histrionics or bombast, the worthies on the walls seem to represent massed ranks of peers from antiquity, who, during the 700 years or so of Parliament's existence, have evolved the *Standing Orders* and the conventions that govern peers' behaviour. For a solitary, living peer to question the rules, they imply, would be to challenge the combined wisdom of the dead. What right has some Johnny-come-lately to second-guess John of Gaunt, Clarendon, Chatham, Rosebery, Lord John Russell,[24] the Marquess of Salisbury, and battalions of dead Lord Chief Justices, Lord Chancellors, bishops and archbishops, many of whom, by reason of their immense distinction, in marble, bronze, gilt or fresco, now gaze blindly down on the insignificant new peer?

The Chamber, gilded and splendid, with sculptures of further worthies between the ribbed and foliate windows, and uplifting frescoes such as *The Spirit of Chivalry* and *The Spirit of Religion* on the walls, is sacred space. On its floor take place elaborate ceremonies, ritualised behaviour and rules incomprehensible to the uninitiated. The strictures governing who may or may not enter it and when are almost inviolable. The little off-white pamphlet of *Standing Orders* is a sacred text, or at least, in common with the law and the *Book of Common Prayer*, becomes so in particular contexts. The law in a Court of Law and the prayer book in a church achieve sanctification by being treated with reverence, by being embedded in ritual and by being so arcane as to need a class of specialist custodians, set apart from others by their dress and training, to interpret or administer them. So it is with the procedures in the Chamber, where priestly clerks in wigs and gowns, the Brahmans of the Lords' caste system, have responsibility for interpreting and administering the wisdom of the irrefutable text. In churches certain symbols of divinity are treated with stylised reverence. In the Chamber the equivalent holy objects are the Cloth of Estate[25] and the Mace – the symbols of monarchy – to which peers bow at certain times. These, and the parliamentary ceremonies surrounding the monarch, create an ambiance so reverential that it can be as difficult for some peers to deliberately break the rules of the Chamber as it would be for believers to act profanely in church. Upon newcomers, these pressures inevitably weigh most heavily even if they do not wholly subscribe to the ideas that underlie them. One new peer boldly avoided wearing a suit on his first few visits, but, although no one alluded to it, he found it impossible to live with the discomfort of nonconformity. He conformed. Informal dress would detract from the dignity and sacredness of the House, and after shell suits and trainers had been spotted in the dining room, the necessity for jackets and ties was conveyed to back-benchers in no uncertain terms by Chief Whips and the Cross-bench Convenor.

In the Chamber, the monarch has iconic status. This reflects rather well on peers, who occupy just one rung down the social ladder. The throne, which dominates, symbolically represents the monarch, and ceaselessly reaffirms this flattering social propinquity. The State Opening of Parliament, when the monarch gathers her lords about her, sheds the stardust of almost superhuman status over them. As they receive no salaries, for most this is their pay cheque. It is also makes very beguiling to individual peers the idea of society as a pyramid, with themselves just below the apex. The more they buy into this view, the bigger their pay appears. To those who do (and it is difficult to reject it wholly), the ceremonies and the whole panoply of the House, which stress the great dignity and elevation of the peerage, tend to engender in individual peers feelings of humility towards the institution and the lowliness of their position within its corporate grandeur. They express their humility in their courtesy toward one another, and their submission to the collective 'will of the House'. Humility toward the collective can make dissent difficult or even impossible to contemplate.

Another principle that provides an incentive to conform is that all peers are considered equals ('peers'). Although hard to believe, socially it works well and is an article of faith to regular peers. Although the group as a whole is defined entirely by social rank, within it, paradoxically, a pipsqueak baron is equal to the oldest duke; a lord without two pennies has the status of a billionaire; and the politically ineffectual are considered to be in the same social position as the grandees and wheeler-dealers. There are few for whom this is not beguiling; in fact, most find it pretty heady. The ethos of equality creates a profoundly attractive, equable society, but puts obligations on its members. The foremost is not to be reckless with the ways things are done. Disdain for the rules and the conventions is felt by other peers, in this context of egalitarianism, almost to be treachery.

The ultimate penalty is to be cast out of the charmed circle, that is, to be put into coventry. Most punishments are mere hints of this, being ignored, for instance, in the corridors for an hour or a day or two. Even those who dislike the Lords' social life are not beyond the reach of the collective will, as political influence depends on being seen to have commitment to the written and the unwritten codes. Back-benchers who do not make enough concessions to them will seldom be listened to in the Chamber. Those who offend only get away with it if their apology is fulsome. Lord Monkswell, who allowed lesbian protestors to enter a gallery as his visitors was as amazed as anyone when they abseiled into the Chamber and fell onto Black Rod's lap, but was never forgiven by other peers, not so much for his mistake but for the tone of his apology. Hansard records this:

> Lord Monkswell: ... four young ladies were admitted to the visitors' gallery in my name ... I tender my apologies to Black Rod and his staff for any difficulties that they had to contend with as a result of my actions. While neither condemning nor condoning the demonstration, I believe that it was understandable, given the results of the vote on Clause 28.
>
> Noble Lords: Oh!
>
> Lord Monkswell: I conclude by repeating the words spoken by a 12 year-old girl yesterday as regards Clause 28: 'It is just what the Germans did to the Jews.'[26]

This was not considered an adequate apology: a peer on his own side complained that his 'personal statement', as it is called, had exceeded the 'bounds of propriety'.[27] In recent years two other peers have been severely censured, at least for a while and by some parts of the House: one for allowing the publication of a book that was indiscreet about colleagues, another for saying to a committee that a handful of peers, who could not be named, had behaved dishonourably.

To be included as a paid-up, participating member of such an exclusive club is, of course, flattering, and it is not the only way in which the vanity of peers is harnessed to enforce attendance and conformity; others include being told how important their role is, and the stressing of the moral obligations attendant on personal merit. A lefty peer nicely described how the humility engendered makes it difficult to be radical:

> "People become absorbed into the establishment. You come here a couple of times a month and it swallows you up. When I am coming down in the train from Manchester, I write these revolutionary speeches. I take the tube to Westminster and as I walk through the portals, my speech seeps away. Then I rewrite my speech. When you are away from it, you have glorious thoughts. In my dream world I thought I was more important than I really was."

An alarming aspect for the newcomer is that it is not only the rules that are incomprehensible; it is also mysterious who polices them, how, and with what authority. The ultimate enforcement agency is, of course, the collective of peers themselves, so in theory the peer is a free agent in his own House. In practice however individual peers find themselves being told off by the usual channels, the 'elders', or the clerks who take the peer aside and say, 'We don't do that sort of thing'. Like many others, Lord Allenby found it like being a new boy at school when he arrived in 1984:

> I was very frightened, particularly when I was taken on one side by the Clerk of the Parliaments and told I was talking too long on the floor of the House and would I shorten my speeches. I thought, my goodness, it's just like being had up before the headmaster.[28]

These admonitions are mere warnings. Behind them is the more subtle but far more dire threat wielded by the collective: if they transgress again, they may be told off by other peers in the corridors or ignored, they will not be treated with respect, nor listened to in the Chamber, and even precipitate a walk-out when they stand to speak. The collective can be unpredictable, as crowds always can, and uncertainty about the results of breaking the rules can make even old hands cautious and, above all, courteous.

Nonconformists

The combination of the unusual influx of new peers since 1997 and the exclusion of most hereditaries in 1999 has changed the complex social ecology of the Lords. A profound shift has taken place, with the persuasive process of assimilation in particular being brought under strain. In the past when malcontents stayed away caucuses of discontent could not form and criticism was rarely voiced. But, in the words of one, the nonconformists are close to reaching a critical mass and "it is like a place turning from a village to a more transitory urban community ... For many new ones it is a hostile environment into which they have been parachuted to fight the battles of the government." A Labour peer who never much liked it put it to me that in the past there were "so few of us, we had to be a member of the club. Now there are so many, we can create our own culture. We don't have to assimilate."

From the viewpoint of most old hands, newcomers are not fitting in as well as they used. As one put it: "the rate of recruitment of new peers has exceeded the ability of the House to instil in them its traditional manners and conduct." Morgan noticed similar pressure thirty years ago when 221 new peers were created during Labour administrations. She reports that senior peers were:

struck by the decline in courtesy, as speeches become longer and more acerbic, and are distressed by the way in which the good manners formerly prevailing inside and outside the chamber have deteriorated as members become 'more professional'.[29]

It was, she observed, particularly those who came from the Commons who were slow to adapt. Accustomed to abrasiveness and political point-scoring, they found it difficult to adjust to courteous and dispassionate debate. Recently blame has shifted from former MPs to those from local government and the voluntary sector, and complaints have focused on long speeches, discourtesy to maiden speakers, using incorrect forms of address and standing or walking at the wrong time or place in the Chamber.

An induction course was set up, where clerks explained that, "those of us who've been here for a long time think that the ropes are worth learning. The ropes themselves are becoming stretched." New peers are taught about the procedures of debate, access to the building and its facilities, the Lords' committees[30] and what behaviour is 'undesirable'.

Despite these and constant official injunctions about respect for the rules, undesirable behaviour has continued. A working group charged with making proposals for improving procedure rejected simplified procedures which would have made life easier for ministers and the government, and instead protected self-regulation, focusing once again on achieving better adherence to the rules.[31] The suggestion that front-benchers should be prohibited from putting their feet up on the Clerks' Table was rejected, but the House adopted most of the group's other recommendations. Those that did not get past concerned training. Baroness Carnegy of Lour opined: 'I slightly regret that we talked about "training" of noble Lords. One does not train people to be parliamentarians. I would have preferred to call it "providing information".'[32] Perhaps peers are too grand for education.

Since then, a few minimal reforms have helped the process of social-isation work its magic on the new intake. Discontented peers expressed their dissatisfaction with the short notice of votes, self-regulation and general resistance to change. They argued for a larger canteen, using forms of address without the titles, the abolition of smoking in the building, taking more of the committee stage of bills off the floor of the House and into a committee room, and for more 'family-friendly' hours of sitting. Defenders of the *status quo* are fewer without the excluded hereditaries and although such reforms were fiercely resisted, hours have been shortened and committee rooms more widely used. Competition at Question Time has become even more intense, complaints about greed with time persist, and the House continues to operate as if peers have no other occupations, but the discontent has subsided. During a debate about the role of the Speaker – precipitated by the government's clumsy announcement of the abolition of the post of Lord Chancellor on 12 June 2003[33] – the majority of peers made it clear that they would not favour more than gentle guidance from the peer on the Woolsack. He or she might be the 'guardian of the *Companion*', but could not decide points of order. The 'maintenance of self-governance', upon which the whole cultural edifice of the House relies, remains overwhelmingly the 'wish of the House'.[34]

Notes

1 Peers insist that the Lord Chancellor (on the Woolsack) needs to be able to see the current or prospective speakers (on the benches), but since the Lord Chancellor's interventions are minimal, clerks have explained that it is more a matter of courtesy. See Chapter 10.

2 Since then Lord Cranborne's father has died and he has inherited his title, the Marquis of Salisbury, but he remains Lord Cranborne in this book because that was his name at the time of fieldwork.

3 Earl Ferrers, HL Deb., 13 May 1999, col. 1345.

4 Only members of the party in government and Cross-benchers receive a call from Downing Street, while others are informed by their own party leaders.

5 Lord Stanley of Alderley, Unpublished diaries 1971–1999, p. 2. These have since been published in Thomas, 8th Lord Stanley, 2004, *The Stanleys of Alderley 1927–2001, A Politically Incorrect Story*, AMCD Press, Cheshire.

6 Lord Stanley of Alderley, *ibid.*, p. 6.

7 Lord Annan, HL Deb., 30 April 1998, col. 414.

8 These titles actually come into effect when the letters patent creating the new peerage is stamped with the Great Seal, but the Introduction Ceremony is the public acknowledgement of the rite of passage from commoner to noble.

9 See Chapter 11 for changes to the ceremony made in 1998.

10 Lord Dubs as quoted by A. Mitchell, 1999, *Farewell My Lords*, Politico's, London, p. 36.

11 Although most hereditary peers have been excluded, some are still taking their seats, so this form of introduction is not yet obsolete (see Chapter 4 for details).

12 Lord Stanley of Alderley, *ibid.*, p. 8.

13 Only two peers claimed to have been unworried by their maidens; both in wheelchairs. They may have had to overcome more and greater obstacles than most peers.

14 As quoted by R. Grant, 2003, 'Nowt so queer as folk', *Guardian Weekend*, 10 January 2004, p. 33.

15 Red Coat is the doorkeeper who stands outside Peers' Entrance and welcomes peers. I was told that Charles II arrived to find no one to greet him at the palace, so he instructed his footman to get down from the coach, open the door and remain there. The current one has naval buttons on his scarlet jacket with tails.

16 Lord Stanley of Alderley, *ibid.*, p. 3.

17 House of Lords, *The Standing Orders of the House of Lords Relating to Public Business* (1994, HMSO, London), *The Standing Orders of the House of Lords Relating to Private Business* (2001, The Stationary Office, London), and the *Companion to the Standing Orders and Guide to the Proceedings of the House of Lords* (2000, The Stationary Office, London).

18 As cited by Lord McNally, in Mitchell, *ibid.*, p. 93.

19 Lord Stanley of Alderley, *ibid.*, p. 10.

20 Lord Windlesham, 1975, *Politics in Practice*, Jonathan Cape, London, p. 140.

21 As evidence of their influence, when a new chair was appointed to the European Parliament's civil liberties committee, the EP clerks recommended reading three documents in preparation, two of which were reports produced by the Lords' European Union committee.

22 P. Bourdieu, 1990, *In Other Words*, Polity Press, London, p. 135. For discussion of titles, see Chapter 11.

23 Sir Giles Gilbert Scott as quoted by G. Stamp, 2000, *The Houses of Parliament: History, Art, Architecture*, Merrell, London, p. 149.

24 Later 1st Earl Russell, Prime Minister 1846–52, 1865–66.

25 See Chapter 10 for details.

26 Lord Monkswell, HL Deb., 4 February 1988, col. 1183.

27 Lord Cledwyn of Penrhos, HL Deb., 4 February, col. 1193.

28 Lord Allenby as quoted by Mitchell, *ibid.*, p. 41.

29 J. P. Morgan, 1975, *The House of Lords and the Labour Government 1964–70*, Oxford University Press, Oxford, p. 42.

30 Select committees deal with particular bills and general topics (monetary policy, economic affairs, the constitution, eight on the European Union and science and technology, delegated powers and regulatory reform). In addition, there are the domestic committees dealing with finance or refreshment under the House Committee, Standing Committees on Liaison (reviewing the work of committees), Selection (choosing members to sit on committees), Procedure, Privileges and Statutory Instruments. There is also a statutory Joint Ecclesiastical Committee on which MPs and peers sit to examine draft 'measures' (equivalent to bills but proposed by the General Synod of the Church of England) before they are put to Parliament for approval (www.parliament.uk/parliamentary_committees/parliamentary_committees26.cfm, accessed 18 July 2004).

31 House of Lords, *Freedom and Function. Report to the Leader of the House from the Group on Procedure in the Chamber.* Session 1998–99, 1st March 1999, HL Paper 34, p. 1. Baroness Hilton of Eggardon chaired the group.

32 Baroness Carnegy of Lour, HL Deb., 22 March 1999, col. 972.

33 This had to be postponed when the consequences and legal difficulties of abolishing this post were pointed out, see Chapter 12 for details.

34 Leader of the Liberal Democrat peers, Baroness of Williams of Crosby, HL Deb., 12 January 2004, col. 390.

3 Performing like a peer

Before the 'execution' of most hereditaries in 1999, about two-fifths of peers attended regularly; that is to say, for at least a hundred days a year.[1] Now, nearer half are regulars. Paid only expenses, with no hope of further honours, they still make the effort to speak in debates, sit on committees or vote, in many cases despite having careers outside the House as well. Those who attend give two main reasons: to influence policy and legislation, and to serve.[2] Hereditaries tend to use the word 'duty' and are more likely to emphasise service to the Crown. Life peers more often talk in terms of 'public service' and tend to see party, Parliament, public or nation as boss.

Plodding through legislation, recommending alterations that may face defeat, or reversal in the Commons, does not appeal to everyone. Lords' proceedings are rarely adequately reported in the press. The political journalist Andrew Marr calls his fellow Parliament-watchers "worshippers of power", and for them, the Lords is a political sideshow: "It is alien territory ... like visiting stuffy elderly relatives, not unfriendly but not our own place."[3] Lords do not seek publicity. The House is derided or ignored by the Commons, and the public hardly knows about it. Some even thought it had been abolished in 1999.

For ambitious peers, it does not have enough influence to be worth the time. Ennobled ex-ministers from the lower House tend to find it unexciting. Some high-flyers stay away because it has too little power. (Many hereditary peers – contrastingly – used to keep away out of diffidence. Other hereditaries became disillusioned by politics, or felt that they did not fit in, or had nothing in particular to contribute; others again were too shy or visited only to vote on three-line whips or occasionally to speak on subjects of which they had detailed knowledge.) The complexity of the rules and the intensity of the social life deter the lazy and the misanthropic. Honours peers (ennobled for their professional distinction) stay away in droves because they are on the whole too busy, or have made their mark on society already, and even some of the intake of working peers since 1997 (ennobled specifically to participate in the work of the House) visit only irregularly. The timetable of debates is agreed only three weeks ahead, so career and family can make participation hugely inconvenient, and the attendance of many life peers decreases as the novelty wears off. Despite all this, enough become committed to the 'legislative sweatshop in which the most elevated in the land are exploited'[4] to carry on the nation's business.

The social life of the palace is extremely attractive to many and utterly addictive to some, who feel it is without parallel. One described it as like "an Oxford college but without most of the back-biting and petty jealousies". Austin Mitchell was told that you 'find yourself at a long table having a discussion with the Bishop of Durham, Lady Warnock and, say, Lord Wilberforce, probably the best judge of the 20th century, and Robert Winston, talking about IVF'.[5] For some it becomes their principal social club and, according to one, peers live ten years longer than the rest of us. Some of the hereditary peers say they are glad that at least they were privileged to have known it for a few years, and a few are so keen to get back in that although rejected the first time, they have put their names down for election in the future.

Other perks which tend to be taken for granted include the lofty gothic of the palace, the sense of ancient power and present privilege, and even, for some, the deference. Peers are cherished like minor royalty by staff, and some begin to feel as they are treated: the accorded status seeps into their identity. It is only within the Lords that they are among equals and, like the rich and famous, or heads of state, they feel comfortable with each other. In this fairy-tale aspect of their identity, the House of Lords is home, they can relax in its comradely, intimate and yet grand atmosphere, and for some it becomes a sanctuary. The House has also the potent characteristic that if peers can occasionally call attention to a neglected issue, improve legislation or contribute to a committee report, it can imbue their lives with moral purpose. It is unsurprising that most peers who regularly attend the House not only claim to be, but give a convincing appearance of being, unusually happy. The exception to this rule may have been the tiny number of hereditaries who, before the reforms, never made any contribution, but attended to claim expenses and kill time in the bars. They were considered the lowest form of life.

Another category that provoked resentment and disdain before the House of Lords Act 1999 were the Conservative backwoodsmen, brought in on three-line whips in emergencies. This quirk of the constitution was abused occasionally. Notorious examples – the votes on Maastricht and poll tax – embarrassed even most Conservative hereditary peers. During one of these charabanc votes, Lord Carter teased the Tories for bringing in so many strangers for a vote on the House of Lords bill. The late Lord Mackay of Ardbrecknish countered that he had spotted a few unknown faces on the Labour benches too. Neither of them knew at the time, to Mackay's good fortune, that they were Conservative backswoodsmen sitting with oblivious complacency on the Labour side. Backwoodsmen could be identified by their ignorance of procedure and of the geography of the House. Stories of their asking whips on the wrong side which way to vote were plentiful. Conservatives argued that their reliance on back-woodsmen was exaggerated and that they habitually exercised restraint.[6] But it was the case that they could win any vote if they wished.

Now the least influential members are infrequent visitors who make ill-informed speeches. They are exceedingly unpopular. Poor speeches may be received politely but the speechmaker's reputation will suffer. Peers can still only do well if they attend regularly and perform well. It also helps to find a niche.

Finding a niche

To find their place in the Lords, most peers adopt certain strategies, of which five idealised examples are described below.[7] There is no peer who consistently exemplifies a single strategy as, like anyone else, all employ whatever means are appropriate to their objectives at the time.

Specialists

Most lords already have some expertise, usually professional, when enno-bled. Even if they don't, many choose to concentrate on a single issue, or two, in order to be taken more seriously by speaking informedly on them in the Chamber. They seek appointment to the select committees related to their field, attend all-party parliamentary groups, keep in touch with relevant interest groups and so on. Until 1999 there was an excess of experts in agriculture, finance and defence. Specialists in law, politics and business still superabound.

Peers who lead their professional fields are taken very seriously: law lords on legal matters, bishops on subjects that are considered 'moral' or 'spiritual', ex-chiefs of the defence staff on defence, and so on. Committee work by peers, which greatly enhances the value of the House, is not known about by most outsiders, but reports from the committees have influence, and inside there is respect for those who give up time for it.

Parties provide briefings to guide members on what to say and whips to tell them how to vote. Cross-benchers, on the other hand, have to form their own opinions, and specialisation appeals especially to them although they have to do their own research. They increasingly receive briefings from interest groups, non-governmental organisations and sometimes ministers. It is often assumed that specialists are more likely to take a non-political view, and peers, sensitive about their lack of democratic legitimacy, press this idea to establish a *raison d'être*. The link made between specialisation and independence may be a chimera but it does help to create a sense of identity to distinguish peers from members of the Commons, who are increasingly generalist full-time politicians. Argument in the Lords is often based on detailed knowledge or long experience.

'A wise man said that the two subjects that really excite this House are badgers and buggery.'[8] This may be an exaggeration, but animal welfare and sex inspire huge numbers of peers to consider themselves expert. Civil liberties and parliamentary reform also lengthen the speakers' lists exponentially. Understandably, hereditary peers were interested in their own execution, and many became overnight *soi-disant* experts on the constitution.

Networkers

Most peers rely on speeches to achieve influence; networkers socialise. Networking tends to be confined to the House of Lords itself, although contact with ministers in the Commons can be important for exerting pressure on the government. Face-to-face contact in all-party groups, bars and corridors is key to gathering support. Letter writing, sending mailshots to all fellow peers, and even the odd peer-led email campaign also figure. They may wish to persuade others to ask questions or to speak in particular debates, to put a particular argument, and, especially, to vote. Some networkers have less instrumental strategies but help oil the wheels, introducing peers to each other, for example, to break down barriers, or providing moral support to ministers.

The Countess of Mar forced the government to recognise the dangers of organophosphates through a prolonged, determined campaign of networking, asking questions and drawing attention to the issue; and others, for instance the lobby defending the rights of people with disabilities, have achieved comparable results. Conservative and Labour networkers usually concentrate on their party colleagues, especially when in government. Liberal Democrats and Cross-benchers may start with their own members but will swiftly work the other parties as particular votes loom. Rebellious government back-benchers rely on networking with other parties as much as their own.

In theory, the Cross-benchers could hold the balance of power and networkers should focus on them. In practice as a large group of unmanaged individuals, each of whom has to be persuaded to attend at the right time and then vote the right way, they are impossible to influence *en masse* and tend to vote mostly when their own specialist topics are under discussion. The fewer but more disciplined Liberal Democrats can deliver more easily but they, or cross-benchers, need to secure substantial support from other groups to get any amendment through.

Some back-benchers are effective at canvassing support and then making deals with the government before the issue is debated. If the minister responsible will not co-operate, peers can network to raise enough votes to force concessions during the passage of a bill, but increased whipping is diminishing the potential for such back-bench alliances.

Party creatures

Until 1830 political parties barely existed in the House of Lords.[9] Now, the only route to office is to ascend the party ladder. Ambitious peers are rare: the few that there are need to toe their party line, keep their noses clean and disguise dissent by absence rather than by voting against their party.

The first step to office is becoming a whip. Besides encouraging members to attend and vote, whips speak on up to three departmental topics each. The champion at addressing diverse subjects seems to be Lord McIntosh of Haringey (a Labour minister), who answered four successive questions on different topics on 10 March 1999, and sounded as though he had mastery of each. On another occasion, when challenged to explain loop unbundling in lay language, his response was received with a cheer.[10]

The next rung up is appointment as a minister (usually a parliamentary under-secretary of state) if in government, or a spokesman if in opposition, to introduce and wind up major debates and respond for their party to bills in their area. Government ministers have administrative responsibilities as well, and salaries and even offices (albeit almost always shared). In the main opposition party, only the Leader and Chief Whip are paid and other front-benchers may have to share offices with three or four colleagues. So, however their ambitions incline them, peers cannot always afford prominence while in opposition. Parliamentary under-secretaries rank below ministers of state, themselves below the secretaries of state who head government departments. MPs take most of the top departmental jobs.[11] The majority of peers do not expect political office. Back-benchers' opportunities for influencing front-benchers are increased by membership of the same party. Parties, and to a far lesser extent Cross-benchers, have funds to employ advisers and researchers to keep their members informed, and party members are kept up to date about plans for legislation and the timing of debates. In addition, parties are sociable organisations, with meetings and events and wider movements outside Parliament, while the Cross-benchers are not. Ambitious, politically uncommitted individuals sometimes join the party that seems to offer the most opportunities and then adopt the politics of that party along with the rest of its culture, often developing the sort of unquestioning tribal loyalty associated with football supporters or units in the armed forces.[12]

What is considered good behaviour by party peers varies according to the party. At the time of writing, Labour peers are the most committed to a party agenda: since 1997 all new Labour members have been required to pledge to attend for most of the votes. Most of the time their own (i.e., government) legislation is at risk, so whipping is forceful and highly organised to get it through. The Conservatives, on the other hand, are only just beginning to catch up with their new circumstances since the 1999 House of Lords Act. Until then, giving their back-benchers independence and rarely demanding their attendance were useful ways of under-playing their dominance of the House. They defeat the government easily when the Liberal Democrats join them, but when on their own, obedience to the whip is becoming increasingly necessary. And as a minority party in the Commons (and not in government for almost a century), the Liberal Democrats are able to afford individualism.[13] But they rally and present a united front on issues such as Europe and human rights and increasingly, since they have held the balance of power, on other issues.

Eccentrics

A more unusual strategy, and one that takes great charm and integrity, is to present yourself as a maverick, a rebel, a comedian or a rogue. It is not a path for the ambitious. Nonconformists may only differ from other peers in certain ways. Breaking the rules of courtesy in the Chamber is off-limits; departing from the usual to make peers laugh, on the other hand, is adored.

Humorous eccentrics are more likely to be hereditary peers. Life peers tend to take themselves more seriously. Although often at the top of their professions and, consequently, fairly relaxed, old habits can die hard and levity may often be an indulgence they feel they cannot afford. Only the exceptional can ignore convention but eccentrics with the ability to perform in the Chamber – Earl Ferrers, for example, or Earl of Onslow – can achieve great influence and people make a point of listening to their speeches. Peers deemed merely odd, who fail to make others laugh, run the risk of being ignored. A little alcohol accentuates eccentric behaviour and increases tolerance of it, but in excess it is treated with scorn.

Political mavericks and rebels also sometimes command respect, or none at all. If they are seen to be sincere and principled they can inspire forgiveness, and even admiration, for ignoring whips. Lord Ashley of Stoke escapes criticism when he votes against his party and has even, on occasion, broken procedural rules without disapproval because of the respect he enjoys. Those with less dignity, popularity or integrity, although congratulated publicly by the opposition, are written off as traitors by their own side and may be seen as "getting above themselves".

Elders

Only time can confer the status of elder, but it carries clout: support and advice from elders are valued and other peers may give way in debate. They are usually regular attenders of many years' standing, who have probably held ministerial posts. Some have reached high office in the Commons before coming to the Lords. Their party managers ask them as often as they dare, which is infrequently, to speak on important issues because they have influence. Lords Carrington (ex-Foreign Secretary) and Callaghan (ex-Prime Minister) are both in this category, as are Conservatives Lord Denham (sitting since 1948) and Earl Jellicoe (since 1935) and Labour peer Lord Strabolgi (since 1953). Such elders tend to have become experts on procedure. Earl Russell has been sitting since 1987, and his knowledge of procedure is hard to rival, but his views are hardly sedate: his championing of gay rights, for example, is seen as youthful. Even so, he is well-regarded across the House. Baronesses Hayman and Symons are highly thought of, but too young. It is impossible for a peer to be too old to be respected, at least until their contributions become too confused, when he or she is gently dissuaded from making more than the shortest speeches.

Nevertheless, the stereotyped view of the Lords as doddering old pensioners is mostly prejudice, though a few resemble the two crusty opera-loving old gentlemen from the *Muppet Show*. The standard of debate in the House is eulogised by peers, and is generally high, but the quality of speeches is not related to the age of the speakers. Homosexuality may be the only topic in which the conservatism of the views expressed seems to reflect the age of peers.[14]

Older peers tend to be conservative about the institution,[15] and to express strong (but not always traditional) views about reform and about obedience to rules. While those who dislike it intensely seldom stay around enough to change the way it works, those attracted to it become regular attenders, develop a stake in the *status quo* and, in some cases, feel alarmed that any change may upset a harmonious equilibrium.

Reputation

Once a niche has been found, all peers (perhaps with the exception of the networkers) have to establish their reputation in the Chamber. To secure the support necessary to move amendments or hold the government to account, reputation is all. It is built by consistent hard work and good performance and there are few who can regularly absent themselves and still maintain respect. To be considered proper peers, they have to be seen to embody the qualities appropriate to the peerage: courtesy, independence of mind, wisdom and expertise, and to be dispassionate, putting national interest above that of party or group.

To be regarded as top performers, peers must perform quite often in the Chamber. It is also necessary to have 'a feel for the House'. It is not enough to excel once; each time they speak they should perform well, responding to the particular nuances of the atmosphere at the time. One astute peer advised: "It is a question of judging the mood. Tell a story with them, show respect, be honest and in tune. They don't like clever speeches, they like you to marshal your arguments." Being clever is no guarantee at all that people will listen to you as the place is stuffed with intelligent peers, and as one said: "Having an intellect only means being wrong with more distinction." Erudition is valued if offered with respect and modesty, particularly in the form of apposite or witty quotations, but what is seen as the paraphernalia of cleverness – such as statistics and surveys – tend to be regarded as unwise and unreliable. Learned speeches do not necessarily sway argument; knowledgeable back-benchers can alienate if they are felt to be showing off or waffling, and analytical contributions from academics are sometimes completely ignored. It may be a House of 'experts' but if knowledge is gained from personal experience it is often taken more seriously than the product of research. A few of the shrewdest conceal their sharpness with humour and feigned stupidity.

Ill-considered contributions do not go down well, slapdash argument is usually detected and honesty, though impossible to define, is greatly valued. Peers should give their own opinions, not parrot others'. They were shocked to hear that one Conservative reads out speeches written by lobbying groups and accepts compliments on his extensive knowledge of many subjects. Government ministers forced to take their party line when it is contrary to their own opinion, can express their position by complimenting another speaker on the force of her/his argument, adding, perhaps with a pained expression, that it is not quite the right time to act on it, making their own stance plain even while trotting out the government's. One minister told a friend in another party that while defending the government's line on Iraq in the House, "my colleagues behind me said that my body language spoke volumes". This goes down well – ministers are seen to be doing their best to maintain personal honesty while making necessary compromises. Back-benchers can be pulled in two directions as well – party whips expect their support, but the unwritten rules encourage them to remain true to their convictions. When the discrepancy is too great, most stay away: rather than voting against party, the appearance of independence is maintained without damage being done.

Most know they will be judged above all by their performance in the Chamber, which partly accounts for their nervousness when rising to speak. Even some front-benchers are frightened, and a minister told me that after many years he still finds the prospect like waking up on the day of an exam and wishing he were ill:

> "As a spokesman you feel it is you against 500 people. If you mess it up your reputation is on the line. Even your own friends can ask extremely difficult questions, it makes no difference which side they are on. If it were noisy and you could get away with bluffing, as you can in the Commons, then it would not be so bad. The problem is that people really listen. And often the questioner knows much more about the subject that you ... However clever you think you are, you realise that there are others here who are cleverer ... Some back-benchers are also ambitious. Most are not but in any case they want to see you fail."

Other factors also contribute to pre-speech nerves. One is the level of expertise that is found in the House. Another is the demanding standard set by some speakers whose contributions resemble polished essays. Even short speeches are expected show mastery of the subject couched with a certain grace and wit. It is a high standard to live up to, and many do not, though most try. One minister was so scared of speaking that she woke at four o'clock every morning to master her ministerial briefs. Ministers' opening replies are written by civil servants, but even sticking strictly to the text can be problematical. One is said to have also read out the civil servant's note at the end of his briefing: 'This is a rotten argument, but it should be good enough for their lordships on a hot summer afternoon.'[16]

It is widely believed that the quality of Lords' debates was higher in the good old days. It almost certainly was not. According to Viscount Sherbrooke, in the 1850s it was like 'addressing dead men by torch-light',[17] and Bagehot famously wrote that the cure for admiring the House of Lords was to go and look at it. Debate seems to have been revitalised after 1958 by the advent of life peers; who brought a new approach and inspired hereditary peers to contribute more, lifting the House from the 'doldrums of the 1950s'.[18] In a smaller 1950s House, the nucleus of regular attenders was only sixty. By the end of the century this had risen to 463, which has created furious competition over time.[19] The most active and committed hereditary peers – many of whom were elected to remain under the House of Lords Act 1999 – were often a match for life peers in intellect, expertise and experience. A tiny number injected alternative, even subversive, views into the House that are difficult to find among the respectable, high-achieving life peers. Since the second stage of reform threatens the remaining hereditary peers, and casts doubt even over the continuance of life peers, the pressure to perform well is felt by many to be a bid for survival. For this combination of reasons, the need to excel as performers has become acute.

Good performance is achieved partly through preparation. Some back-benchers work in the Library (often using library clerks to conduct research), maintain good contacts with interest groups, or (rather fewer) consult with those affected by legislation. Sadly, to date, back-bench peers can get away with claiming expert knowledge more on their own personal experience and selected contacts rather than by broad consultation, but that may change in the future. Lobbies have been sending more briefings and providing more assistance;[20] as a consequence, peers are being obliged to take greater notice of a wider range of interest groups.

One method for holding government to account is to ask questions during Question Time.[21] Ministers always have advance knowledge of questions and so can prepare themselves with a good reply from their civil servants. When minister and questioner are of the same party, she or he may also have forewarning of any follow-up questions. In opposition, back-benchers want to catch the minister out but it is difficult to get full and honest answers out of the government: "You have to stack the questions up and get them into a funnel", advised one Cross-bencher, in a bid to trick them into being more candid about difficulties than they intend. Those who can pull such tricks off are respected for it.

Wily back-benchers give or send briefings to those who are likely to speak on their side during questions or debates, or they may have a word with them in the Bishops' Bar, or write personal (preferably hand-written) letters. It is vital to choose the moment carefully for controversial speeches. One caused outrage by arguing that the Oxbridge special fund should be abolished: with over 300 Oxbridge graduates among peers, such a recommendation should not be made recklessly. He could have made sure in advance that enough sympathisers would be present to back him up. Successful performers avoid appearing to champion a party political position, especially if they sit on the cross- or bishops' benches.[22]

The audience never cheer, clap or stamp their feet, they listen in silence, so declamatory orators jar. Courtesy is prized; the content can be savage as long as the form is courteous. The General Synod of the Church of England is apparently a bear garden compared with the Lords. When a peer violently disagrees with the speaker she or he should say that it is an honour to follow the noble lord, whom she admires and disagrees with in equal measure; or, at the extreme, 'the speech we just heard, by the high standards that he's always set himself, did fall somewhat short'.

Insults, noise or cleverness attract the wrong attention. Wit is what works. Whether it is an astringent exchange between two members in the Chamber, or persiflage in the corridor, humour in the House is energetic and everywhere. It is used to humiliate, to distract attention from weak points in an argument, to compliment and cajole, but above all to get and keep attention. A Liberal Democrat peer explains: "When listening to a twelve or fourteen hour debate it can be deathly boring. One is constantly looking for ways to use a can opener to a closed mind, any way to break down peoples' defences, but also just to get them to listen." More unusually, humour oils the wheels of ritualised debate by overcoming procedural difficulties. On one occasion a minister, Lord Williams of Mostyn, was delayed by traffic after lunch with the Queen. Lord Carter, the then Government Chief Whip, was desperately flannelling in order to fill the procedural gap, when Earl Russell inquired, 'My lords, in the circumstances, would it be either in order or welcome for me to follow the example of Winnie the Pooh and wish the noble Lord a very happy Thursday?' Lord Carter replied gratefully: 'When he asks that kind of question, I am always reminded of the Danish proverb which says that you have to walk behind an ostrich for a very long time before you pick up the feather of a wild duck.'[23]

Humour is an almost constant background to business. Teasing punctuates debates and there is a very thin line between acceptable and unacceptable jibes, Lord Williams got away with mocking racists by saying that 'some of my very best friends are hereditary peers',[24] but another went too far when he referred to the homosexual tendencies of a Second World War general. Even the House itself can be a target: Lord Ashburton, following a peer who suggested that it be renamed the House of Revision, mused perhaps '"House of Correction"?'[25]

Humour is particularly a feature of 'parliamentary occasions' (or POs). These are controversial votes or debates that aim to defeat the government and attract media interest. You can tell if it is a genuine PO if the car park is full of Rolls Royces and Baroness Thatcher is present. The atmosphere sparkles and buzzes with peers and their friends joking and chattering. Since there is nearly always a huge audience, peers who are trying to make their mark should perform if at all possible. During my research the topics that inspired them usually concerned reform of the Lords, homosexuality, hunting and civil liberties.

Most peers believe themselves to be experts on these issues, and a certain amount of waffle and hyperbole are delivered, but what POs lack in intellectual content, they tend to make up for in drama. It is imperative that the peer aspiring to popularity does not speak for long. There is no point. A contribution that helps to build the tension a little, and make gentle fun of the other side, will go down well; merely rehearsing the arguments yet again will not.

Status as a performer has solid advantages. It obtains for its holder preference in speaking: when several peers rise to speak, there is a surprising amount of agreement between peers about who should be called, and those with status as good performers have an immense advantage. Well-respected peers are often put at the beginning or end of speakers' lists by some parties; lesser ones whenever a smaller audience is expected.[26] Acting disrespectfully can also alter your position. A former cabinet minister repeatedly failed to attend the whole of debates in which he was speaking. He was moved from his normal prominent place and put at the very end to force him to sit through the wind-up speeches.

Peers rush to the Chamber to listen to a high-status peer, while poor performers provoke a walkout. The latter are perceived as too outspoken, greedy with time, and out of touch with their audience. But there is hope for them – just as you can lose your parliamentary status in one poor speech, so too you can elevate yourself by making a good one. Reputation is made, sustained or broken by performance in the Chamber.[27]

Democratically elected politicians with their eye on the next election can be more concerned with their constituents and the media. The contrast with the United States Congress highlights this difference. Senators (subject to re-election), who are 'big men' in Congress, are realising huge ambitions; most peers, in contrast, find themselves in the Lords after their ambitions have ceased to burn brightly, if they ever had them. Even those who are ambitious have a place in Parliament for life so have no need to court those outside. But although most peers are uninterested in a political career, nearly all want to make their mark. While senators consolidate power by appearing to contribute to debates, controlling powerful committees, using the press and building huge empires of staff,[28] peers rely on using their specialist knowledge, asking probing questions and performing with courtesy, independence and wit to impress others.

Notes

1 Out of 1166 peers, 463 attended for 100 days out of a possible 228 in the unusually long session of 1997–98. In 1999–2000 327 peers out of 714 attended for 100 days or more and of the 92 elected hereditaries as many as 72 were regulars. Source: House of Lords Information Office.

2 In a questionnaire sent out as part of this research in 1999 and returned by 177 peers, see Appendix 2.

3 There are exceptions – Matthew Parris appreciates the peers' tradition of ignoring ideological fashion and listening to the argument; he describes it as an 'another place with a different ethos and less attention to the wind' (Features, *The Times*, 24 June 1998).

4 A. Mitchell, 1999, *Farewell My Lords*, Politico's, London, p. 49. The average in the 2002-03 session was 362 peers.

5 Baroness Hollis as quoted by Mitchell, *ibid.*, p. 43.

6 For example, see The Earl of Carnarvon, The Lord Bancroft, The Earl of Selbourne, The Viscount Tenby and Douglas Slater, 1995, *Second Chamber: Some Remarks on Reforming the House of Lords*, Douglas Slater, London.

7 J. P. Morgan clustered peers into slightly different groups: 'apprentices', 'innocents', 'adventurers', 'legalists', 'politicians', 'elder statesmen' (1975, *The House of Lords and the Labour Government 1964–70*, Oxford University Press, Oxford, pp. 27–44). The idea of 'apprentices' has diminished during the last four years and been replaced by the more neutral category of 'new' peers who may or may not be successfully assimilated.

8 Lord McNally, HL Deb., 12 March, 2001, col. 527.

9 E. A. Smith, 1992, *The House of Lords in British Politics and Society 1815–1911*, Longman, London, p. 93.

10 This took place on 28 March 2001.

11 The Lord Chancellor is always in the Lords, as is the Leader of the Lords. Other relatively recent exceptions include posts taken by the Lord Carrington, Lord Gowrie, Lord Cockfield, and since 1997, Lord Young of Graffham, Baroness Amos, and Lord Williams of Mostyn. Lord Williams of Mostyn was the first Attorney General, head of the Law Officers' Departments, in the Lords for 400 years; and the post is now held by another peer, Lord Goldsmith.

12 See Chapter 9.

13 See Chapter 9 for details.

14 See Chapter 7.

15 The 'elder statesmen' Morgan writes about appear to have been more involved in the House during the 1960s in contrast with their present relative aloofness (*ibid.*, pp. 40–4).

16 Quoted by Lord Holme, 1996, 'The way the wind blows', in A. Jay (ed.), *The Oxford Dictionary of Political Quotations*, Oxford University Press, Oxford and New York.

17 As quoted by Smith, *ibid.*, p. 39.

18 Morgan, *ibid.*, p. 19.

19 House of Lords Membership and Attendance Session 1997–1998, Journal Office, House of Lords.

20 R. Rogers and R. Walters, 2004, *How Parliament Works*, Pearson Education, Harlow, pp. 120–1.

21 See Chapter 10 for details about this ritual.

22 In 1845 when Bishop Samuel Wilberforce took his seat in the House, Prince Albert gave him the following advice: 'A Bishop ought to abstain completely from mixing himself up with the politics of the day, and beyond giving general support to the Queen's government, should take no part in the discussion of state affairs, but he

should come forward whenever the interests of humanity are at stake, and give boldly and manfully his advice to House and Country (I mean questions like the education of the people, the health of the towns, measures for the recreation of the poor, etcetera.)' As quoted by the Bishop of Norwich, HL Deb., 24 June 1997, cols 1492–4. Bishops still tend to speak on subjects with obvious moral content (not wholly unlike those recommended by the Prince), such as marriage, sex, housing, education, overseas aid, and business ethics (though legislation of exclusively moral or political content seems now a rather nineteenth-century concept).

23 Earl Russell, HL Deb., 13 April 1999, col. 627, and Lord Carter, HL Deb., 13 April 1999, cols 627–8.

24 Lord Williams of Mostyn, HL Deb, 15 October 1998, col. 1160. Not all hereditary peers understood the joke.

25 Lord Ashburton, HL Deb., 30 March 1999, col. 366.

26 While the opposition parties decide the order for their own party members, the Government Whips' Office orders the government and Cross-bench peers, and then issues the whole list of speakers.

27 See Chapter 7 for more on the difference between peers.

28 J. McIver Weatherford, 1985, *Tribes on the Hill: The US Congress Rituals and Realities*, Bergin and Garvey, Westport and London. For further discussion of this comparison see Chapters 10 and 12.

4 Restless natives

Until 1999, the British Parliament included several hundred lords and a handful of ladies who were legislators solely by heredity. In that year, an Act of Parliament abolished their automatic right to sit in the House of Lords.

The 'execution' (as they called it) aroused almost hysterical emotion among peers, comically remote from the near-indifference of the rest of the nation. Opposers of the bill tended to see the House – or even in some cases the hereditary peerage – as a vital, beleaguered bastion of decency, family values and national backbone; and in its historical continuity they perceived the sound and majestic foundation of this island's stability and moral fabric (see Figure 4.1). Among the bill's supporters were a number of life peers who saw the aristocracy as a class of hereditary criminals. For them, inherited titles were a blood-stained relic of ancient oppression, expropriation and exploitation, and the pompous rituals and even the sumptuous, pinnacled fabric of the Palace of Westminster itself, symbols of privilege and ostrich-like lack of reality.

In the event, banishing the hereditary peerage was a polite, acquiescent affair, and towards the end the dominant emotion was not political passion, but sadness and hurt. Some qualities that do not do well in the democratic process – humour, irreverence and eccentricity – largely left Westminster with the hereditary peers. Although a political triumph for the government (because the Conservative party in the House was halved, creating near parity between the two main parties), the Act itself was a fudge and a disappointment. Horse-trading enabled ninety-two assorted hereditary lords and ladies to slither into the third millennium still, improbably, as members of the legislature. In addition, the government has so far failed to complete its reform.

TO ALL HEREDITARY PEERS

This is a

CALL FOR ACTION

We can and we must

KILL THE BILL

Four days of intensive debate in your Lordships' House last week and last October have failed to show up any alternative that GUARANTEES the independence of spirit, the breadth of skills and experience, the spread of age and the minimum of party political bias and patronage more securely than does the present composition of the House of Lords.

WE ARE NOT AGAINST REFORM
WE SUPPORT THE ESTABLISHMENT OF A ROYAL COMMISSION

BUT the Commission should examine the workings of parliament as a whole and should not exclude from debate the 700 year old role of hereditary peers.

We accept that the in-built Conservative Party majority is a problem. BUT several acceptable suggestions have been made as to how this might be resolved - including the proposal that our votes should be recorded but not counted in the amendment of legislation.

OUR DUTY IS TO THE CONSTITUTION AND TO THE SOVEREIGN

We sit in the House of Lords by right of Letters Patent signed under seal by the Sovereign.

These grant us and our heirs successively that we "may have hold and possess a seat place and voice in the Parliaments and Public Assemblies and Councils" of the Sovereign within the United Kingdom.

THESE RIGHTS CANNOT BE LIGHTLY SURRENDERED

Together we have a majority in the House. We can defeat this Bill. This is not a matter for party whips: it is a matter of personal conscience and constitutional duty. We should not be bound by any Salisbury convention in a matter of such constitutional importance.

YOU MUST ATTEND THE SECOND READING DEBATE

AND

KILL THE BILL

"The game's afoot"   5th. March 1999

Figure 4.1   Freedom in Action poster: Kill the Bill.

The lion and the unicorn

'In their lust for power, New Labour has slaughtered the sacred cow of socialism and trampled on the beliefs and shibboleths of Old Labour. So, to placate the dogs of the Left, they have thrown them the bone of the hereditary peerage.'[1] But New Labour was, at last, grasping an elusive nettle. Reform had been shirked by a century of governments not just because it was difficult to reach agreement on what was to follow, but, unedifyingly, because it is convenient for any government to have an upper House perceived as democratically illegitimate, as it makes it easier to ignore.

British constitutional history has been a struggle for power between Crown, Lords and Commons. The Crown ceased to be a contender in the seventeenth century, after which competition was between the two Houses of Parliament, and the powers of the Lords are defined principally in relation to the Commons. The Great Reform Act of 1832 ended the Lords' control of the Commons. According to Bagehot, this was when it became a House of revision.[2] By the end of the nineteeth century, through gradual widening of the franchise, power had unequivocally transferred to the Commons. The problem then presented by the Lords was not so much its hereditary component, but the overwhelming size of the Conservative party in it following the Liberal split over Ireland. On the other hand, the fact that it was widely seen as illegitimately constituted made peers diffident about using their veto, and their advice easier to disregard, thus increasing the power of the Commons and acting as a disincentive for reform.

In 1909, the defeat by the Lords of Lloyd George's anti-poverty 'people's budget' turned what had been merely a political debate on the budget into a constitutional crisis between the Lords and the elected government. Re-elected in 1911 with a mandate for constitutional reform, the Liberal government threatened to swamp the Lords with Liberal peers unless the Lords accepted a parliament bill restricting their powers. Reluctantly, peers backed down and the Parliament Act 1911 changed the Lords' power of veto into one of delay. In 1945, to prevent the Lords mangling the Labour programme of reforms following World War II, the Salisbury-Addison Convention was formalised, debarring the Lords from rejecting any legislation proposed in the government's election manifesto.[3] The 1949 Parliament Act, passed under the terms of the Parliament Act of 1911, reduced the Lords' power of delay from two years to one.[4]

The Life Peerages Act 1958, introduced by a Conservative govern-ment, was possibly the most significant reform of the twentieth century:[5] it empowered the Crown, on behalf of the government, to create life peers of either sex, and they revitalised the House. The Peerage Act 1963 allowed women hereditary peers to sit and enabled hereditary peerages to be disclaimed.

In 1967 Harold Wilson's Labour government reached agreement with the Conservatives that hereditary peers should either become non-voting members or be created life peers. This was approved by 251 votes to 56 in the Lords, but in the Commons an unlikely alliance of back-bench MPs led by Enoch Powell (a Conservative right winger) and Michael Foot (of the Labour left) were able to sabotage it. Edward Heath describes what happened:

> the reason why the measure fell was that it was opposed by Michael Foot, who said, 'Away with an upper House – we don't want an upper House at all.' He got a lot of support. On the Conservative side, the measure was opposed by Enoch Powell, who said, 'Let's go back to the 14th century with the upper House.' He got some support. Faced by the two of them, the Government lost their nerve and Harold Wilson said, 'Let's pack up.'[6]

It remained illegitimately constituted even in the eyes of most peers.

By 1996, the House comprised 403 life peers and 769 hereditaries. Of the latter, only seventeen sat on the Labour benches. Although 226 life peers were regular attenders in the House (sitting for more than one day in three) only 205 hereditaries were; and quite a few of them sat on the cross-benches. On a day-to-day basis the Conservative preponderance was thus not always noticeable; but the problem remained that on issues that excited them (or their party leaders) they could always carry the vote. The result was that government defeats were markedly more rare during Conservative governments (see Table 4.1).

In addition, although less than a quarter of the hereditary peers attended regularly, and some made extremely useful contributions to the House, it had long ceased to be possible to justify their being there at all on grounds acceptable to the overwhelming majority of people. In the 1997 general election the Labour party promised in their manifesto to abolish the right of hereditaries to sit in the Lords as 'the first stage in a process of reform', and in 1999, up to a point, they did.

The spaniel

Much of the following narrative took place in secrecy, behind closed doors. Most principal actors in it were immensely helpful in interviews, but each, inevitably, tended to cast himself as hero of his own story. The discrepancies that resulted were reconciled by information from a variety of other sources, and by constant observation in the House.

A Cabinet sub-committee charged with making proposals about

Table 4.1   Government defeats 1974–2003[7]

Government party	Session	No. of defeats
Labour	1975–76	126
	1976–77	25
	1977–78	78
	1978–79*	11
Conservative	1979–80	15
	1980–81	18
	1981–82	7
	1982–83*	5
	1983–84	20
	1984–85	17
	1985–86	22
	1986–87*	3
	1987–88	17
	1988–89	12
	1989–90	20
	1990–91	17
	1991–92*	6
	1992–93	19
	1993–94	16
	1994–95	7
	1995–96	10
	1996–97*	10
Labour	1997–98	39
	1998–99	31
	1999–2000	36
	2000–2001*	2
	2001–2002	56
	2002–2003	83

*Election year, often a shorter session.

reform met in January 1998. Lord Cranborne, Leader of the Opposition in the House, plotted his response. He knew the battle to save all hereditaries could not be won. Neither the public, the Commons, nor the press were sympathetic. Cranborne bluffed. Using his only trump, the Conservative preponderance in the Lords, he threatened the government's whole legislative programme unless compromise was agreed. The Conservative leadership publicly pretended they were losing control of their back-benchers: the hereditaries were up in arms over reform, they said, and might do anything – the Earl of Onslow, terrifyingly, had promised to behave like a football hooligan.

Lord Richard, then Leader of the House,[8] hoped to give the House legitimacy by expelling the hereditary peers and introducing a substantial elected element. He called a meeting in which he and his Chief Whip, Lord Carter, formed one side, and Lords Cranborne and Strathclyde (Opposition Chief Whip) the other. They circled around the tricky subject. Cranborne asked for some ideas on paper; Richard refused. They all met again in Cranborne's home in Chelsea for lunch. Carter and Cranborne talked about farming in the West Country but little progress was made on reform. Subsequent meetings between Lords Richard and Cranborne began to achieve momentum. The Prime Minister looked as if he might agree to a two-thirds elected and one-third nominated house at a meeting on 3 February (that is, about a month after the cabinet sub-committee on Lords reform first met), but other members of the sub-committee (Peter Mandelson, Jack Straw and Nick Brown) pressed for a nominated upper House.[9] When Prime Minster Blair was asked what should be done, he replied: "Try to flush them out but keep your cards close to your chest." Lord Richard mistook this for endorsement and pressed even harder for a part-elected house. The Prime Minister, reput-edly alarmed at the prospect of a more legitimate and therefore stronger second chamber, or perhaps exasperated by Richard's bullish approach, sacked him.

He was replaced by Baroness Jay. This meant that both Labour and Conservative leaders had their fathers in the House: Viscount Cranborne, as the son of the Marquess of Salisbury, had been given a 'writ in accel-eration' enabling him to sit before his father's demise; and life peer Baroness Jay's father, former Prime Minister Lord Callaghan, was also a life peer. The irony that the Labour Leader killing-off the hereditary prin-ciple had her father there with her was enjoyed.

In stricter secrecy, and without the press leaks of earlier talks, Lord Cranborne and the Lord Chancellor (Lord Irvine) began meeting in a private house in Lord North Street to thrash out a more modest agree-ment on reform, focusing on stage one (execution) only. Cranborne was resigned to the expulsion of most hereditary peers if it was agreed that some should remain. He had decided that the election by hereditaries of a proportion of their number would not only retain some of the most useful members until further reform but also exert pressure on the govern-ment to press ahead with stage two (introducing an elected, appointed or hybrid house); and if there were no further reform, the hereditary prin-ciple might last in perpetuity. If the Lord Chancellor failed to agree, the Conservative hereditary peers, Cranborne claimed, would wreak 'Somme and Passchendaele' for this session and the next. Rather than risk their whole legislative programme, the Lord Chancellor, with the Prime Minister's consent, accepted this.

Parliamentary debate of the principle of abolition took place in the House of Lords in October 1998, prior to the introduction of the bill. Baroness Jay opened with a broadside, frostily delivered. Hereditary peers, she told them, were anachronistic and inappropriate for a modern parliament.[10] She warned those who threatened to stand in the government's way that they would be in breach of the Salisbury-Addison Convention. Battle had begun.

There were 114 speakers. The themes and vocabulary of debate quickly became established. During the year-long passage of the bill, and in defiance of Lords etiquette, the same arguments were repeated time and again by different speakers, almost as if they gave reassurance to those preparing to depart. Many equated heredity with family, and, as Baroness Strange put it, 'the family is what civilisation, as we know it, is based on'.[11] Others argued that since the monarchy is a good thing and hereditary, so too should the House of Lords remain. The refrain, 'if it ain't broke, don't fix it', came up more than a few times, and the dangers of meddling with the constitution also recurred, dramatically introduced with a quotation from Talleyrand: 'if the English Constitution is destroyed the civilisation of the world will be shaken to its foundations.'[12] Nor were supporters of the bill innocent: the aphorism that arguing for the preservation of hereditaries was like turkeys arguing against Christmas became wearisome.

Sometimes the debate, though earnest, seemed to lack gravitas: when Baroness Kennedy of the Shaws argued that she would not employ a hereditary plumber, Lord Mackie of Benshie replied that he would because they would have received such good training, and the Earl of Buchan rose to observe that hereditary plumbers and hereditary peers were both splendid. Several suggested with relish that, having her father in the House, Jay herself was an honorary hereditary peer. She looked bored and disdainful. The admirable and often glorious or heroic public service records of hereditary peers and their ancestors were exhaustively explored, but when Labour Lord Williams of Mostyn wound up debate with his own family's service as teachers, enlisted soldiers and tenant farmers, some Conservatives and Cross-benchers dismissed it outside the Chamber as class envy. Claims of the hereditaries to rise above partisan politics were effectively rebutted by Lord Richard: 'I accept that large numbers of them sit independently; they listen independently, they weigh the arguments independently, and then they independently vote Conservative.'[13] The serious arguments had all been put two centuries earlier by Edmund Burke and Thomas Paine;[14] but the debate did serve as a reminder that no two peers agree on how the House should be constituted, so abolishing hereditaries before replacing them at least had the advantage of pragmatism.

Later the same month, at the State Opening of Parliament, the Queen read out the government's legislative proposals from her throne in the House of Lords. Assembled peers and bishops, enrobed and seated, and MPs standing squashed together at the bar of the House,[15] listened with customary respect, until she announced the hereditary peers' eviction. Labour MPs murmured 'Hear, hear'. The Queen appeared shocked; interruption was unprecedented. Peers growled 'Shame, shame' in response. It was a jolt for many of the hereditaries.

Cranborne and the Lord Chancellor had privately agreed on retaining some hereditary peers;[16] now they were haggling over numbers. Cranborne wanted 100 and asked for 150. The Lord Chancellor offered fifteen life peerages in addition to four more for hereditary peers of first creation, as well as places for the Duke of Norfolk and the Marquess of Cholmondeley who would continue as Earl Marshal and Lord Great Chamberlain. Cranborne pushed him up to seventy-five elected hereditaries (10 per cent of the total), and then dreamed up a ruse. The committees, he suggested, and the pool of deputy speakers would be short of members unless fifteen further hereditaries were elected to continue in those positions, making ninety elected and a round total of a hundred. When told, according to Cranborne, the Prime Minister said: 'Well, that all sounds alright but I have to ask Alastair.'[17]

The Conservative Leader, William Hague MP, did not share this view; he was more interested in press coverage of Tories sabotaging Labour legislation than in saving hereditary peers. Repeated defeats in the Lords of the European Parliamentary Elections Bill, intended to warn the government of the dangers of Tory hooliganism, had given him a taste for guerrilla warfare. He insisted the deal should be put to the shadow cabinet. Cranborne knew that would end the secrecy and persuaded him that a constitutional committee of Tory MPs would be preferable. They leaked nothing but rejected the deal. Despite this, however, Cranborne, behind his leader's back, continued secretly negotiating, counting on being able to present Hague with an irreversible *fait accompli*. In December, Hague told Cranborne he planned to taunt the Prime Minister that Labour, having promised an end to hereditary peers sitting in Parliament, was now planning a 'U-turn' by hanging on to a hundred of them. Cranborne's priority was saving the hereditaries, not his party leader, and he lost no time in warning the Lord Chancellor. They decided that, with Alastair Campbell's help, they could save the deal by presenting it as a Cross-bench initiative. Cranborne insisted that Baroness Jay as Leader of the House should approach Lord Weatherill, the Cross-bench Convenor, to front it. (It later became known as the 'Weatherill Amendment'.)

Accordingly, on Wednesday 2 December, Alastair Campbell was to make public the deal at a press conference just after the beginning of Prime Minister's Question Time. That morning, Cranborne told Hague of this, wrongly supposing that he would not raise the taunt at Questions if he knew about the simultaneous press conference. Cranborne added that he was going to tell the Association of Conservative Peers at 4.30 p.m., and would have a signed letter of resignation ready. Hague was furious and did raise it at Question Time. Blair made mincemeat of him, even revealing that Cranborne had finalised the deal without his leader knowing.[18] Later, Hague and Conservative party Chairman Michael Ancram MP, stormed into the Conservative peers' meeting while it was in session, but Cranborne had already succeeded in convincing his colleagues. Hague was obliged to listen to a number of senior Conservative peers argue in favour of the deal, and by the time he spoke, he need not have bothered.

Shortly afterwards Lords Cranborne, Strathclyde and Carrington (former Foreign Secretary) met MPs William Hague, Michael Ancram and Sebastian Coe[19] in Cranborne's office. Cranborne asked whether Hague would like him to resign or to be sacked. The latter. Cranborne and Strathclyde stood by the window concealing their laughter at Hague's anger. Hague asked Strathclyde to take Cranborne's place as Opposition Leader in the Lords but Strathclyde, out of loyalty to Cranborne and the Weatherill deal, declined. Carrington tried emollition, saying that there must be some solution, but none could be found. In fact Hague's predicament got worse. On hearing Cranborne had been sacked, the whole Conservative Lords front-bench resigned.

By 8.45 p.m. Hague was desperate for anything positive to say to the *9 o'clock News*. Finally Strathclyde, knowing Cranborne wanted him to, accepted the leadership provided he could remain free to honour the deal. This was accepted. At 10.30 Hague met the other Conservative front-benchers in Strathclyde's office. Sitting in armchairs in partial darkness with drinks and the television soundlessly on, the room had a vaguely nightclub atmosphere. Hague was trying to restore his credibility with a speech about 'having faith in us' when his audience started giggling. 'Am I saying something funny?' he asked, irritably. They pointed to the TV screen behind him showing soft porn.

The front-bench would not withdraw their resignations unless Cranborne's deal became Conservative policy. Hague, done for, relented. Cranborne later told the press that in Hague's position, he too would have sacked him(self) for, as he put it, 'behaving like a badly trained spaniel'.

The four horsemen

Later in December 1998, in a white paper, the government reiterated its manifesto pledge to do away with hereditaries but its intention to make the second chamber 'more democratic and representative' was overshadowed by opaque promises of 'modernisation.' It mentioned that some hereditary peers might be permitted to stay in an interim House.

Debate of the white paper in the House did not, in general, reach a very high standard. It began with Jay at her most patronising: reform, she said, brought in the Tory backwoodsmen and confused their front-bench. Strathclyde counter-attacked, accusing the government of putting class prejudice before constitutional reform.[20] From this low point debate went downhill. Describing the House of Lords that she first knew in 1986, Baroness Strange said: 'it was like a Victorian children's story which my grandmother used to read to me called The Angel of Love, in which every person is a house and his eyes are windows out of which looks the little angel of love ...'[21] Lord Nunburnholme (who had been thrown out of the Conservative party for his excessively right-wing views, and had told me that he viewed Ghengis Khan as liberal) enigmatically related an obscure Turkish saying: 'If you spit in an Englishman's eye, he will smile; if you spit in his eye a second time, he will say thank-you; if you spit in his eye a third time, he will kill you.'[22]

Backwoodsmen who had never taken any interest in the House and knew nothing about it, stood in the Chamber and pontificated on the constitution like saloon-bar bores. The Lords would unravel, they said, once they were no longer part of it, and a House appointed by patronage could only lead to tyranny. Even regular attenders were panic-stricken. Lord Morris warned that ancient Greek democracy collapsed once the legislative power was nominated by the executive.[23] Lord Glenarthur saw the constitution as a stool with five legs – monarchy, Lords, Commons, judiciary and church – change one leg and the whole stool will rock.[24] Others, too, foresaw destruction. Lady Saltoun of Abernethy was not alone in predicting that the bill would bring about the apocalypse:

> the high road to dictatorship, tyranny and totalitarian government, and, in the end, to civil unrest, rebellion and revolution which we have seen, over the past 200 to 300 years in almost every other country in the civilised world, with all the suffering and misery that such upheavals bring.[25]

Besides Conservatives and Cross-benchers predicting catastrophe, differences were increasingly being expressed by back-benchers in moral terms; each side struggling with desperate passion to establish the superior moral substance of their view of the nation and even the cosmos. Tradition, custom, stability, God, monarchy and the family were weapons on one side; democracy and equity on the other. However, for the government front-bench, democracy had become a tricky zone: if applied to the Lords, the primacy of the Commons might be challenged. Ministers focused instead on a 'modern chamber for the twenty-first century', as if 'modern' – a key New Labour term – had intrinsic value.

There was an emotionally charged sub-text too, more evident outside the Chamber than within. Hereditaries were beginning to show hurt. Some accused the government of cynically manoeuvring for political advantage to reduce the number of Conservative peers, though the Labour objective of political balance between parties was neither unjustified nor concealed. Many saw the plan to exclude them as being motivated by spite and felt the Labour side were gloating, and some Labour peers were smug and even occasionally appeared to be enjoying the hereditaries' discomfort; but the Labour counter-charge of Conservative arrogance had truth in it too.

A working group of party advisers, civil servants and the Clerk of the Parliaments began considering how to elect the hereditary survivors. It was named the 'O Group' by Lord Weatherill. Each party representative pulled in a different direction from the others. The government wanted the instructions to be in *Standing Orders*, rather than in the bill, which could be more easily changed; the Conservatives wanted an elaborate, possibly permanent, electoral system, while the Liberal Democrats were unimpressed by the whole idea. While the O Group worried away, the bill began its course.

It was introduced in the Lords at the end of March. Baroness Jay began the debate, trying to set a more polite tone by acknowledging the contributions made by some hereditary peers, but she also pointed out the absurdity of their presence: 'In this chamber we still confront an ossified system whose days were numbered in the 1900s.'[26] Most hereditaries, too, seemed to be adjusting to the changing tide by adopting a slightly more conciliatory tone, but jokes about guillotines and 'ermine euthanasia' were now considered only marginally amusing. On the second day the Lord Chancellor, who had already angered peers the night before by chatting rather too blithely on the front-bench during opposition speeches, further infuriated them by pompously threatening that if the legislation were disrupted, the Parliament Act would be invoked and the Weatherill Amendment lost.

Conservatives talked of New Labour pandering to the old left, and of constitutional vandalism (the UK constitution being under threat, they said, not only from this bill, but from regional assemblies, the EU and other reforms). Lord Inglewood claimed, fairly typically, that the bill: 'strikes at the very heart of our nation's historic constitutional arrangements which have been in place since the Middle Ages.'[27] It was claimed that the denial of hereditary peers' right to vote in the House was an infringement of their human rights or would devalue the validity of the Great Seal.[28] Again, hereditaries gave themselves credit for guaranteeing political stability, protecting the citizens against abuse of power by governments and defending the monarchy: they warned once more that the whole system would unravel once they had gone. Alarm was expressed that without their restraining influence the floodgates would be opened to an inundation of destabilising socialist measures. In reply Lord Shore of Stepney (Labour) pointed out, very gently, that hereditaries actually weaken the Lords because government is able to dismiss the upper House whenever convenient because of its illegitimate element; and Lord Thurso (Liberal Democrat) observed that it is ridiculed for this reason every time it tries to do its job.[29]

On firmer ground, hereditary peers argued they should not be sacked until the government had a plan for the future. 'No stage one without stage two' became a slogan. There was frustration and a sense of injustice that they would not be among the designers of the new House, and distrust of the life peers as its architects. The point was also repeatedly made, with the hurt of the unappreciated, that the hereditary peerage had done a good job and behaved with restraint. This was only partly true. Those whose angst drove them further, claiming they had never abused their Conservative majority, went too far. Occasionally but regularly, on subjects particularly close to their hearts, or when fiercely whipped (such as for the Poll Tax), Tory backwoodsmen had swamped the vote. Furthermore, since agreement on stage two would have delayed the bill for many years, or possibly indefinitely, the two-step approach made some sense. The painful truth for the hereditaries was that neither the public nor the media had come to their defence in sufficient numbers.[30] Individual hereditary peers who had come to terms with their expulsion, began one by one to make their scaffold speeches – thanking, complimenting and remembering – some, like Lords Carrington and Shepherd,[31] unnecessarily because they were given life peerages later.

Among the enraged, indignant or despairing, some hereditary peers calmly spoke out in favour of their own abolition, like Lord Hardinge of Penshurst, a Cross-bench hereditary who succinctly said: 'clearly I have at present a right, in a purely legal sense, to be standing here making this speech, but I cannot see any philosophical or moral underpinning of that right or any reason why it should exist.' There were abolitionist hereditaries on the Conservative benches too, such as Viscount Blakenham; and the Earl of Clancarty (a Cross-bencher) felt the government should consider more radical forms of democracy such as a peoples' lottery. Similarly, some Labour life peers swam against their tide, such as Lord Winston, the celebrated fertility specialist, who enraged his party by saying that he was not convinced that the government had a clear idea of what the second chamber should do.[32]

One-hundred-and-eighty-three peers put themselves down on the list of speakers. Many referred to the role played by hereditaries in the past. The winding-up took place in the small hours of the second day and many of the previous self-justifying speeches were made superfluous by Lord Williams of Mostyn pointing out: 'the question is not whether the hereditary peers do a good job, but rather by what right they do the job at all.'[33] There was no division after the second reading, but 318 peers stayed after debate to vote at 3 a.m. on a motion about whether the bill would make the House more democratic. This symbolic protest was won by the opposition.

Excluding those that were withdrawn, about 120 amendments were tabled to be debated over six-and-a-half committee days. (These take place in the Chamber and all peers can contribute, see Chapter 10.) One amendment argued that the 1949 Parliament Act was illegitimate; another opportunistically tried to increase the number of peers to be elected; a third proposed the abolition of titles (amusingly rejected by the Labour party). Lord Randall of St Budeaux (also Labour) drove the government to distraction by suggesting a system of weighted voting in the Chamber (to compensate for the Conservative majority) of mind-boggling complexity that would, he proposed, have made the abolition of the hereditary peers unnecessary. When he added that the Clerk of the Parliaments could work out the details of his formula,[34] a peer on the front-benches consoled the clerk quietly with, 'that's just spoilt your day'. One which inspired entertaining exchanges between Earl Ferrers and Lord Williams, concerned whether 'a' or 'an' hereditary peer was grammatically correct. Baroness Jay agreed with the opposition: 'I was brought up to say an hotel', she said.[35] Perhaps only in the House of Lords could this have been carried to a vote, but it was, and at 1.09 a.m., thirty-one members voted for and sixty-three against – another symbolic protest.

Attempts were made to defer the bill until after a Royal Commission, or after stage two had been agreed, or even after a referendum had been held. Were these merely delaying tactics? If passed they would have postponed 'execution' which was the (rather futile) aim of many. But some had a point. Those who argued that stage two was necessary immediately because the House might otherwise collapse into formless anarchy were wrong. Others, however, worried that once the government were rid of most hereditaries, incentives for stage two would not be enough to overcome the political difficulties, and they have been proved right to date. Other amendments were attempts to signal that the House would never be the same again: it was for instance suggested that either the titles or the name of the House should be changed. Only the Weatherill Amendment got through both Lords and Commons. The usual channels[36] had agreed that voting on this should be relatively early in the evening to ensure that plenty of Cross-benchers were still there to vote. Proceedings were hurried along by Jay (to the inevitable ire of Conservatives) and the vote was over-whelmingly in favour of the amendment.[37]

On 17 May, as the end of the committee stage approached, tempers seemed to fray. The usual channels had been unable to agree what time to finish. The Conservative front-bench knew the Cranborne deal obliged them to deliver the bill whatever their back-benchers' feelings, but the threats they had made had ominously come true and they were now really struggling to control some, who were angry, mortified and despairing at their leaders' acquiescence to the bill. Conservatives spoke with elaborate preambles, detail and repetition and withdrew amendments and then tabled them again later; but it became clear mere dawdling was not going to sustain morale. Their leaders needed to give them, and the Conservative managers in the Commons, a treat. A spectacle had to be laid on. They planned a dramatic government defeat.

However, their massive majority had not given Conservatives the useful habit of discretion. Lord Carter (Government Chief Whip) learned via leaky Tory peers that their back-benchers had been told to ready them-selves to vote for an adjournment at 10.30 p.m. He therefore knew precisely what was coming. A little later than the appointed hour, and red in the face, the Tory Chief Whip Lord Henley[38] duly suggested an adjournment on the grounds that the constitution should not be debated late at night. Carter protested that after a go-slow all week, an adjourn-ment would merely waste more time. But Henley pressed his point and, after some increasingly irritable exchanges, the Conservatives won the vote, to the immense satisfaction of their back-benchers. Carter knew what was required of him: theatrically, he looked thunderous and slammed his folder on the despatch box saying crisply that the govern-ment would have to consider how to proceed. His colleagues patted him on the shoulder and murmured consoling words; they assumed his fury was genuine. Journalists reported Carter storming out angrily over this 'unprecedented' action.[39] In fact he had not only known what would happen, but had already put aside the following afternoon to complete the committee stage. In co-operating to provide a little drama he had yielded only an insignificant victory, and helped Strathclyde placate his troops.

On the following day the price had to be paid and the Lord Chancellor began debate tetchily saying that the patience of the country was being tested to destruction. (In fact the country did not seem to notice what was going on, though some people had the impression the whole upper house was being abolished were a little surprised). Exchanges of threats in the Chamber between the parties ensued, covering no useful ground, until each side publicly reminded the other how problematic making deals in public is. The usual channels resumed their secretive control and things ran smoothly once again.

Government ministers disagreed over timing amongst themselves. Baroness Jay wanted to get the final stages of the bill out of the way in July, while others argued for making it the very last piece of business so that the threat of cancelling the Weatherill Amendment could act as a Damoclean sword over the departing hereditary peers who would have no other incentive for restraint. Damocles won.

In June, Strathclyde announced that the Conservative front-bench intended to push only three amendments at the next stage of the bill, which concerned: (1) replacing, by election, elected hereditaries who die; (2) the establishment of a Statutory Appointments Commission; and (3) the validity of the writ. Some of his back-benchers, however, were hell bent on tooth-and-nail resistance. A fighting fund had been established, some of which was used to disseminate information. Money was also raised for a legal challenge to the bill – £25,000 by one peer in an evening in the Bishop's Bar.

Off-the-wall opposition to the bill was led by 'Freedom in Action', whose director was the son of the Duke of St Albans (noble by descent from Nell Gwynne and Charles II), enjoying the courtesy title of the Earl of Burford (see Figure 4.1). A surreal public conference was held at which a pompous QC obsequiously addressed his audience as 'My lords'. The Parliament Act 1949, he said, was invalid, and the House of Lords Bill was hybrid and could be thrown out. Lord Renton pointed out flaws in this analysis but was ignored. Another peer inconsequentially mentioned that he had been conceived in Jamaica and had written to the Jamaicans to ask whether they might help save the hereditary peers. Even the QC thought this unlikely. Freedom in Action, and its representative in the Chamber, Lord Clifford of Chudleigh, struggled for credibility. They sent out 3,500 letters advising peers to vote against the bill and their heirs to protest, but few took any notice. Meanwhile, though the Tory front-bench knew they had to preserve the deal, their back-benchers tried to delay: so whips had to prevent Tory rank-and-file voting for their own party's amendments.

The government had insisted that since the interim House would be temporary, runners-up in the elections should replace elected hereditary peers who died.[40] This would allow the arrangement to fizzle out after all the runners-up had died. At Report Stage, extraordinarily, the Lord Chancellor, under pressure from Lord Strathclyde, but against the wishes of others in government, reversed this. To secure Conservative cooperation in other legislation, or, according to some, because he was not bothered either way, he conceded that by-elections for replacement hereditaries could take place after the first session of the next Parliament (until then, runners-up would do.) This meant a permanent hereditary presence until further reform was introduced. Although many in the Labour party saw by-elections as an unnecessary concession and one that compromised their manifesto commitment to remove the hereditary peerage from Parliament, this went through at third reading.

A motion was passed to refer the bill to the Privileges Committee, to test whether it would breach the provisions of the Treaty of Union between England and Scotland and whether the bill could remove the right of hereditary peers to sit when their writ of summons referred to the whole Parliament (that is, until the next general election). This might have killed it. The buzz around the Moses Room, when they delivered their verdict in October, was as intense as it gets. Esoteric arguments about the validity of writs and the absolute rights of Scottish peers were a sharp contrast to the simple result: the government won.

As peers were taking their places in the chamber for the third and final reading, a bizarre act of protest took place: the Earl of Burford jumped onto the woolsack shouting, 'This is treason'. The doorkeepers hesitated: if he were a fully fledged peer they would not have had the right to oust him until the House said so. The Earl of Onslow – the very man who had threatened to behave like a football hooligan a year earlier – looked horrified and pulled him by the arm. But Burford's script quickly ran dry and after ranting a bit and shouting a few more slogans, he quietly let the doorkeepers lead him out. Government peers were amused, and pleased that the outburst tainted the opposition; many of their opponents, in whose supposed interest Burford had demonstrated, were aghast.

The third reading debate dealt with further amendments, and amendments to amendments. The government saved time by letting through Conservative motions that would be reversed by the Commons in any case. After a rush of peers attempting to speak towards the end, Labour back-benchers lost patience and called for a division. Only eighty-one peers finally voted against the bill. Most knew that exclusion was inevitable, as the Parliament Act would have been used if they defeated the bill. For others, resistance had been emasculated by the promise of resurrection for a few. Even some of those most bitterly opposed to one-stage reform could not bring themselves to jeopardise the chances of survival for colleagues who so badly wanted it and who might stay to defend Parliament.

The installation of a tribal chiefdom

Hereditary peers had been campaigning for their elections for some months: appearing active in the Chamber and at party/Cross-bench meetings, holding drinks parties, or even assigning other peers as campaign managers. As it became clear the bill would be passed, the process of electing ninety hereditaries began in earnest. A closed Procedure Committee meeting (at which I was present) was held in a deathly atmosphere of mistrust to discuss the O Group's proposals. A Cross-bench proposal that the hereditary peers should be elected by the life peers as well as hereditaries was brusquely dismissed by a minister: 'Exploring the metaphysical questions is neither here nor there, it was a deal.' The Tories also rejected it: whether they were trying to avoid a situation where blackbirds elect the cuckoos or trying to ensure that the government moved on to stage two by refusing to help make the system appear more legitimate, they wanted hereditaries to elect hereditaries. Labour did not care, so the three parties were not going to waste time in discussion of the merits of the idea. A suggestion that the bill should be passed before *Standing Orders* were changed, in case it was defeated, brought the response, in clipped tones, that if 'ludicrous fantasies' came about then the *Standing Orders* could be changed back.

The office of the clerk preparing for the elections became the hub of the House. Through the kindness of clerks, I was co-opted as one of their assistants and helped to register peers as candidates and electors. The office was alive with rumour and gossip and had such zing that even peers who came in sad and hurt, left buoyed up. With dignity and wit, lords presented themselves as candidates to face the embarrassment and perhaps humiliation of being publicly ranked. Lord Carter observed to me that it was "the installation of a tribal chiefdom". The country may have been not much moved by it, but for hereditary peers it was life or death. Some made immense efforts to take part. The father of one had died only three weeks before; he had managed to prove his right, take his seat and oath, and register as a candidate, while another came from Australia to do the same. Journalists, peers and senior clerks dropped in to get the latest (it was suggested that a particularly glamorous student working in the office partly accounted for this). One peer registering as a candidate knew so little of the House that when the division bell sounded eight minutes before a vote, he asked me, "What *is* that noise?". (I mentioned this to a peer, it went round the House and to my embarrassment it was in the newspapers the following day). When journalists asked questions about the elections, we smiled and said not a word.

There was indecision. Vacillators were persuaded to stand at the last minute; one decided he was definitely too old to put himself down – until he changed his mind on the last morning; and one registered twenty minutes before the deadline. Another changed his mind when it was pointed out that if he were a runner-up he would get in once one of the successful candidates had died (when asked if he was Conservative, he replied 'just').

There were only eighteen Labour hereditaries in the House, and none registered as candidates until party managers intimated to some that candidacy was their only route to survival. Seven submitted their names. A few, on the other hand, knew that they would be offered life peerages. They were not allowed to say, and acted mysterious. Lord Shepherd pulled out when informed that he, and other former Leaders of the House, would be metamorphosed into life peers. A Conservative told us his decision depended upon whether he was offered a safe Commons seat as he wanted to be where real power was. Front-benchers pondered aloud on whether they would be offered life peerages, but then again, what if they were not? Lord Cranborne decided not to stand, changed his mind and put his name down only to find he was ineligible,[41] and was given a life peerage in any case.

Electoral statements of up to seventy-five words were permitted. Thriller writer Frederick Forsyth wrote one for a friend; Earl Ferrers, grandly, did not submit one (and was elected); Lord Pender used only one word – 'Duty'; Baroness Strange wrote that she brings flowers and loves the House of Lords (she was also elected); Viscount Monckton of Brenchley stood for the Queen and for muzzling cats to stop the torture of mice and small birds. Cross-benchers tended to stress that they were independent; Conservatives, Labour and Liberal Democrats emphasised their contributions and attendance records.

Proportions, meanwhile, were being discussed. The allocation of the seventy-five places were to be in ratio to the number of hereditaries in each party and the Cross-benchers: forty-two Conservatives, twenty-eight Cross-benchers, three Liberal Democrats and two Labour. These numbers had been agreed and voted on. The Conservative voters had to rank their forty-two best candidates in order of preference, the Cross-benchers' twenty-eight, and so on. Many of the latter gave up and called their Convenor for advice. He noted his preferences on the back of an envelope and made suggestions if asked. Unfortunately, one of his inner circle became fed up with consulting the envelope every time someone asked and not only typed, but photocopied and handed out the list with the favourites starred. Those not starred were apoplectic. One threatened to sue and another railed that if it reached the press it would "blow the Cross-benches out of the water". But, because some without stars were elected, it was allowed to fade quietly away.

The remaining fifteen places in the elections, which were for chairmen of committees (as the Lords still calls them) and deputy speakers, were still up for grabs. Since these were to be voted by the whole House, they could all easily have been gobbled up by the Conservatives, but they generously agreed that they should not. The usual channels wrangled, settling on eight Tories, with the Cross-benchers having three, and Labour and Liberal Democrats two each. In the event, for reasons of their own, the Tories decided to allocate nine places to themselves and only two to the Cross-benchers.

On the last evening of registration, as we were finishing off the paperwork, Sir Michael Davies, the Clerk of the Parliaments, bought us champagne, the sassy American television presenter Ruby Wax put in an incongruous appearance, and I had a final drink in the Lords' Bar with a colleague and a 'Stalinist' from the Refreshment Department who favoured guillotining hereditary peers, even though he felt there was "nothing wrong with them as individuals".

Voting took place quietly and rather formally in committee rooms under the supervision of the Electoral Reform Ballot Services. Peers do not have the right to vote in parliamentary general elections, and looked rather ill-at-ease in the little plywood voting booths. 410 voted for 214 candidates. It was a complicated ballot as candidates had to be ranked in order of preference; Conservatives had to choose and rank forty-two. The doorkeepers called out voters' titles as they entered ('His Grace the Duke of Rutland', etc...) so it sounded like an unbelievably grand ball, which was helpful as we crossed off those who had voted.

The count for the deputy speakers' election happened first – in a barren office block in Turnpike Lane, a couple of miles from Westminster – and was subdued, merely a run-through for the real thing. The second count, for the seventy-five, was painfully tense. The scrutineers were peers. One argued that spoilt ballot papers should be allowed where the intention was obvious, but the rest insisted on sticking to the rules. The fifth and sixth positions in the Liberal Democrat election were tied and it was agreed to draw a lot. The numbers 1 and 2 were written on two business cards. The Clerk Assistant picked the card that decided their fate.[42] When it was over the scrutineers visibly relaxed and joked about how Americans get mixed up about titles: chat-show hosts asking a baroness 'Do I call you Bar or Nessie?', and hotels refusing to allow a Baroness and husband with different surnames to share a room.

We returned to the House of Lords, sworn to secrecy about the results. In the attendants' office, one was insisting warmly that the exclusion of hereditaries was exactly like the transition from the Weimar Republic to the Nazi Reich. Hereditary peers had died in world wars for us, he said, and should not be treated like this. Another protested that "we" (enlisted men) died in larger numbers and it was time for their aboli-tion. While they argued, the atmosphere in the Peers' Lobby pinched tighter.

Peers looked embarrassed as they filled the chamber to hear the results. It was one minute to 1 p.m. but the Clerk of the Parliaments did not rise. The Clerk of the Journals had signalled to him that copies of the results were not yet available in the Printed Paper Office. Lord Judd began speaking on an intensely dry subject and the minutes ticked by. Carter sent a message to across the floor of the House to Strathclyde, which was passed down the Conservative front-bench and made them all smile: it explained that there could be no announcement until the photocopier could be made to work. Peers packed into the chamber. The tension rose. Lord Judd said that he had just five more points to make in conclusion, everyone groaned and then laughed. More peers came in.

At long last, in total silence, after an agony of waiting, the Clerk of the Parliaments got up, as if in slow motion. It was the last moment of hope for some. He read out the names, starting with Labour. Then it was the turn of the Liberal Democrats. Earl Russell's bald head looked pink as he leaned forward, his whole body apparently rigid with antici-pation. His name came first, then Avebury and finally Addington, whose hunched shoulders collapsed with relief; he smiled and Russell patted him congratulations. Some names were greeted with approving 'Hear, hear'. As he made his way down the long list of Conservatives, the Clerk got slower and slower, anxious not to make a mistake, adding to the sense of quiet doom.

Peers rushed out to congratulate, console, gossip and to spread the news to the press who were circling like vultures in the Peers' Lobby, but they looked increasingly shocked as the day went on. Proceedings had to be suspended when Lord Montague of Oxford had a stroke and died (presumably in the ambulance as dying is not permitted in the Palace of Westminster). Doorkeepers, already fraught at good friends being expelled, carried his body silently to the ambulance and were virtually unable to speak for hours. There was anger. Baroness Jay's dismissiveness toward hereditaries had reached a new high in absenting herself on that day. One said: "She's at Chequers but I don't care if she is at Buckingham Palace, she is the Leader of the House and she should be here." They vowed to get rid of her.

There was much speculation about how people had voted. A few claimed that Catholics voted for each other. Others pondered the results; one thought 80 per cent of those elected might be useful. A clerk, emotionally, thought it might have been better if all hereditaries had gone: after all, the election personalised the exclusion and admirable people had been lost. The Channel 4 news that evening was respectful, departing from its usual ridicule of the Lords. Just for the evening, because they had voted for their own abolition, hereditaries were heroes.

Lord Cranborne held a memorial party, bussing peers to Hatfield House, his father's seventeenth-century ancestral palace not far from London, like a school trip. Over-sensitive souls accused him of celebrating hereditaries' demise despite his success at saving so many. Black Rod (who had taken infinite pains to be tactful) got into trouble for sending out – on the day the results were announced – a letter with instructions for departing peers, asking them to hand in their passes, empty their desks, lockers and cloakroom hooks. His civil service-like position prevented him from expressing regret in the letter but hereditaries were enraged; they even complained to the press that he sounded like a nanny. On a lighter note, Lord Grenfell, in response to the offer of a cardboard box for papers, quipped, 'I trust it will be large enough to sleep in on the Embankment?'[43]

On 10 November, peers waited impatiently for the return of the bill from the lower House. At 10.30 p.m. the Commons were still debating it, and key back-bench peers who had been killing time with a drink or four in the Bishops' Bar decided it had became the wrong moment to tackle consideration of Commons' amendments. They warned their front-bench that they might have problems with anything they did not like, and the usual channels, seeing they were tipsy, postponed debate to the next day.

The 11 November was not only the final day of the bill, but the last day of the session, and the last day the hereditary peers would sit in the House. It was also Remembrance Day, perceived by some to be more of a Conservative than a Labour event, and was all the more so that day as they felt they had much to remember. In the afternoon the Chamber over-flowed. Peers were in a touchy, difficult mood and a despondent atmos-phere prevailed. I was sitting below bar when a doorkeeper surprisingly but politely insisted on searching my handbag; Black Rod had heard a rumour that someone planned to release a fox into the Chamber and, although we were on friendly terms, he thought it might be me. Moments later Lord Ampthill just managed to stop Lord Nunburnholme drunkenly handing a white feather to Lord Cranborne.

Debate began smoothly. Lord Stanley of Alderley, proposing an amendment to an amendment, looked to the future, hoping people would pay close attention to what followed once the hereditaries had gone. This was echoed by others. Lord Strathclyde made a good-humoured and appropriately partisan speech and Baroness Jay addressed the Chamber with the refrigerated hauteur expected of her. Then proceedings unravelled. Lord Strathclyde spoke to the wrong amendment; Lord Clifford of Chudleigh compounded the error by rising to speak too soon. The Chairman of Committees, absolutely barred by procedure from intervening from the Woolsack, did so, but failed to sort out the muddle, and for ten or fifteen minutes there was pandemonium. The government had done nothing incorrect, but peers were angry and the feeling that blame lay with the executioners was made clear. The Government Chief Whip and others rose to give their own interpretations of what should be happening and the Chairman of Committees tried to intervene again, but every intervention only increased the confusion and mistrust. Baroness Jay rose to try to clarify the situation and to absolve the government front-bench, courteously, but with a patronising air, blaming procedure ('I agree that the procedure is a little complex. One has to have GCSE in double negatives to understand …'), but peers continued trying to speak out of turn. Lord Erroll shouted at Jay 'You guillotined me last time so I do not dare let you get up', but the House was having none of that and checked him with a menacing growl of 'Order, order'. At this critical moment Strathclyde rose and gallantly took the blame for the muddle. A sigh of relief quivered tentatively in the air. He asked that Lord Clifford of Chudleigh, a departing peer, be allowed to speak, which was granted, but immediately he had finished disagreement arose again about which amendment they were discussing. Lords Williams and Ferrers, genial heavyweights from opposing sides, suddenly cleared the atmosphere with this quirky exchange:

> Earl Ferrers: My Lords, I say this with trepidation, but I think there is confu-sion in the noble and learned Lord's mind. I believe we are dealing with Amendment No. 13.
>
> Lord Williams of Mostyn: My Lords, if the noble Earl is right – and he invari-ably is, most of the time – I always agree with him. He is living testimony to that. In fact, we are having lunch together next week.
>
> Earl Ferrers: My Lords, the week after. The noble and learned Lord has misdirected his mind again. He will have to look not only at his brief but also at his diary.[44]

The inordinate laughter of awful tension being released unexpectedly charged the Chamber with good humour. The Chairman of Committees made a pleasantry that it had been appropriate that amendment 13 had caused pandemonium, and the session fizzled out; there were no grand valedictory speeches, no vote, no fox and no final protest. In the adjourn-ment speeches that followed Baroness Jay unbent wholly in a graceful tribute to hereditary peers; and the last speaker in the old House was Lord Weatherill, who had fronted the saving of the ninety-two.

After a half-hour break the House reconvened for the ceremony of Prorogation. The principals were dressed up in red robes and tricorn hats for the occasion. The session's last bills became acts, one after the other, as the Clerk of the Parliaments called '*La Reine le veult*' (Norman French for "the Queen so wishes") for each. This was the moment the axe finally fell for hereditary peers.

Afterwards, peers' offices and the corridors seemed filled with children coming to see their fathers and grandfathers at the Lords for the last time. They walked around the building pointing out pictures of their ancestors, or to their banners in the historical tableaux, or their coats of arms carved and gilded on the walls, some taking leave with difficulty of an ancient historical connection.

Later still, a few hundred milled about and drank a glass of wine in the Royal Gallery. Baroness Jay seemed genuinely sympathetic to those who were departing and pleased some by saying goodbye with feeling, but it wasn't much of a do and soon everyone had evaporated. The anti-climax left the place barren; it seemed odd that they should have departed with their box files but with no ceremony. While the government team went to celebrate the execution and the end of the session, hereditary peers drifted out of the House for the last time.

The morning after

Politics is perceived to be about winning, so discussion of the 1999 reform usually asks, who won? Cranborne achieved both his declared aims of saving some hereditaries and ensuring that government remained under pressure to complete its reform. The Lord Chancellor also won: he managed to kill off the Conservative majority and secured Tory co-operation for one parliamentary session. Although a less co-operative Tory front-bench would have been an irritant to the government, threats of Somme and Passchendaele were hyperbole. The Conservatives would probably not have killed that bill, or others, because hereditary peers did not have public support and the government could have used the Parliament Act to force legislation through. Such resistance would have given the government the excuse to 'modernise' procedures by giving back-benchers less freedom to speak. However, the government did get an additional bill through. (Lord Carter told me that when he went to Lord Strathclyde with the programme of bills for the 1998–99 session he asked for a peace dividend, the Food Standards Bill. Strathclyde replied in a surprisingly easy-going fashion, 'Alright then').

If numbers were all the Cross-benchers would now hold the balance of power, but in practice they are unwhipped and usually vote only in their fields of specialisation, so seldom decide results (particularly after 7 p.m. when they tend to drift away). This leaves the Liberal Democrat party with a critical role. They seem to have won the battle of Lords reform so far, a small compensation perhaps for their under-representation in the Commons.

Parliament and public did less well. While the prospects for further reform appear to be receding, bogged down by dissent, the presence of ninety-two hereditary peers, although admirable as individuals, does nothing to help the credibility of the upper Chamber. When replacement hereditaries were elected from outside the Lords by the remaining hereditaries in the House,[45] media mockery was less than expected but did not do much for the standing of Parliament.

The main thrust of the bill, abolishing the right of 90 per cent of hereditary peers to sit, created rough parity between the two main parties, as the figures in Tables 4.2 and 4.3 show. Since most of the lost hereditaries did not participate very often, and most of the regulars were elected to remain, the day-to-day composition of the House has changed little. For instance, the core group using the library, about 400 peers, was approximately 30 per cent hereditaries before the Act, and is only slightly changed after it. The average attendance dropped from 417 in 1997–98 to 352 in the session after the Act, but around 370 was normal during the 1990s until the new administration in 1997.

However, the House has become more serious and more political, and peers more earnest since the hereditaries' departure. The opposition is showing signs of getting braver, as government defeats shot up to eighty-three in the 2002–03 session, an amendment to the Queen's Speech was won by them in 2003 and a major constitutional bill was referred to a committee for scrutiny by an alliance of Cross-benchers and Conservatives on 8 March 2004. In addition to the increased party activity arising from government and opposition being evenly matched, peers feel they have to prove themselves individually.

Following a strange, sad calm after the 'massacre', the hereditaries who were saved have renewed confidence. They feel more legitimate. Yet another failed attempt to secure agreement on a plan for reform, with the government abandoning a draft bill to remove the remaining ninety-two in March 2004, means that their final abolition, assuming it happens, may take a long time.

Culturally too the House of Lords is changing with the departure of most of the hereditary peers. The absurd constitution of the old House made it easier to understand and forgive the snobbery; it seemed an inevitable part of the colourful, eccentric tapestry. The spoilt arrogance of a few hereditary peers could be maddening but most of those I met were courteous and considerate. Many often passed the time of day with me with affable sociability, generously giving their time and often conveying interesting stories and quirky opinions; countless others greeted me and asked after my family whenever they spotted me lurking in the lobbies.

Table 4.2   Party and peerage of all peers in the House of Lords before the House of Lords Act 1999 (August 1998)[46]

Party	Life	Hereditary 1st creation	Hereditary by succession	Archbishops/ bishops	Total
Con.	171	4	296		471
Labour	147	1	17		165
Lib. Dem.	41	0	24		65
Cross-bench	118	4	199		32
Other	25	0	87	26	138
Total	502	9	623	26	1160

Male: Female = 1056: 104
Lords without writs of summons = 67, Peers on leave of absence from the house = 68
Prince 1, Archbishops 2, Dukes and Dukes of Royal Blood 25+3, Marquesses 34, Earls 169, Countesses 5, Viscounts 103, Bishops 24, Barons/Lords 830, Baronesses 96, Ladies 3*, Total: 1295.
* When a few particular hereditary peerages are held by women, they are referred to as 'ladies' rather than 'baronesses'.

Table 4.3   Party and peerage of all peers in the House of Lords after the House of Lords Act 1999 (January 2000)

Party	Life	Elected hereditary	Elected hered. office holders	Hered. royal office holders	Bishops	Total
Con.	179	42	9	1		231
Labour	195	2	2			199
Lib. Dem.	57	3	2			62
Cross-bench	132	28	2	1		163
Other	7				26	33
Total	570	75	15	2	26	688

Male: Female = 578:110
(Not including 3 peers on leave of absence from the house)
Archbishop 2, Dukes 2, Marquess 1, Earls 27, Countess 1, Viscounts 17, Bishops 24, Barons/Lords 505, Baronesses 108, Lady 1, Total: 688.

Hereditaries' most peculiar feature as a group was their relationship to history. Some – though they knew that personally they were mere insignificant individuals – saw themselves as embodying history. Others had a more wry and realistic attitude to the fact that their family stories embrace the nation's – sometimes even the world's – most well-known turning points. Whether it was Lord Napier and Ettrick recalling his family being excluded from Cromwell's Act of Grace and Pardon, or the numerous peers whose relatives held absolute powers of life and death over vast tracts of Empire, or won prodigious battles by land or sea, or Viscount Oxfuird telling us his ancestors split the atom and married two American presidents,49 the fund of anecdotes was inexhaustible and often funny. Such stuff rests lightly on the shoulders of most hereditaries, merely an archive of amusing tales. For others, possibly with too little else in their lives, it has vastly exaggerated, almost spiritual, significance.

Earl Ferrers asked the bill's supporters not to make their pleasure in trashing the hereditaries too obvious: 'War-whooping for joy or vitriol is rather like kicking spaniels ... Even those accused of the most heinous murder are given the best possible breakfast before they go to the gallows.'50 Now that they have gone, it seems that the second Chamber could usefully retain some of their style. Their perceived democratic illegitimacy inspired humility in many. Their leisurely courtesy, wit and irreverence also seem unlikely to be sustained, to the impoverishment of the nation's political life. The life peers (almost) on their own are creating an atmosphere that is suddenly more professional, serious and work oriented, but the deference demanded by some lifers is no more palatable than the snobbery of some of the hereditaries.

Notes

1 Lord Stockton, HL Deb., 30 March 1999, col. 286.
2 W. Bagehot, 1867, *The English Constitution*, Chapman and Hall, London.
3 An agreement made between Lords Salisbury (Cranborne's grandfather) and Addison that the Lords would not reject government bills proposed in their general election manifesto. Salisbury suggested during the Lords debate on the King's Speech in 1945 that 'it would be constitutionally wrong, when the country has so recently expressed its view, for this house to oppose proposals which have been definitely put before the electorate'. He later specified that the House should not throw out a bill on second reading. See House of Lords Library Notes LLN 97/004, 1997, The Salisbury Doctrine, pp. 24, 31.
4 Apart from this, the Parliament Act 1911 has been used on four pieces of legislation since 1949: the War Crimes Act 1991, the European Parliamentary Elections Act 1999, the Sexual Offences (Amendment) Act 2000 and the Hunting Act 2004.
5 The 1958 Act opened the door for reforming composition, the 1999 Act pushed it further open by creating near parity between the two parties. It is only once further reform is enacted (to abolish the remaining hereditaries and secure either independent appointments or elections or both) that the process will be complete and the relative significance of each step can be judged.
6 Edward Heath MP, HC Deb., 2 February 1999, col. 761.
7 Official parliamentary website, http://www.parliament.uk/faq/lords_govtdefeats.cfm, accessed 10 March 2004, and House of Lords, 2003, *Public Bill Sessional Statistics for Session 2002–2003*, Public Bill Office, House of Lords for the 2002–03 session.

8   That is, Leader in the House of Lords of the party in government.
9   John Morrison, 2001, *The House of Plots in Reforming Britain: New Labour, New Constitution*, Pearson Education, London.
10 Baroness Jay, HL Deb., 14 October 1998, cols 922–4.
11 Baroness Strange, HL Deb., 14 October 1998.
12 As quoted by Lord Belhaven and Stenton, HL Deb., 14 October 1998, col. 1033.
13 Lord Richard, HL Deb., 14 October 1998, col. 946.
14 1790 and 1791 respectively.
15 The railings directly in front of the entrance from the Peers' Lobby and at the opposite end to the throne.
16 The source of this idea is unclear. Some report that the idea was dropped into the Cross-bench suggestion box at the time that a group of Cross-benchers were reviewing options for reform in 1995. In their report they mention that hereditary peers might elect a small number of their order, based on early systems used to elect representatives of the Scottish and Irish peers, but admit it may become impractical. (The Earl of Carnarvon *et al.*, 1995, *Second Chamber: Some Remarks on Reforming the House of Lords*, Douglas Slater, London.) Others have been credited with the idea of elections of hereditaries, one of whom is surprisingly elevated but wishes to remain anonymous.
17 Alastair Campbell, then Director of Communications at 10 Downing Street.
18 At this low point for the Conservatives, Tony Blair was surprised to learn that Lord Cranborne had been spotted carrying two magnums of champagne through Peers' Lobby. It was not clear what the Conservatives had to celebrate, and so caused consternation for Labour. It turned out that the whips had been promised a magnum for each week they delayed the end of the session. They had pushed it from 14 to 26 November.
19 He was ennobled in 2000.
20 Baroness Jay, HL Deb., 22 February 1999, cols 841–2; Lord Strathclyde, HL Deb., 22 February 1999, col. 851.
21 Baroness Strange, HL Deb., 22 February 1999, col. 874.
22 Lord Nunburnholme, HL Deb., 22 February 1999, cols 1051–2.
23 Lord Morris, HL Deb., 22 February 1999, col. 1058.
24 Lord Glenarthur, HL Deb., 22 February 1999, col. 1038.
25 Lady Saltoun of Abernethy, HL Deb., 22 February 1999, col. 970.
26 Baroness Jay, HL Deb., 29 March 1999, col. 12.
27 Lord Inglewood, House of Lords, HL Deb., 30 March 1999, col. 249.
28 Lord Norrie, HL Deb., 30 March 1999, cols 171–2; Lord Glenarthur, HL Deb., 30 March 1999, col. 89.
29 Lord Shore of Stepney, 30 March, 1999, cols 267–8; Lord Thurso, HL Deb., 29 March 1999, col. 125.
30 In a MORI opinion poll, carried out in 1998, only 21% wanted to keep the House of Lords as it was; the rest would have replaced it with appointed peers (11%), elected peers (25%), or a mixture (23%), or abolished it (12%) (http://www.mori.com/polls/1998/t980721.shtml).
31 Lord Carrington, HL Deb., 29 March 1999, col. 27; Lord Shepherd, HL Deb., 29 March 1999, cols 60–3.
32 Lord Hardinge of Penshurst, HL Deb., 29 March 1999, col. 923; Lord Blakenham, 30 March 1999, cols 334–5; The Earl of Clancarty, 30 March 1999, col. 253; Lord Winston, 30 March 1999, col. 154.
33 Lord Williams of Mostyn, HL Deb., 29 March 1999, col. 425.
34 Lord Randall of St Budeaux, HL Deb., 27 April 1999, col. 241.
35 As quoted by Michael Cockerell, 2001, 'The politics of second chamber reform: a case study of the House of Lords and the passage of the House of Lords Act 1999', in

N. D. J. Baldwin, and D. Shell (eds), *Second Chambers*, Frank Cass, London and Portland, p. 128.

36 The Leaders and Chief Whips of the three main parties as well as the Cross-bench Convenor; see Chapter 9 for details.

37 At Lord Onslow's suggestion, the procedural difficulties of trying to deal with amendments to the Weatherill Amendment before it had been passed were overcome by persuading a large number of peers to withdraw their amendments, pass the Weatherill Amendment, and then retable them.

38 When Lord Strathclyde replaced Lord Cranborne, Lord Henley took over as Opposition Chief Whip.

39 Robert Shrimsley, 1999, 'Fury as Tory peers block the Lords reform bill', *Daily Telegraph*, 18 May, p. 2.

40 This system, suggested by a Labour peer, is used by the National Executive Committee of the Labour Party.

41 He was there under a writ of acceleration not a hereditary peerage, so was not eligible to stand, but would lose his right to sit as Lord Cranborne after the House of Lords Act because he was there 'by virtue' of a hereditary peerage. He subsequently sat as a life peer (Baron Gascoyne-Cecil) but then took a leave of absence.

42 Only the first three Liberal Democrat peers got back into the House, but since 'fastest losers' would take the place of those peers that died, their relative position could have been significant in due course.

43 An area in London well-known for its homeless population.

44 Earl Ferrers and Lord Williams of Mostyn, HL Deb., 11 November 1999, col. 1463.

45 In the case of the election of a new Labour hereditary peer, it was not quite as embarrassing as anticipated because the one remaining hereditary peer was joined by two hereditary Labour deputy speakers as electors.

46 See the parliamentary website: www.the-parliament-stationery-office.co.uk.

47 The 1998–99 session had an average of 446 but was probably atypical because the House of Lords Bill made it a particularly interesting year and for many, it was their last. See www.parliament.the-stationery-office.co.uk/pa/ld199798/ldbrief/ldfaqs.htm, accessed 25th April 2001.

48 See Chapter 12 for details.

49 Lord Napier and Ettrick, HL Deb., 30 March 1999, col. 349; Lord Tanlaw, HL Deb., 15 October 1999 col. 1138; Lord Oxfuird, HL Deb., 23 February 1999, col. 1024.

50 Earl Ferrers, HL Deb., 23 February 1999, col. 65.

5 A social directory

Lords and Commons

Back-bench and Cross-bench peers rarely meet MPs. Except for front-benchers and ex-MPs, lords and commoners are kept apart socially; neither visits the other's bars or dining rooms and there is no common meeting place. There are two exceptions: the Lords' Bar is a popular meeting place for MPs who are having illicit affairs, and the newly formed Parliament Choir includes MPs, peers and even staff. Besides these, members of the same party from the two Houses attend the same party political meetings and work together on particular bills; and joint committees and some all-party groups entail regular contact between members of the two Houses. Nevertheless, the two bodies (peers and MPs) in the same palace are separate enough that one can almost forget the existence of the other at times; and it is probably healthy: after all, they are structurally opposed and the function of one is to hold the other to account.

The unpredictable and unsociable working hours, comparable proce-dures, abundant bars and dining rooms, rigorous questioning of minis-ters, noisy back-benchers and so on, make the two Houses appear similar. But universal suffrage and media interest have put different pressures on them, and they have evolved accordingly. The paramount interest of many MPs now is ensuring their own re-election, so in the Commons party-political point-scoring often replaces reasoned debate. For them, entries in Hansard are desirable, their constituency press is better, and nationwide publicity a huge boost. Peers, on the other hand, have no constituencies, are influenced by lobbying groups but have no need to be accountable to them, and remain almost untouched by the media. They have life tenure; most are unworried about outsiders, seldom court publicity and influence each other usually only to improve legislation.

While Commons debate is often raucous, the Lords are decorous. Most see their proceedings as understated and considerate, and as one peer put it: "A sharp intake of breath here is the same as a yah-boo there." The observation, "That vicious tribe down the corridor – now they are cannibals", reflects a typical Lords attitude, as does, "If there is a difference between the Commons and the Lords, the former is like jungle warfare while the latter is like being parachuted into the desert. In both places, it is war."[1] Lords' wit can be fierce but tends to be dry. Self-regulation functions through courtesy: peers give way to expertise, insisting on fairness in the allocation of speaking time between parties and the Cross-bench group. Many suppose it is like a Quakers' meeting. It is pointed out by MPs that the Lords can afford to be courteous because it has less power.

Neither House holds members of the other in high regard. Peers complain that the quality of MPs has declined. An ennobled ex-MP felt: "The House of Commons has sadly been infiltrated by a generation of politicians who are not too sure what they believe in or why", and former Foreign Secretary Lord Howe warned that 'clones of the clowns' are not wanted in the upper House.[2] MPs, for their part, mostly assume that the Lords remains sleepy, if not moribund, dull and stuck in a time warp. I was asked in the Commons: "How can you stand that place, doesn't the stink of urine get you down?" All parties are uncomplimentary:

> There is bred into every member of the House of Commons a contempt for the House of Lords. They always think – particularly Tory ministers in the House of Commons – that their House of Lords colleagues are, one: very stupid, two: unversed in the ways of the world and three: completely igno-rant about politics.[3]

Most of the time, there is little antagonism between parties in the Lords; they have less to hide from each other, and, perhaps because whipping is milder, peers of different persuasions fraternise amicably. Most are no longer ambitious and have no time for the exaggerated party loyalty necessary in the Commons for promotion. They owe whips nothing. No one can sack them, the only incentives that can be offered them are well-placed offices, committee places, and overseas trips, and the only threat available to whips is to inform the party leader of disobedience. Peers who reliably toe the party line do so because they want to, usually because they are convinced that their party is pursuing (or preserving) the highest moral aim, and out of loyalty.[4]

Peers' ranks and background

When I first ventured into the palace three main types of peers could be found:

- life barons and baronesses, including law lords;
- hereditary peers of various ranks, including those of first creation;
- archbishops and bishops.

All life peers are barons or baronesses. Hereditary peers may be (in ascending order of rank) barons, viscounts, earls, marquesses, dukes, and dukes of royal blood, or, if one of the women peers by succession, baronesses, ladies or countesses.[5] The oldest extant peerage was created in 1264 and is held by the 28th Baron, Lord De Ros, an upholstered furniture-maker. Even before the House of Lords Act 1999, most regular attenders were either life peers (52 per cent) or had succeeded to peerages created during the twentieth century.[6]

Although the three groups were distinct, there were always anomalous creatures, such as Lord Cranborne, who received a writ of acceleration enabling him to sit in the House while his father remained alive, and is now a life peer but on leave of absence, and Lord Selkirk of Douglas, who disclaimed an Earldom but later accepted a life barony. The House of Lords Act 1999 complicated matters by adding new categories: hereditary peers who, elected by other peers, retained the right to sit as members; all the hereditary peers of first creation (except for most of the royals), who were given life baronies and so never left the House; and excluded hereditary peers who were given life baronies and returned.

During debate on reform Baroness Jay drew attention to the restricted background of hereditary peers:

- 60 per cent were landowners/farmers;
- 42 per cent had careers in the armed forces;
- 1.4 per cent described themselves as workers;
- 45 per cent went to Eton;
- 37 per cent went to Oxbridge.[7]

Although farmers, financiers and the services were over-represented greatly before most hereditaries were swept away, there was more occupational heterogeneity than now. Peers included civil servants, economists, writers, insurance or stockbrokers, teachers, architects, accountants, doctors, artists, police officers, engineers, clergy, and, more unusually, restaurateurs, dentists, art dealers, publishers, market researchers, and nurses. A golf club proprietor, a racing driver, a racing

Table 5.1 Peers' work experience after the House of Lords Act 1999 (1999/00)[9]

Experience	Regulars*	All peers**
Voluntary sector (unpaid)	218	462
Company director	94	235
Former MPs	90	185
National Service + WWII	74	179
Local councillor	80	133
Barrister	39	117
University lecturer/professor	37	93
Judge	15	66
Researcher	34	62
Governor (school, college)	29	56
Adviser to political parties	29	54
JP	28	46
Manager	26	45
Civil servant	16	45
Finance	16	40
Arts	17	40
Trades union official	24	37
Theatre	13	32
Journalist	18	31
Editor	16	30
Business	13	29
School teacher	15	25
Solicitor	15	24
Voluntary sector (paid)	14	23
Armed forces (career)	11	23
Farmer	15	22
Engineer	9	17
Accountant	8	17
Marketing	8	14
Writer	8	12
Banker	4	12
Doctor	2	11
Publisher	5	7
Police officer	2	7
Ambassador	1	7
Social worker	4	6
Economist	5	5
Stockbroker	3	4
Architect	1	3
Dentist	2	2
Labourer	1	1
Total	1059	2249**

* Regular peers attend for more than 100 days a year. Those arriving during the parliamentary session have been put into the category of "all peers" even if they attended regularly.

** Most peers fall into more than one category so the total greatly exceeds the number of peers in the House. (Source: Crewe and Kruger, see p. 129, n. 28.)

Table 5.2   Type of university by party/group 1999/2000

Tertiary educational	Con	Lab	Lib Dem	Cross-bench	Other	Total
Oxford	55	32	19	43	13	162
Cambridge	52	34	12	43	15	156
Other university	51	77	19	52	4	203
All universities	158	143	50	138	32	521

Source: Crewe and Kruger, see p. 129, n. 28.

manager to the Queen, a zoologist, an electrician, a theatre manager, a photographer, a pilot, and a grocer were all one-offs.[8] Among both hereditaries and lifers there are large numbers of company directors, media people, political party workers and voluntary sector managers. Disproportionate numbers of life peers are or have been in academia, industry, law, business, trade unions, banking, local government or the House of Commons.

Until the end of the nineteenth century, most titled people owned land. This number had been declining and the exclusion of most hereditaries reduced it further. The proportion with artisan and artistic occupations also reduced, and that of professional people increased (see Table 5.1).

Lawyers, company directors, former MPs and academics now dominate. The emphasis has shifted since the 1980s when the main categories of all peers were: landowners/farmers (44.4 per cent), public service/administration (29.4 per cent), industrial (17.7 per cent) military (15.4 per cent), financial (10.3 per cent), and lawyers (10.2 per cent).[10]

Of course members of the House of Lords cannot sit in the Commons,[11] but they may be members of other parliaments, such as the European Parliament or devolved assemblies. In 2002 all three presiding officers of Scotland, Northern Ireland and Wales were peers. Although old hands complain that the 'new' House is over-crowded with peers from the voluntary sector, there are, in fact, rather few working in charities or voluntary organisations. Peers are now a well-educated lot: the vast majority are graduates, most still from Oxford or Cambridge (see Table 5.2).

Hereditary peers are more likely to live abroad (sixty-two before the House of Lords Act), while life peers (or their parents) are more likely to have their origins in other countries. There are, for example, life peers who originally come from Antigua, Australia, Bangladesh, the Caribbean, the Czech Republic, Germany, Hong Kong, Hungary, India, New Zealand, Ruthenia, South Africa, Tanzania and the United States.

'The office'

'The office' is a principality, independent of the rest of the civil service, run by the Clerk of the Parliaments, who is appointed by the monarch and dismissible only by an Address of the House of Lords to the Sovereign. He and his four hundred staff serve the House of Lords not the government or Parliament as a whole. The office has two parts: the Parliament Office, run by clerks, and Black Rod's Department.

The elite, twenty-five graduate 'career clerks', manage the Parliament Office departments, which are those most directly concerned with the legislative, judicial and committee work of peers. There are also various semi-independent fiefdoms headed by specialists who have either worked their way up or have been brought in after a career elsewhere. Hansard (the Official Report) produces a written account of proceedings; the Library offers research services, publications and other materials; the Accountant's Office has expanded over the years to deal with the Treasury's demands for greater financial management; and Parliamentary Archives (until recently named the Record Office) stores parliamentary documents in the Victoria Tower, making them available to peers, staff and, where appropriate, the public. The House of Lords Refreshment Department encompasses three restaurants, one canteen, three bars, three function rooms and a gift shop.[12] Staff in these fiefdoms tend to remain outsiders, even after many years and, although not treated unkindly by the career clerks, never become 'one of us'. Security, office facilities, building maintenance, ceremonial events and practical services for peers are provided by Black Rod's Department, with the Gentleman Usher of the Black Rod and Serjeant-at-Arms (one person) as its head, and door-keepers, attendants and housekeepers as his troops (see Figure 5.1).

The title 'Clerk of the Parliaments' was first used in the sixteenth century when the job became continuous from one Parliament to the next.[13] Before that the responsible official was the Clerk of the Parliament and the first was probably John Kirkby in 1280.[14] There are several different kinds of clerk in the Lords, but the Clerk of the Parliaments, like other senior clerks, is appointed only from the cadre of career clerks, the elite of Lords administration.[15] Once recruited, clerks' prospects rest in the hands of the Clerk of the Parliaments, who may promote and keep them in the loop, or not. Until the 1960s these clerks were male, usually ex-public school and Oxbridge, and often had relatives and friends among the hereditary peerage. An older clerk commented wryly that he and others like him had spent their whole lives under finials. Another observed, loftily, that when applying for a clerkship, "you had to have a good degree, so that they knew you were a superior person". It was expected they would spend their whole careers in the House. Fitting in

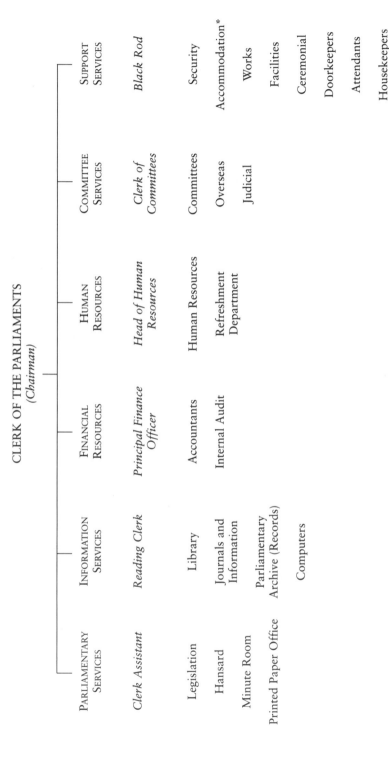

Figure 5.1 Organogram (House of Lords Human Resources office, July 2004).
*Accommodation means office facilities for peers.

CLERK OF THE PARLIAMENTS
(Chairman)

PARLIAMENTARY SERVICES	INFORMATION SERVICES	FINANCIAL RESOURCES	HUMAN RESOURCES	COMMITTEE SERVICES	SUPPORT SERVICES
Clerk Assistant	*Reading Clerk*	*Principal Finance Officer*	*Head of Human Resources*	*Clerk of Committees*	*Black Rod*
Legislation	Library	Accountants	Human Resources	Committees	Security
Hansard	Journals and Information	Internal Audit	Refreshment Department	Overseas	Accommodation*
Minute Room	Parliamentary Archive (Records)			Judicial	Works
Printed Paper Office	Computers				Facilities
					Ceremonial
					Doorkeepers
					Attendants
					Housekeepers

required good manners, dressing well and "having breeding". New recruits were given an office, but no work for weeks or months, until they could confidently look as if they knew what they were doing even when doing nothing. They took luncheon together at their own long table in the peers' dining room, and familiarity with lesser orders was unknown. Most had private incomes and wore tweeds on Fridays, if they worked at all, ready for the weekend in the country. The work was light: administration was less demanding and committees did not exist. When they wanted something they called clerical staff, all former naval petty officers, for any trifle: to riddle the fire or fetch paper, water, coffee, envelopes, and coal. As one former clerical officer put it: "The clerks were upper crust. We called them 'sir' ... You even took their clothes to the laundry."

The 1964 Labour government brought with it a less hierarchical culture, and by the 1970s longer sitting hours and the introduction of committees made reform urgent. Until then the Clerk of the Parliaments made appointments as he chose. (In fact, the civil service open competition system of recruitment had been introduced in 1870, but it was probably never systematically applied[16]). Employment and equal opportunities legislation led to professionalisation of the personnel work and applicants to clerkships have had to take 'fast-stream' exams since 1974. Those who came in by the previous 'hit-or-miss' system describe the new intake as less grand, more serious, ambitious and hardworking. When committees subsequently proliferated, 'retreads', fast-streamers who had already had careers in the civil service, were recruited to work in the Committee office. Women clerks, arriving in the early 1980s, reputedly broke down much of the traditional formality of clerkly culture. By the mid-1980s, tweeds were rare and clerks and staff working closely together usually addressed each other by first names. By the middle of the 1990s younger clerks would even socialise with non-clerks, eating together, meeting for pool evenings and inviting each other to functions.

Working practices have developed more slowly. This is attributed to the complexity of Parliament as an organism and to the fact that, geographically, it is dislocated. Reviews and reforms periodically take place within each department, many of which are highly efficient, but physical fragmentation inhibits overall management consistency and there is a tendency towards conservatism as far as the whole is concerned.[17] Until very recently, there was no management board so that, aside from the top three clerks, few staff had had much idea of what went on in other parts of the organisation or in the office as a whole. The trio of clerks at the top met daily, but regular meetings did not take place between senior departmental managers. The Parliamentary Archives, so staff told me, knew no more what the Information Office was up to than a member of the public.

The management structure was changed in 2002. Lord Tordoff (then Chairman of Committees), introduced a management board and streamlined the domestic committees to make the Office more coherent, efficient and responsive. Clerks were delighted, but some resistance had to be overcome among peers.

Most changes undergone by British public institutions have also taken place in the Lords. Information technology has revolutionised communication and the production of documents. Financial management has been overhauled:[18] the budget of the House has been divided into twenty-three areas and the Clerk of the Parliaments (Accounting Officer since the 1880s) is responsible for making sure each meets its aims and objectives. A new system of performance-related pay has been introduced. The effect of recruitment by open competition has been profound: besides the clerks, secretaries are less 'sloaney',[19] attendants and doorkeepers are no longer all former cavalry non-commissioned officers (the infantrymen went to the Commons), and no clerical staff are ex-navy petty officers.

Efforts have also been made to improve promotion prospects. The Human Resources Office (formerly the Establishment Office), responsible for personnel, has introduced opportunities for training and study for new qualifications. Obstacles remain: the independent fiefdoms tend to work so separately, and with so little contact between each other, it can be difficult to cross between departments. Jumping into the college of career clerks would be the trickiest feat of all. No one has yet done so, although the recently appointed Clerk of the Printed Paper Office (a clerk by title, but not a career clerk) has come close. He is allowed in the sacred precinct (the Chamber), doing division duty (crossing off the names of peers as they vote) but does not deal with the most sacred area of all, parliamentary procedure. A senior clerk has expressed determination to break down barriers by recruiting more graduates to lower management who might then be encouraged to apply for clerkships.

The Human Resources Office has also made some progress recruiting and promoting black and ethnic minority staff, but none has yet risen beyond middle management, and the vast majority are at the bottom of the hierarchy.[20] Those who stick it out are highly thought of, but at a cost. They are 'put in their place' by some peers or ignored in favour of white staff, and the peers who do not assume that black staff are less efficient are rewarded with lightning speed service. The occasional racist joke, and giving the worst jobs repeatedly to black or Asian staff, reveal that a few are ill at ease with black and Asian colleagues.

Strides have been made in eradicating sexism. Twenty years ago a woman head of department would have been a dream, but as women peers have become increasingly important their example may have altered preconceptions held by staff. Now there are three female department heads, and in addition two women clerks have recently held the vital and challenging post of Private Secretary to the Leader of the House and the Government Chief Whip, and a fifth of the career clerks are women. Male peers are gallant to women staff, opening doors for them for example, but some still tend to assume that they are secretaries.

Working in the palace

On the whole, staff enjoy working in the palace: they describe it as steeped in history, a showpiece, magnificent and breathtakingly impressive. Some spend their first weeks getting hopelessly lost which adds to the mystery and awe. They make comparisons between the Lords and a public school, an Oxbridge college, a family, a town, a theatre, television, a ship, a high-profile military headquarters, a sacred place, or Fawlty Towers. Some are ambivalent about the building as a workplace as it is "not always suited to a modern-day working environment", and chronically short of space. It is pointed out that most staff now work in outbuildings while some of the peers' offices are empty most of the time.

They also enjoy the long holidays, camaraderie, courtesy, the friendliness of the peers, the happy atmosphere, their colleagues' dedication to public service, the buzz of being at the centre of politics, 'getting a show on the road', and the antiquated but entertaining style. Some consider it an honour to work there. Those who have taken early retirement from the civil or armed services tend to be particularly content. Some junior staff complain about pay, lack of prospects among non-clerks, lack of career planning for clerks, the deference expected by peers, resistance to change, old-fashioned attitudes, hierarchies, late nights, long hours, and slow or impenetrable decision-making systems. An executive officer wrote that he had 'never worked anywhere with such a tendency for "precedents" to be a governing factor in all matters'. A clerk pointed to the 'inertia of certain practices and conservatism of some staff – at all levels. Though an initial hostility to change of any kind can ultimately give way to acceptance, it can be hard work.' Many clerks act with alacrity when faced with problems and are impatient for updated working practices, but some revel in the traditionalism of the institution and its members.

Those who have worked elsewhere report favourably on Lords management. The civil service is a little less formal, but adopted a hard-nosed attitude to staff during the 1980s, according to former civil servants. The Lords, to its credit, did not. Relations between junior and middle-ranking staff and the upper echelons are mostly cordial. It is not democratic, there are no effective channels for communication from bottom to top, and it is old-fashioned and paternalistic, but it is not a stressful place to work and, while it is not, on the whole, a berth for slackers, it is less macho and competitive than the commercial world, according to those who have worked in both.

In the Commons, the larger office means that senior and junior staff rarely train together or even meet, whereas in the Lords all grades attend some training courses together. The Commons federal structure, with its departments all responsible to a commission, contrasts with the simple hierarchy of the Lords, where decisions are easily and quickly made, at the top. According to a staff member who had worked in both, the Commons is a collection of disputatious oligarchies while the Lords is a benevolent dictatorship.

Though the Commons has political primacy, the Lords' staff tend to prefer working where they are. Those who have spent time in both report that peers are friendlier, more polite and more appreciative than MPs, who infuriate staff by their disregard of rules. Senior Lords staff view their Office as more liberal and progressive than their counterparts in the Commons, whose top officials are said to be highly resistant to any change, and, in particular, to ideas originating in the Lords.

Lords and Commons staff work co-operatively together, but on rather few occasions (except for the two top clerks and the Private Secretaries to the Chief Whips from both Houses, who work closely with each other).[21] The separation in work is echoed in leisure; social interaction between the two is minimal. The 'E Club' was set up to transcend barriers, and does so for a few. Founded just after World War II, it was so named because members thought, wrongly, that they had been using dining room 'E'. The members are not necessarily officers or even the most senior staff (but tend to be or become heads of departments) and are invited to join because they are thought to be congenial people. They meet two or three times a year for lunch, or to go on a trip, such as tours of the Foreign Office and of the parliamentary sewers and boilers. Whoever is chairing the occasion usually says a few lighthearted words about their job but otherwise their activities are social. Plenty of non-members did not know about it until suspicions arose that it was a kind of freemasonry, which led to the publicising of its limited and innocent role. However, some non-members remained unconvinced.

Like any institution, the House of Lords has its rascals. Until recently, one group of junior staff covered for each other so that every day one could take an illicit paid day off. Another group spent more time drinking in the Sports and Social Bar than working. It was not unheard of for a few staff to sleep in the building, though it was against the rules, and to take money on the side by charging for jobs done during work time. But the scale of the problem was minute and new systems have been introduced to prevent repetition. The vast majority of staff would be horrified to learn about this modest sleaze, even if alcohol is surprisingly widely tolerated.

Both the separation of fiefdoms and the status hierarchy are accentuated by geography. The offices nearest the Chamber tend to have the grandest occupants; so the Principal West Front is like Knightsbridge, where the three top clerks and Black Rod reside. This is followed in descending order of status by the Library Corridor, First Floor West Front, First Floor Committee Corridor, Second Floor West Front, Second Floor Harcourt Corridor, Basement, where you find Printed Paper Office staff, and finally 'Estabs' – accountants, committee clerks and others outside the palace – the equivalent, perhaps, of Tower Hamlets. Geographically the most detached of all is the Parliamentary Archives, situated in and beside Victoria Tower, and its denizens feel most distant from the business of the Lords.

It is essentially culture rather than geography that separates the two main divisions of Lords staff: the Parliament Office and Black Rod's Department.

The Parliament Office

Clerks

The word 'clerk' most particularly applies to the twenty-five[22] career clerks at the top. They tend to see themselves as belonging to an exclusive college; and in fact, they do. Although even the most senior clerks are far more accessible and visible to junior staff than their equivalents in civil service departments, and clerkly stuffiness is much less now than it once was, some still display a certain aloofness. When one retires, traditionally only clerks were invited to the retirement function. A few continue to use the clerk's private table in the peers' dining room. One said he would feel awkward finding himself beside non-clerks, as, with little in common, they would run out of conversation. Only a few years ago 'baby clerks' were still instructed not to talk socially to more junior staff, and a few still claim that familiarity makes managing those beneath them difficult. Clerks habitually clubbed together to buy wedding presents, until recently when other staff asked to be allowed to contribute to a clerkly gift. The dispute that ensued had to be adjudicated by the highest relevant authority below the monarch: the Clerk of the Parliaments decided that anyone could contribute to wedding-gifts for clerks. Several non-clerks advised me never to criticise a clerk; they may do so themselves but if an outsider attacks they close ranks. Even clerks complain that some of their colleagues are tradition-bound: they resist giving up mundane tasks on the grounds that they have been done by clerks for hundreds of years. A review by civil servants suggested that the whole office, including clerks, was overgraded, but nothing came of it and the report is not available.

Rivalry between clerks is stupendous. Where once they progressed effortlessly toward the top job, now Buggin's turn[23] is no longer the rule and clerks vie for the few plum posts. The peculiar clerkly culture undoubtedly increases their competitiveness. With the exception of a handful of younger ones, they still compete at being 'clerkly', meaning precise, politically neutral, clever, but above all, infallible. Clerks should never make mistakes. They work hard and fast, with awesome efficiency and intelligence. One of them, the current Reading Clerk David Beamish, surprised no one when he won the TV programme *Mastermind*. Older clerks are often tough on mistakes made by their juniors: in Oxbridge tutorial style, they write acerbic or furious comments in the margins of documents. A polytechnic-educated clerk disliked such abrupt ways of communication which was, reputedly, partly why he left after only a few years. Non-clerks find the focus on grammar and spelling, rather than content, maddening. One recalled the comment on a report: "You have had no classical education but data is plural." The clerkly response is that mistakes are distracting. Their method of communicating advice has softened greatly in the last few years, and in any case, a culture of perfectionism, however irritating to those not part of it, may be necessary for the work they do in the Chamber and committees.

Their particular pride is in serving all peers impartially. On occasion they give advice to one side about a tactic in the Chamber and then, if asked, tell the other how to thwart it. Some are reactive and minimalist about how much information to give to peers; their advice tends to be conservative. Others are more pro-active, intervening to give procedural advice before they have been asked for it, and tend to be more reforming. Lords clerks probably have more influence than their counterparts in the Commons, as one explains:

> "Part of the reason for this is that there is much more room for manoeuvre. In the Commons clerks are much more like policemen, the rules are laid down and they have to advise about them only. But in the Lords the flexibility means that clerks can say 'You could do this, and then that might happen. Alternatively, you could do that.'"

Some relish the ceremonial and the court dress, and most look forward to their duties at the table in the centre of the Chamber during legislative sessions. One was asked by an outsider, at which point in their career they can give up dressing up in silly clothes and paying court to peers. He explained that that is the state they aspire to. Of the nine clerks who undertake table duty, one, in an admission of self-doubt rare for clerks, said: "It is gruellingly boring and hideously worrying, one might not know the answer." A few find the flummery a waste of time.

Clerks are often given managerial responsibility shortly after they arrive. Staff are not always happy with this and report that they may be brilliant at handling amendments, proof-reading, or summarising a discussion but can lack management skills. Some staff claim that the younger clerks have to prove their worth and find it difficult to ask advice, particularly from non-clerks. They get around this by asking 'How would you do this?', then pronouncing 'That's given me something to think about' and adopting it as their own.

Clerks as a group are criticised for their snobbery, privileges, exclusiveness and intolerance of mistakes, but critics are almost unanimous that these have declined enormously in recent years, and clerks are deeply appreciated as individuals. They are, with few exceptions, perceived as intelligent and easy to work with. It is not the individuals but more the membership of the clerkly college, with its practices and stuffy attitudes, that grates the nerves of other staff. The Clerk of the Parliaments during my time, Sir Michael Davies, was both respected and liked.

The independent fiefdoms

The four semi-autonomous fiefdoms – the Library, Parliamentary Archives, Hansard and the Refreshment Department – are officially part of the Parliament Office but function quite separately. Staff within them tend to identify with their departments rather than with the House of Lords.

The Refreshment Department

Refreshment personnel describe themselves as one family despite its multicultural and cosmopolitan character. The relatively high proportion of foreigners, however, has caused resentment. One black British member complained: "These foreigners come in and are taking our jobs, and they don't even have any English at all." Some groups are perceived as particularly volatile. After a manager stopped a fight in the kitchen he explained: "It's just a Spanish problem ..." They see themselves as separate from, and livelier than, the rest of the Parliament Office. Most feel they are working in a restaurant with school holidays and, as one put it, the atmosphere of a ship. The refreshment managers, almost all catering specialists brought in from outside, are a cohesive group. They lunch together at 2.30 p.m. and have other regular meetings. They have little time for socialising but between them they know everyone in the Lords because they serve them all.

The Library

The Library has research clerks but they are not in the college of career clerks. Although more highly qualified than career clerks when first recruited, as specialists they are lower in the hierarchy and have fewer opportunities for promotion. They take pride in their demanding role, providing information for peers to use in revising laws and holding the government to account. Library staff socialise with each other but rarely with others. Every week a large group meets in the Lords' Bar. Within, there is a significant gulf between library clerks and assistants; the former conduct research for peers while the latter provide library services and handle peers' enquiries. Managers try to avoid factions forming by rotating those who do research with those on the desk.

Hansard

Hansard harbours an even clearer split between two groups of staff. Despite the intensity of their work and their common goal in producing (very quickly) the Official Report of parliamentary proceedings, reporters and editors scarcely speak to each other. They sit in adjacent rooms and, for meals, the reporters go to a canteen while the editors use the press dining room. Both groups work extremely hard and take few breaks, if any, which leaves little time for socialising; and since even their work does not bring them into direct contact with any other staff, they are isolated. Most of the editors were once reporters, and most of the reporters are women who used to work in the courts. The reporters tend to complain that editors see themselves as superior. Editors view reporters in general as a hive of revolution and anti-establishment attitudes, while they perceive themselves as calm and uncomplaining.

Parliamentary Archives

Newcomers to Parliamentary Archives take a long time to gain recognition among Lords' staff. They work at a distance, in the upper storeys of the huge but inaccessible Victoria Tower, and venture into the palace so seldom that even doorkeepers, who know almost everyone, often do not recognise them – they can get ticked off for being where they are perfectly entitled to go. They are quite remote from the House in spirit too: several feel uncomfortable with its formality and grandeur. The idea of being part of the Lords tends to be far outweighed by their feeling of membership of the Parliamentary Archives team, cataloguing, preserving and accessing records for the public ranging from original Acts of Parliament from 1497 to recent copies of Hansard.

This relationship is changing, however. Parliamentary Archives staff are updating record management, cataloguing and storage throughout the House. This has been described as a third revolution following those of financial management and information technology, and arises partly from the need to comply with the Freedom of Information Act. But the process has not always been smooth. When new staff ask why records are catalogued in a certain fashion, older staff tend to reply: 'Because it's always been done like that.' Clerks often take old records with them or throw them away when they change post. Some mark certain files with 'Only open by permission of X', which may present problems once they have moved on. Secretaries and clerical staff tend to be attached to their own well-worn systems. Not all Lords' staff have a sense of the historical importance of some of the documents they produce, so do not necessarily see the Parliamentary Archives' work as central to Parliament.

Black Rod's Department

The substantial cultural differences between the Parliament Office, which facilitates the business of the House, and Black Rod's Department, which looks after the building and the peers, stem partly from their different roles, but much more from the backgrounds of their staff. The Parliament Office is civilian, while Black Rod's Department is run by ex-servicemen. Historically, the staff of the latter were all ex-non-commissioned officers; now there are civilians as well. The sonorously entitled Gentleman Usher of the Black Rod and Serjeant-at-Arms (a former general) heads the department, with his two deputies (brigadiers), and the Administration Officer (a major.) If their armed forces ranks had not matched their relative Lords status, I was told, it would have caused difficulties. Once a general, always a general. Former servicemen like working with others from the same background – one former naval non-com explained it was like going back on board ship: "We spoke the same language: run ashore meant go out for dinner, dobeying meant washing ..." But civilians remain baffling: "Everyone was so polite and nice unlike the army where they bark orders. When I was first told off, the hint was buried in a pleasant conversation about several matters. I left thinking 'I think I have just had a rollicking but I am not sure'."

Armed services style contrasts with the donnish discursiveness of the clerks. Black Rod officers' meetings are known as 'prayers' and have a certain structured rigidity: they follow an agenda closely and comprise a series of unilateral decisions by the senior officer present, often followed by an order. Clerks' meetings are unstructured, conversational and reach decisions by consensus. Black Rod officers find clerks waffly and inefficient, while the clerks think of their Black Rod colleagues as rigid, old-fashioned and over-concerned about hierarchy. One clerk expressed the feeling that some of Black Rod's Department are so different from other staff that they might as well be from the planet Thorg. Clerks have mastery over words and rules; Black Rod's staff excel at ceremony.

Co-operation between the departments is required most of the time, and both sides show great flexibility. They often like each other as individuals and, since all behave with exquisite Lords courtesy, problems seldom arise. Slight tension has arisen over equal opportunities policies, exposing differences of approach over the need to comply with the law versus the value of tradition. The responsibility for recruitment into Black Rod's Department, once entirely in Black Rod's hands, is now shared with the clerkly Human Resources Office, which insists on open competition rather than recruitment by word of mouth. If the best candidate were a woman with no services background, they would insist on that person (although this has yet to happen at a senior level). Some of Black Rod's department think this is mere political correctness and feel undermined by it; and some within the Parliament Office feel that there are too many 'Rods', as some call them.

Doorkeepers

Most doorkeepers love working in the House of Lords. Known to some as 'the uniformed branch', they are splendid in white ties and tails, large gold badges on their chests conferring authority and dignity. Doorkeepers are the face of the House that peers see most of, and it is necessary not only that they recognise peers (to avoid mistaking them for mere members of the public), but that they are able to address by name and unerringly carry messages to all but the most infrequent attenders. Novice doorkeepers once learned names by spending their first three years on Peers' Entrance to the palace. A senior doorkeeper greets the peers as they arrive, so the junior hears their titles. (Each peer has a peg with his name on. This means that for evermore doorkeepers know peers by their pegs, and will occasionally spot one and think, 'I know she's somewhere in the Es.') There are of course uniformed police both outside and inside the House, but doorkeepers are in charge of security in the Chamber, as well as the good order and seating of visitors, and, of course, like all the other staff, with the peers' well-being.

All doorkeepers have had a previous career: in 1999 there were seven who had been in the army, two in the navy, five in the Royal Marines, six in the air force, as well as some "poxy civvies" – a policeman, a prison officer, a fireman and a coroner's officer. Some go back a long way with individual peers, having served in the forces under the command of officers who are now members of the House, which makes for a subtle closeness between the two groups difficult to describe or even understand. With the respect for office and status inculcated by the services, door-keepers' attitudes to the peerage tend to verge on reverence. At the same time, their perception of individual peers is open-eyed and realistic. They express respect for the high rank of every peer with unfailing courtesy. This is accompanied by a lighthearted and extremely personal banter that would in more pompous contexts be taken as disrespectful in spite of the affectionate warmth it conveys; in the Lords it is accepted as an expression of the paradox created by, on the one hand, the respect commanded by peers as legislators and men of high social rank and, on the other, their common human frailty. Notwithstanding their wit and directness, doorkeepers seem never to overstep the mark into disrespect. Most peers reciprocate in kind, and both sides patently greatly enjoy this affable badinage. It is also extended to peers' visitors, and is enjoyed most intensely among and between the doorkeepers themselves.

Rivalry between forces and regiments hardly fades in the move from the services to Parliament. Those who were musicians are deemed "poofters"; those who were not, it is countered, are "philistines". The Long Range Artillery are "drop-shorts", the Marines are "dense as bricks", and the Guards, "classy". Mess rules apply, meaning that no matter how badly a doorkeeper behaves in the mess room no colleague would ever sneak on them. They can criticise each other – particular indi-viduals are considered grumpy or "old dinosaurs" – but their loyalty to each other is colossal. The pageantry, continuity and humour of the place suit the doorkeepers' style, and they have plenty of opportunities for imbibing alcohol during their breaks.

Doorkeepers approach 'strangers', that is visitors, with business-like gravitas that can be, and is possibly meant to be, intimidating, and at first they seem strict and formal. However, once trust is established, decorum evaporates. If women are prepared to banter with them, doorkeepers humorously flirt with them or show ostentatious avuncular concern. Early in my research the Principal Doorkeeper, then Mr R. M. Skelton but known as Mick, called me Sarah by mistake; it stuck, and I am flattered when he remembers to call me by my nickname. Two of the doorkeepers remained formal, even abrupt. When I asked another what I should do to get into their good books, he told me to call one 'Colonel'. It worked a treat; from that moment he treated me most kindly, as if I were an annoying but favoured niece. One never thawed. He steadfastly refused to budge from formality with me, possibly because he thought the other doorkeepers allowed me to break the rules too much. After a year of visiting, asking permission to go into the Chamber had become a joke: I was just told, "You've got a season ticket, go where you like." Once, when the best galleries were full, a senior doorkeeper saw my Strangers' Gallery ticket, normally given to members of the public, and asked with mock irritation,

"What are you doing with that?"

"They're booked up in all the galleries. Mr X told me to go to Strangers."

He ripped up my ticket and said, "If anyone asks, you're Australian. I'll put you in the Commonwealth Gallery."

Any member of the public will be admitted to Strangers' Gallery so long as "they do not smell or have fleas". They are asked to fill out a ticket so there is a record if they cause a disturbance. If anyone were to make real trouble, Black Rod has the power to lock them in a cell, and a choice of two cells to lock them in. Children are allowed in if they can write their own ticket, but even that rule is now often relaxed and I was allowed to take in a baby only a few months old.

During the study, three women were recruited to the doorkeepers, one naval nurse and two civilians. The first only realised the novelty she was when peers congratulated her on being the first woman and the first ethnic minority doorkeeper. The Principal Doorkeeper gave her his unreserved support. She was put through her paces by others with stern discipline, and referred to as 'Mr' by one, but with her services background she was not fazed by it. She gained her colleagues' respect, and, now that two other women have joined them, the other doorkeepers are no longer exacting.

I was told that women doorkeepers have softened the atmosphere. The men and women have a separate mess for breaks, which suits both, but when they come together doorkeepers are apparently merrier, less secretive and more like a family. Swearing and smutty jokes are in a decline but that is not a cause of particular regret. Some still feel that "females are treated with slightly more respect than their rank would call for – much like in military circles", although another casts doubt on this in a questionnaire sent out during the research:

'Ladies, fine – I believe in equality. I've got daughters. Lady doorkeepers is an excellent idea, for example in case a Baroness is ill and needs a woman to help. But can they carry the mace? Can they reach the letters, the tables etc? The political position is that they'd like a black woman whale but they would cause a problem of quality, however. No insult intended.'

But he is in a minority. Most doorkeepers, during my research led by the highly effective and adaptable Mr Skelton (since replaced by one of equal calibre), may not care for change but adjust to it, if slowly, when they have to.

Attendants

The functions of attendants are several: handling mail for peers (though part of that has shifted to the Parliamentary Post Office), maintaining the supply of stationery in peers' offices, helping with office machinery like photocopiers, checking the fabric of the building and the work of contract cleaners, certain security duties; and of course, looking after the well-being of peers. They, too, used to be recruited from the armed services but now are mostly civilians (though they tend to share a certain scepticism about the need to enforce equal opportunities legislation). Putting civilians under quasi-military command seems to have caused problems within the department: differences of style have not always been accompanied by a corresponding desire to reach accommodation. Most bristle if Black Rod officers refer to 'orders', 'troops' or 'discipline'. Some Black Rod officers, military style, are punctilious almost to a fault about neatness in certain areas: the fringe of the Throne in the Chamber has been a peculiar source of discord: an officer wanting it brushed up to five times a day; attendants not seeing the point.

Attendants are aware, and resentful of, their low standing in the House. One fumed that the senior staff in other departments are capable of "treating us like trash, the lowest of the low". Until recently, for example, alone among Lords' staff, the attendants' and the housekeepers' spouses were not given places in the Royal Gallery during State Opening. But although there is resentment among some, other attendants share doorkeepers' reverence for the peerage and will go to almost any lengths for them. They sometimes have to provide menial services. If peers' status were not so respected by some attendants, peers might find it more difficult to get certain extra-curricular jobs done so easily, like changing car tyres or going to the bank. Like doorkeepers, many attendants engage in friendly, humorous badinage with peers, but they are not so renowned for their wit or forthrightness.

According to some, attendants' standing improved during the 1990s, although there is some debate about whether their uniforms did. They used to look like undertakers, but now, with blazers and red ties, look like 1950s' game-show hosts and still envy the doorkeepers. An amicable division exists between those who work in the palace itself and those on security duties in its various outposts. The latter have a quieter life but have to deal with tourists, skateboarders, schoolchildren eating their sandwiches on the steps, cyclists chaining their bikes to railings, and peers or staff who have lost their keys for the outbuildings or car park. Whether in an outpost or the palace itself, attendants often talk of their love of the parliamentary buildings that they check for problems each day. Those working in the palace collect discarded paper from the floor of the Chamber every evening and often find exquisite doodles and drawings.

Housekeepers

Cleaning in the House is the responsibility of the housekeepers. Among the warmest and most humorous people you can meet in the Lords, they are straightforward enough to slightly resent the euphemistic name they have recently been saddled with. They were content to be known as 'housemaids', but it had to be changed to comply with the law. Pragmatically, they chose to be called 'cleaners' but this was considered untraditional. Housekeeper, they feel, implies dealing with linen, which is only true of the head and her deputy.

Housekeepers work an early shift, finishing at 10 a.m. Few peers, mostly those who use their Lords offices for private business, regularly show up early enough to meet them and pass the time of day. Since house-keepers clean the same patch, they get to know their regular early peers whom they find polite, warm and friendly. More than their appreciation of peers, however, they enjoy the building. It is over-run with mice. So many peers are active in animal rights, no agreement on mouse-control seems within reach. They find them in the rubbish bins or running across the floor or even jumping out of filing cabinets. Ghosts also make frequent appearances. The palace is scary, strange, but marvellous, and the housekeepers work with scrupulous care.

They share with the attendants some problems arising from being under military-style command. While I was with them, a manager appeared to ask how many men it took to iron a shirt (the answer was none, as it is women's work) and then sent another housekeeper to order them not to talk to me while working. Consternation has been caused by an attempt to offer a promotion structure within the housekeeping department. Leaders were appointed to each team to supervise, but the choice of leaders was not invariably considered sensible and tensions emerged between some team leaders and the members of their groups. They remain, however, fairly close-knit overall and hostilities are kept to a minimum by different sub-groups taking their tea breaks in different rooms. They used to be even closer knit: almost entirely Irish, and recruited by word of mouth from relatives and friends. Over the years they have been joined by people with origins in the Caribbean, Africa, Germany, Morocco, Malta, Turkish-Cyprus and the Philippines. Fifteen out of forty-two Housekeepers are black or Asian, a proportion matched only by the Refreshment Department.

Lords staff welcomed me with trust, curiosity and courtesy, and, above all, they made me laugh. I confess that I never expected such hospitality among British informants and will always feel respect and affection for them. Some of the groups – clerks, doorkeepers, attendants, and housekeepers – seemed peculiar to Parliament in their behaviour or duties, which is why they have received most attention here.

Notes

1 In World War II, barbarous atrocities characterised the jungle war in Asia, while the desert war in North Africa, though equally hard-fought, was distinguished by scrupulous decency on both sides.

2 Lord Howe, HL Deb., 10 January 2002, col. 699.

3 Lord Cranborne, as quoted by A. Mitchell, 1999, *Farewell My Lords*, Politico's, London, p. 65.

4 See Chapter 9 for more on whipping by political parties.

5 Primogeniture applies to most peerages, and if there is no male heir, the peerage becomes extinct. Some Scottish titles are inherited by a son if there is one, but if there are only daughters, one of them may claim and they decide themselves who should do so.

6 House of Lords, March 1996, *Information Sheet No. 2, The House of Lords at Work*, Journal and Information Office, House of Lords, p. 7. They define peers as part of the 'working house' if they sit at least one sitting day in three.

7 Baroness Jay, HL Deb., 14 October 1998, col. 923.

8 *Dod's Parliamentary Companion*, 1998, Vacher Dod Publishing, London. Some peers do not mention their profession so this list is far from exhaustive.

9 These figures were compiled for this research project by Julia Kruger in 2002. The main sources were *Dod's Parliamentary Companion* and the notes from this research.

10 Donald Shell and David Beamish (eds), 1993, *The House of Lords at Work: A Study Based on the 1988–1989 Session*, Oxford University Press, Oxford, p. 37. These figures are different from Baroness Jay's earlier in this chapter both because of the different date, and because they refer to all, rather than just hereditary, peers.

11 However, excluded hereditary peers can sit in the Commons: Viscount Thurso has been the MP for Caithness, Sutherland and Easter Ross since 2001.

12 Departments which extend across both Houses are not on the official House of Lords staff list and were, therefore, not included in this study, they include the Pass Office, Parliamentary Works Department, police, postal service and the palace's own fire service.

13 Michael Davies, 1999–2000, *The Office of Clerk of the Parliaments*, Peterhouse Annual Record.

14 Others claim that his role was different and William Airwyn was the first in 1316.

15 In contrast, the post of Private Secretary to the Chief Whip, which was always filled by a clerk seconded from the House of Lords' Parliament Office, has recently been opened up to competition so that external candidates can apply.

16 Sir John Sainty, former Clerk of the Parliaments, personal communication.

17 Hansard only works while the House is sitting and reporters may get up to twenty weeks leave a year, while the computer office and housekeepers get six. Pay is not adjusted to reflect these differentials; and while this causes resentment, it has been accepted to date because it occurs between offices, not within them, indicating how very separately the different parts function.

18 This was partly as a result of the Ibbs Enquiry, a review of the management of the Commons carried out by Sir Robin Ibbs in 1990.

19 These were people (especially women) who lived (or aspired to) the lifestyle of the upper/upper-middle classes living around Sloane Square. For details see Ann York and Peter Barr, 1983, *The Official Sloane Ranger Handbook*, St Martin's Press, London.

20 Of the twenty-five black and Asian staff who responded to a House of Lords questionnaire in January 2003, all but one were grade C or below and ten were in the lowest grade. (The grades are judicial group 4, senior bands, A, B, C, D, E. 274 out of 419 staff responded. Human Resources Office statistics, 2003).

21 There is, however, a 'Study of Parliament Group', composed of academics as well as clerks from both Houses.

22 In addition to these, there are five 're-treads', i.e., civil servants who have moved from government departments to work as clerks for the Lords' committees.

23 Whereby the person who has been there the longest moves up when a position becomes vacant.

6 Hierachies

Anthropologists used to search for the 'social structure' of communities, that is, a single system regulating relationships within it, as though society were a building whose weight-bearing components could be identified. In fact, societies are never organised by one structure alone; multiple identities and interlocking structures are always found. The House of Lords is a complex web of relationships, some aspects of which are obvious to all (such as party political membership), while others are taken for granted or disguised. Informality and warmth mask hierarchies that go unnoticed even by some natives. Social hierarchies encompassing staff as well as peers are the subject of this chapter.

Separation

The Palace of Westminster has some peculiarities in common with a Hindu temple, and the behaviour of parliamentarians and staff shares some features with that of members of Hindu castes. The separation into caste-like groups in the Lords is, in some respects, more rigid than is usually found in Asia, but while in Asia higher castes deliberately avoid lower ones for reasons of ritual purity, separation in the Lords is so taken for granted most people are hardly aware of it. For instance, peers and the sixty-odd officers may visit certain designated areas that have attributes of sacredness, where access for staff below a certain status is restricted, and the closer to the sanctum – the Chamber – the fiercer the regulations. There are similarities also in that the occupational groups, whether priests and kings in Asia or clerks and peers in the Lords, are visibly ranked in status through rituals and socialise mainly within their own groups.

In the scheme idealised in ancient Hindu texts, castes fell into four occupational categories: 'Brahmans' (priests), 'Kshatriyas' (rulers and warriors), 'Vaishyas' (merchants), and 'Shudras' (service providers or labourers). Lords occupational groups fit this pattern quite closely. Clerks are priestly Brahmans; peers, holding temporal power, are princely Kshatriyas while Black Rod's officers and doorkeepers are warrior Kshatriyas; staff in the Parliament Office fit into the Vaishya castes, trading information rather than goods; while attendants, waiters, and housekeepers are Shudras.

The word 'clerk' has the same Greek root as cleric and clergyman and used to mean priest. It is no coincidence that both parliamentary clerks and Hindu priests are the possessors of arcane knowledge. Both enjoy privileged access to the sanctum; senior clerks even sit at one of its altars – the Table. Mundane tasks at the altar, writing down peers' names for instance, are invested with gravity just as washing an idol is in a Hindu temple. Both priests and clerks derive their authority from their closeness to sacred texts, and especially from the fact that their interpretations over-ride everyone else's; for clerks these are the *Standing Orders*, the *Companion to the Standing Orders* and *Erskine May: Parliamentary Practice*[1] (the name is that of the now immortalised clerkly author). Members of both groups are conspicuous by their distinctive costume: eighteenth-century court dress and wigs in the Lords, and dhotis and a sacred thread in South Asia.

Peers preside over the system, making laws and fighting moral wars with each other and with the more tumultuous rulers at the other end of the palace. They are protected by the other castes, which provide security, information and services.

Except for hereditary peers, membership of these groups is not by birth; yet, once recruited, it is exceptional for an individual to change to a different category. Only one has ever jumped into the priestly caste by becoming a career clerk from another staff group: a Hansard reporter from the Commons who took the civil service exams and, exceptionally, joined the clerks.[2] But no Lords' staff member has become a fully-fledged Table clerk. At least four clerks from the Commons or Lords have made the leap into the peers' caste: the first being the sanctified Erskine May in the 1880s, and the most recent being the late Lord Henderson of Brompton in 1984.

Endogamy – marriage or sex within your own social group (caste, class, clan, tribe or whatever) – is a common social phenomenon every-where. No explicit rule exists in the House of Lords but in practice people marry and have sex within their own group. There are two pairs of clerks married to each other, a high proportion for less than twenty-five people of whom only five are women (in 2000), and rumoured clerkly affairs have been within the caste. There are at least five married couples among peers, although unsurprisingly (with the average age nearly seventy), three couples were married before they were given peerages. Affairs between peers, or peers and peers' wives, are not unheard of; although usually within the same party, one Labour whip and Conservative back-bencher had a long-standing relationship in the 1990s. But romance is more common among MPs.

In three marriages that have occurred between male peers and female staff, the women involved have left. In one case it was found confusing when a woman staff member exercised the privileges of a peer's spouse. At a social function, when someone made a pass at her, she is said to have replied: 'How dare you? Don't you know that I'm Lady X?' Her hybrid category – part peeress, part staff – was problematic, and she resigned. During my time in the House affairs between staff were the subject of much speculation, as in any office, and, in all the cases I knew about, stuck to endogamy or hypergamy (a higher status man associating with a lower status woman).

Different groups in the Lords seldom eat, drink or socialise together. Although clerks and other officers have the right to use the peers' dining rooms, and even to invite guests, they rarely do and almost never eat with peers. In another part of the dining room, attached to the peers' main restaurant, there are two 'long tables', one for peers and the other for officers and clerks, where the custom is for people to take the next seat available. No guests are allowed. When the Clerk of the Parliaments asked me to lunch at the officers' table, I felt as honoured as when a Brahman friend in India sneaked me into the kitchen (her most sacred room). But it was more formal and alarming: would I drop food, keep up with the conversation, should I pay for my own lunch? (A flattering indication of my temporary 'insider' status was that I did pay). Only a few clerks or other officers eat at this exclusive table anymore, so perhaps the social hierarchy is gradually weakening; on the other hand, although most go to the more informal eating places, even there they often sit with other officers.

A combination of restrictions on where people may eat and the different preferences of particular groups means that in the staff canteens and bars, occupation groups (or sub-groups) often sit together and socialise almost exclusively within their group. Attendants drink in the Sports and Social Club, Hansard editors eat in the press dining room, and library staff meet in the Lords' bar. This separation largely applies outside the palace as well. Clerks, for instance, hold retirement parties in a London club to which outsiders are not invited.

A few events bring all the inhabitants, even peers, together. The staff Christmas party excludes only refreshment staff and housekeepers. The newly created Parliament Choir bars no one and has a Commons door-keeper as one of its officers. A senior clerk holds an annual party at his home for his whole office, and a monthly pool session in a pub welcomes anyone from the Parliament Office, but these examples are exceptional.

Although the House of Lords forms a perfect hierarchic pyramid, like South Asian caste systems the relative status of each group is not straight-forward: the ranking of categories is fluid and depends upon whom and when you ask. For instance, staff involved in providing information tell you that they are graded higher than doorkeepers in the official hierarchy, but doorkeepers put themselves higher on the grounds that they are closer to peers. If you ask attendants and doorkeepers about their ranking rela-tive to each other, each would say that they are closer to the peers and so higher. And some hereditary peers may assume superiority in ancestry, but clerks feel and are widely regarded as superior in brains.

To rely on people's own view of their position in the hierarchy is to risk being misled. It is more reliable to watch how they behave in sacred places – the kitchen and the temple in South Asia, and the eating rooms and the Chamber in the House of Lords. Peers have their own dining area, and only peers, officers and doorkeepers are allowed within the Chamber, at least during sittings. (A rule that smacks of ritual purity ordains that no one but a peer is ever allowed to put their posterior upon the red leather of the benches.) The steps of the Throne may be occupied by a diverse group of present, potential and excluded peers, including the eldest child of a peer, peers of Ireland, diocesan bishops who have not yet seats, retired bishops, and an assortment of other dignitaries: privy counsellors, the Clerk of the Crown in Chancery, Serjeant-at-Arms and his deputy,[3] and the Dean of Westminster. Also in the chamber, but behind the bar, there is standing room for MPs and younger sons of peers. In the same area, on the spiritual side, peers' spouses may sit; on the temporal side there are seats for peers' guests and distinguished strangers. Above the chamber, the shallow galleries are sectioned into areas for peers' children, ambassadors and foreign diplomats, important commonwealth visitors, and more peers' guests and distinguished strangers. At one end there is a gallery for the press, another for MPs and their guests, and still higher up, we find the Strangers' Gallery for members of the public. What this adds up to is that the higher your status the closer you sit to centre of the Chamber, where the sacred symbol of debate – the Table, Mace and Woolsack – reside.

The proceedings that take place on the floor of the House create the sacredness of the whole House – the rigid rules about movement, the ritualisation of debate, and the priest-like behaviour of the clerks all emphasise this sanctity which diminishes the further you are from the blue carpet that separates the two front benches. Thus front-benchers, privy counsellors and the top five bishops all sit on the lowest of the peers' benches, closest both to the action and (*ipso facto*) to the epicentre of the sacred space that runs through the middle of the chamber; the Lord Chancellor or Chairman of Committees, their deputies and the Table clerks sit at the epicentre itself; and lowly visitors can only sit in distant galleries above.

Like Brahmans, clerks are supreme in matters of ritual. Brahmans claim authority from God; clerks derive their status from the peers, though in theory they are responsible to the monarch. The Clerk of the Parliaments is appointed directly by the Crown. When introduced to the House, the Clerk's rite of initiation is as formal as that of peers and also entails swearing an oath of allegiance to the Queen:

> ... I will also well and truly service Her Highness in the Office of Clerk of Her Parliaments making true Entries and Records of the things done and passed in the same. I will keep secret all such matters as shall be treated in Her said Parliaments ...

In the rituals of debate in the Chamber, clerks are not mediating, as priests do, between humans and the spiritual world, but between members of Parliament. Their relationship is one of service to peers, but their ritual knowledge is superior and it is they who know what behaviour is off limits or 'undesirable', even if it is the peers who decide in practice. Clerks advise on what these elevated beings can say, when and how, and they derive their status from those they serve. A clerk put it like this:

> "We are upper servants, rather like courtiers in court in the eighteenth century – like 'women of the Bedchamber'. Because they were serving the King or Queen it was an honour to perform what would be menial in other circumstances. Similarly clerks even when doing rather mundane work, like minute taking, are doing an important job because of the importance of those they are serving."

Symbols of class

What does the distinction between 'officers' and 'staff' in the Lords achieve? It is presented as a bureaucratic device to avoid overcrowding in peers' dining areas and private rooms. Although it largely coincides with civil service grade six or seven and above, officer status is in the gift of the Clerk of the Parliaments. He can bestow it on any member of staff he chooses: in practice, to all clerks and most of the senior managers. This group of fifty or so, of whom over half are clerks, have almost the same privileges as peers: they can work in the library, eat in the same restaurants, drink on the terrace, marry and have children christened in St Mary Undercroft chapel, and belong to some all-party groups. Other lordly privileges they can use only with discretion: officers are not normally expected to use the Peers' Entrance or staircase, should not sit on the armchairs in the library, and should avoid the Bishops' Bar when it is busy. In the words of one clerk they should be "discreet and unobtrusive". Other staff, of course, may not go near these places. Restrictions are policed by lower status officials: doorkeepers, restaurant staff and police officers. Most staff and younger officers now question the rules that distinguish between them; they doubt their value or see them as divisive.[4] Traditional officers, on the other hand, see them as unavoidable or useful in encouraging staff to better themselves. This view is revealing. The system appears to be more symbolic of class status than of bureaucratic efficiency. To achieve the latter, an efficient set of rules might be based on other considerations (such as work roles, length of service and position in the building) rather than a division into two groups. But, as in any society, the social and cultural is usually as important as the practical or functional in regulating social behaviour.

An important principle underlying Lords administration demands that those in proximity to peers behave 'properly'. Officers have to be (or become) 'gentlemen': well-mannered, well-dressed and well-educated. These things come naturally to clerks, who traditionally came from upper middle-class/upper-class families, fee-paying schools and Oxbridge.[5] Black Rod's senior staff, former army officers, come from similar class backgrounds. Clerical staff are mostly middle/lower-middle class, with mixed educational backgrounds, while doorkeepers, attendants and the lowest grade staff tend to be lower-middle/working-class and/or have their origins outside Britain.

Thus, those with the right to enter peers' private areas tend also to have the 'right' class credentials. An officer with a working-class background told me that if he uses officers' privileges, he catches surprised and even resentful looks from some, of 'What are you doing here?', as if he were diluting their position. According to officers from his background, there is a distinction between officers who come from the right class and "officers who are not gentlemen", revealed by patterns of behaviour that may not be codified nor even conscious, but reflect assumptions about what constitutes appropriate behaviour. An example is found in attitudes to lunch. Staff and officers from the 'wrong' background regard it merely as sustenance during a break. Peers and 'posh' officers, on the other hand, see it more as a social event and even an opportunity to entertain (although in practice workloads are making the latter increasingly difficult for officers). There is also a rough correlation between social class and time of eating: the posher you are, the later you eat. Policemen eat at noon while clerks tend to break at 1.30 p.m. This is not a precise pattern, but a pronounced tendency. Class also enters into the choice of who to eat with. But class is not a simple question of birth; it needs sustenance by particular forms of education, profession, social networks, accumulation of symbolic capital and so on. Thus, one hereditary peer (an ex-police sergeant and the son of a Labour MP) felt so out of place in the Lords that he spent much of his leisure time with police officers and doorkeepers in the Sports and Social Club. This kind of anomaly is far from unique.

My position in relation to peers varied according to context and was always reflected in their behaviour, and mine. Peers who had been strangers to me when I arrived, who knew me only as a researcher with a staff pass, usually gave me tea, coffee or a drink when I interviewed them, and tended to make me feel my position was one of distinct social inferiority. A few invited me to join them in the canteen or on the terrace, but I did not usually eat meals with peers. I would not have dared to invite one to lunch, whereas I often took staff to meals. I was, however, given meals by the few peers I already knew. We met as equals on those occasions, as if I belonged to the same class for lunch. Peers who were academics – nearly always professors – usually inspired my respect but simultaneously were, as fellow members of a relatively egalitarian profession, my social equals. In private we talked as equals; in public, and especially with other peers, I deferred to them. Women peers stood on their dignity less than men so it was easier to forget about status.

Two other areas that often reveal class distinctions are dress and terms of address. These tend to be prescribed in the Lords, but there is often room for manoeuvre. Staff are obliged to address peers by title, but dukes exemplify how the forms of address differ according to the speaker. Lower status groups would probably address a duke as 'Your Grace'. Those in a higher position (including other peers) are most likely to say 'Good morning, Duke'. An earl can correctly be addressed as Earl Ferrers, Lord Ferrers or My Lord, but only those with a relatively low class status would use the last. Even if a clerk did not know a peer's title, he would avoid addressing him directly rather than resort to My Lord. It reveals whether you are, as one informant put it, "upstairs or downstairs" in the House of Lords. A non-clerk graduate commented that he did not "go in for that Milord, Milady business. I talk to them as if they were normal human beings. They look uncomfortable with all that grovelling business."

As recently as the 1990s a senior clerk stuffily refused to agree to 'Esq.' being attached to the names of non-officers in the official proceedings, so the honorific had to be abandoned for all. Clerks used to write to each other putting just the surname of the recipient after 'Dear', but most have stopped on the grounds that the practice is, in the words of one, "snobbish and divisive because we would not do it to lower ranking people". Some male clerks still answer the phone with their surname only, a habit that many see as old-fashioned and a signal of class affiliation. But in general, social interaction is becoming increasingly informal.

Names and titles are not fixed, but, like most systems of social ranking, relative and situational. I called the former Clerk of the Parliaments 'Michael' to his face, 'Mr Davies' in front of a peer, and 'the Clerk of the Parliaments' if I was talking about him to a doorkeeper. Similarly senior staff would address Black Rod by his first name if speaking to him, but if there were attendants present would revert to Black Rod. A senior manager, who had derived his sense of hierarchy from the army showed the most acute consciousness of this when, meeting the Clerk of the Parliaments after his promotion, he asked:

"What should I call you now?"

"Michael."

"But you are Clerk of the Parliaments now."

"Yes, but my name is still Michael."

Status is not made up of grade and class distinctions alone; gender can be critical: doorkeepers' suave dignity demands that all address them as 'Mr'; except junior female staff who use their first names. The first woman to become a doorkeeper has always been called by her first name by all staff and even some peers (aside from the colleague who addressed her as 'Mr').

Some staff allow peers to use their first names, some do not. Waitresses and attendants generally do not mind, but doorkeepers are uneasy: "familiarity breeds contempt", explained one, adding that since they are like butlers, serving and advising, distance is necessary. Peers might use their first names in the bar, but doorkeepers seldom respond in kind – a Lord remains a Lord even over a whisky. One woman peer has, with difficulty, managed to persuade three doorkeepers to address her by her first name but only when no one else is listening.

The subtleties of systems of address are like grammar: complex, evolving and usually noticed only when someone gets it wrong. A complication is that emotional elements are also sometimes expressed in terms of address, such as people veering towards formality when irritated or offended. And, because rigidities of hierarchy have lost their edge, where once there would have been the limpid clarity of class differential, there is now sometimes confusion. Some clerks find it confusing when peers write to them by their first name; they would prefer to respond with the usual 'Lord Y', but fear it may appear stuffy. Younger ones have got accustomed to using first names, particularly when working closely with

Labour ministers since 1997. Black Rod's officers address members of their staff as 'Mr Z', as they would have done with junior officers in the services, but those who were not in the forces can find it formal and alienating. The House is moving – more slowly than other British institutions – from formality to informality. While in other contexts strangers simply bounce straight to first names, peers and senior staff still tend to ask permission first.

When peers are sitting (meaning debating), everyone in the Chamber and in the peers' restaurants is required to look smart. Tie-less peers are directed to the attendants' office to borrow one before entering the Chamber. Again, there is room for a range of approaches, from the formality of dinner jackets when men have come from some function to vote, to the scruffy jacket and running shoes favoured by the late Lord Longford. The most untidy dressers tended to be hereditaries. Secure enough in the sense of their own status, they felt able to appear like unmade beds if it suited them, and no one in the House held it against them. On the other hand, visitors to the Peers' Dining Room dressed in shell suits and trainers caused outrage; these clothes are not associated with the 'right' class of people. It seems, therefore, that looking smart may be about not looking too obviously lower class.

To sum up, while not all the boxes have to be ticked in every case, education, eating habits, dress and terms of address all tend to be symbolic indicators of both bureaucratic status and social class.

Hierarchy and belonging

The comparison with Asian caste systems emphasises how impervious the groups in the House of Lords tend to be. New members can easily be accommodated, but moving to a new occupation within the Lords is extremely difficult. It is this that the Lords has in common with Hindu practices. But the analogy should not be taken too far, as differences outweigh similarities: the marriage and eating patterns in the Lords are the result of preferences more than of prescriptive rules, and kinship – a cornerstone of caste – is now only minimally relevant. ('My noble kinsman' was a common form of address between hereditary peers, but has almost completely disappeared since 1999.) The comparison shows principally how culture is relevant to social interaction in the political domain in twenty-first-century Britain, as it is elsewhere. Social hierarchies, such as those based on class, have to be understood to make sense of how people operate in the Lords.[7]

What does class mean in Britain these days? Although its existence is denied by some peers, Cannadine points out that British people still tend to articulate their identity and their sense of where they belong in society in terms of class, in at least three ways: (1) class as hierarchy, as in the graduations of the hereditary peerage and so on down; (2) two groups, such as 'upper' and 'lower'; and (3) three groups: 'upper', 'middle' and 'lower'.[8] It is the first of these that has abiding appeal in Britain, and seems to prevail in the Lords. The natives there do not neatly divide into the two most obvious groups: peers and non-peers; nor the convenient three-fold division of peers, officers and staff. Peers may form a coherent group much of the time because of their peculiar and unique status there, but they are not necessarily considered socially superior to all others: clerks are equal to peers in some contexts so division into two groups does not hold water. Three groups do exist – peers, officers and staff – but again not very neatly: many non-clerk 'officers' do not feel they are full members of that category, and, more importantly, the terms 'officers' and 'staff' hold less meaning for most people than, for instance, membership of the teams that they work with.

More significant than these dual or triple divisions, or the four-fold caste hierarchy, is a fluid pecking order that adjusts according to context. When asked, informants say they see themselves as belonging to one of these main discrete groups in the following descending order of bureaucratic rank:

1   Peers
2   Clerks
3   Black Rod's officers and Parliament Office non-clerk officers
4   Parliament Office staff[9]
5   Doorkeepers
6   Attendants
7   Refreshment Department
8   Housekeepers

The pecking order is more fluid than this ranking implies because senior members of the lower groups are higher than junior members of the higher ones, and within the higher groups there are those with 'breeding', which has cachet in the Lords, and those without. The bureaucratic hierarchy is thus overlaid with another defined by the class you arrive with. Status changes so much according to context that some doubt whether there is a clear hierarchy at all, but what should put it beyond doubt is the ability of any individual to know her or his status relative to anyone in the building. Doorkeepers would claim a higher status than many in category 4; attendants perceive themselves to be as important as doorkeepers, and so on. They may not all agree, which is why it is necessary to allow several rankings to emerge according to context rather than one, but the existence of status hierarchies is beyond dispute.

This may give the impression of divisions within the institution; but the House of Lords is a courteous, harmonious place. This is partly because a sense of belonging is easily engendered by the village-like ambience of the House – in which both peers and staff, once recruited, tend to remain until death or retirement – its relative isolation, and the importance of its work to the political health of the nation. The last is a source of almost palpable pride to both peers and staff; and they are proud too of the service they give it. The disdainful attitude of the press, the executive and the public only serve to increase solidarity among those who work there, who hold up Parliament as the most precious institution in the kingdom. While the Commons provides the nation with a noisy Theatre of National Confrontation, in the view of the Lords, their Chamber, contrastingly, is a place where courtesy and accommodation are valued and often found. So it is in the House as a whole.

Pride in their collective importance creates coherence, so that even if divisions lie at the heart of the House, resentments felt by those at the bottom are rarely expressed. Another related but even more important force drawing all inhabitants together is that almost all – peers and staff – find their proximity to (other) peers seductive, if not irresistible. In what sometimes seems a somewhat isolated community, the status of lords is even higher than in wider society, with the ceaselessly deferential behaviour of staff towards them building and maintaining the peers' status. It is, above all, the peers' status that makes the House different, exalted and unique. This creates a lively centripetal momentum within the whole House, so that staff behaviour bolsters the position of peers, which elevates the whole House. In elevating the peers, staff are elevating themselves. An apparent paradox is that in behaviour that apparently raises the peers far above themselves, staff are simultaneously drawing all members of the community, including peers, closer together. Staff do not feel equal to peers, they feel more like their servants, but the inequality is perceived (in the main, on both sides) as social and structural rather than personal. In day-to-day conversation, there is a prevailing sense of the equal humanity of all. So while staff, and peers, show respect for the elevated rank of peers, and for their embodiment of the upper (and noble) House of Parliament especially when they are fulfilling their role as legislators, it is not because they are regarded as superior human beings. It is the rank and not the person that is superior. Individuals can inspire respect if not awe: but at the same time staff gossip about which peers are a waste of space, who tells good jokes and who is pompous or boorish. They privately ridicule individual peers, and peers among themselves can be equally ribald about staff; but in public, and in particular when there are inequalities of status between individuals present, the part-charade of deferential status relations is played out seamlessly. Staff have to iron out the anomalous unlordly Lords by complaining about them behind their backs. Characters with no manners are not proper lords or real House of Lords men or women.

Most peers understand that staff respect their status rather than their person. There is a certain tension between treating peers according to their rank, and responding to them as individuals. The deference paid to peers by the lower ranks is often expressed partly through humorous chaff, which appears to be a way of letting off steam by expressing resistance to the hierarchy in an acceptable form. Doorkeepers, in particular, tease nearly all, particularly those who deserve mockery, joke with those they like, and admonish those who step out of line, irrespective of their rank. Peers who share an armed forces background, or learn quickly, are able to discern the humour; some, perhaps accustomed to the more earnest bureaucratic hierarchies found in many British institutions – where senior staff feign egalitarian attitudes while controlling those beneath them most effectively – are perplexed and sometimes offended. Meanwhile, more observant peers notice that you earn more respect from doorkeepers if you learn their names and recognise and greet them when off duty – it demonstrates that you do not take them, or their status, for granted. So not only do people disagree about their relative ranking, different groups operate according to different definitions of what behaviour is respectful.

The high overall standard of politeness is partly because most inhabitants are in awe of the status of peers, including peers themselves. Breaking the rules of courtesy can cause shock. This, of course, is most true in the Chamber because there the rules of debate combine with the eminence of peers to require that they should show the highest respect to each other. While the rest of society learns informal egalitarianism, the House has retained both rigid hierarchies and forceful rules of etiquette. Good manners are a way of reminding peers of their social eminence, their reward for the unpaid grind of revising legislation. The courtesy flows down from the Chamber; it is both an obligation towards the peers, and a benevolent infection emanating from them.

Notes

1 Mark Hutton *et al.*, 2004, *Erskine May: Parliamentary Practice*, Butterworths Law, London. Although this mainly describes Commons' procedure, and peers rarely consult it, it does also refer to Lords' procedure and clerks in the Lords use it as a reference book.
2 See Chapter 5 for details about clerks.
3 In their roles as Serjeant-at-Arms and Deputy, but these posts have been merged with the Gentleman Usher of the Black Rod and the Yeoman Usher of the Black Rod. In those roles the former has his own box while the latter sits in the officers' box.

4 According to a questionnaire carried out in 2000, see Appendix 2 for details.
5 The pattern is now breaking down, with several state-school and non-Oxbridge clerks.
6 For a study of the importance of cuisine in maintaining class distinctions, see J. Goody, 1982, *Cooking, Cuisine and Class: A Study in Comparative Sociology*, Cambridge University Press, Cambridge.
7 This adds another challenge to Dumont's much-disputed idea that while hierarchy permeates Hindu ideology, egalitarianism underpins Western ideology and practice. L. Dumont, 1980, *Homo Hierarchicus: The Caste System and its Implications*, University of Chicago, Chicago and London, p. 233.
8 D. Cannadine, 2000, *Class in Britain*, Penguin Books, London, pp. 22–3.
9 In the Committee Office, Judicial Office, Journal and Information Office, Parliamentary Archives, Human Resources Office, Hansard or the Library.

7 Are peers equal?

Members of the House of Lords often say that all peers are equal. That, they tell you, is the meaning of 'peer', and they sometimes add that the Lords is, therefore, a meritocracy. Anthropologists, of course, observe that natives stick to cherished beliefs even when they are confounded by their behaviour.

Procedures emphasise equality between peers. So too does the courtesy whereby all peers seem to be treated with equal respect. By such means an appearance is maintained that there is only one social class present among peers – the nobility. The lordly behaviour expected of individuals, particularly in the Chamber, reinforces this. The 'independence' of peers means that ideally none should identify themselves in debate too closely with interest groups, but should speak with dispassionate objectivity and independence of mind. None therefore is first and foremost a woman, or a Christian, or a farmer, but all are peers, bound in equality by their unique lordly status before all other considerations. Even on the occasions when peers mention such other identities in debate, they tend do so deprecatingly, sometimes observing that the point of view they are expressing as women, Christians, farmers or whatever, may not be the only point of view relevant to the debate, nor even perhaps the most important.

Earl Russell told me, "peers rise as equals but how they sit is up to them", meaning that all will be listened to with equal respect in the Chamber but the impression they make depends on how they perform. Lord Strabolgi expressed the general view: "You are judged by the contribution you make and not by your family background." However, even this equality of opportunity has limits. Within the white male majority, certain groups seem to find it easier to gain influence – well-connected members of the upper or upper-middle class for instance, former secretaries of state and law lords. Others, such as black or Asian peers, have to work harder to establish their reputations. If they fail, it is apparently their ethnicity that is to blame. So while peers agree that rank, peerage type and class do not divide them, they turn a blind eye to the fact that some have advantages not enjoyed by others. Other peers have related that whatever happens in the Chamber, every kind of snobbery can be found – although you have to look quite hard – in the corridors and bars, and, as one woman peer observed: "Just beneath the surface ... lurk racism, homophobia and deeply old-fashioned attitudes to women, blacks and foreigners." Antagonism on these grounds is only very rarely expressed, but underlying assumptions colour some relationships in the House of Lords as elsewhere.

There are, of course, official hierarchies based on position in government, in the opposition, the judiciary or the church; and there is the stubbornly persistent ranking of ancient protocol in which the Lord Chancellor and archbishops take precedence over the Prime Minister and the Speaker of the Commons. These are dealt with in a later chapter. Informal inequalities, expressed mostly in private conservations and the way peers behave, are the subject of this.

Peerage

It is often offered as evidence of the equality of peers that even dukes are accorded no more respect than others in the House, and that the peerage pecking order from dukes (top of the tree), through marquesses, earls and viscounts to barons, baronesses and ladies lost its significance.[1] It was a Labour peer who observed how important this was because, if peers were too overawed by the social distinction of certain groups, they might be frightened to speak. And a Cross-bencher said typically: "Those minding tradition make sure that the front-benchers do not dominate and that dukes, for example, do not get more deference."

That peers roll out dukes to demonstrate equality is surprising because they appear to be the one group that do inspire awe. Dukes have rarity value: there remain twenty-eight in total, (only two attending the House since 1999), and they are addressed differently from other peers. You can write to other peers 'Dear Lord X', but a letter to a duke starts 'Your Grace' or 'Dear Duke'. Above them there is only royalty. The late Duke of Norfolk in particular – the Premier Duke and Earl of England and Earl Marshal and Hereditary Marshal and Chief Butler of England – possibly increased the general admiration of dukes by the respect he earned personally. But, while he was proud of having achieved the rank of general in the army, he was realistically unimpressed by his dukedom: it happened by chance, he told me, and had nothing to do with him. Not

so other peers. One asked me before the hereditary peers were excluded –
"Will any really important people accept a peerage once the grand peers
like the Duke of Norfolk have gone?" – and a Labour lifer said to Lord
Cranborne:

> the truth of the matter, Robert, is that, if I'm honest with myself, the reason
> I really love being here is because here am I from a humble background in the
> same assembly as the Duke of Norfolk and without the Duke of Norfolk I
> won't enjoy it nearly as much.[2]

Peers are dazzled by the wealth of the Dukes of Devonshire and
Westminster, it is said, though other very wealthy peers are not necessarily
so admired. The perception of an aura around dukes might indicate that
some peers are more moved by the ranking of peerage than they choose
to admit even in private. But in the Chamber even a duke commands no
greater attention than any other peer.

On a day-to-day level rank was the subject of endless badinage,
usually concerning who had the higher or lower status, as in "you'll prefer
talking to him; he's an earl", but since the exclusion of most hereditary
peers, this has been rare. Few non-barons remain and peerage rank is of
no apparent political significance.

Law lords and bishops are treated differently from other peers and
their position remains unchanged by the exclusion of hereditaries. Law
lords are the ultimate court of appeal and work in one of the committee
rooms, perfectly separate from the legislative work of other peers.
Perhaps incongruously, they are entitled to contribute to law-making in
the Chamber (but possibly not for much longer because the government
plans to establish a separate supreme court). Their interventions are
infrequent as they tend to feel compromised by making laws in the House,
and then interpreting them in the courts, and they are, in any case, too
busy to spend time in the Chamber. On occasion they feel it necessary.
Because they are the most senior lawyers in England and Wales, and
because of their rarity on the benches, and because of their practised
competence in discussing the law in public, their contributions can be
influential. When Michael Howard MP was Home Secretary from
1993–97 and began playing, in the words of a Cross-bench lawyer, "fast
and loose with the law", law lords made a significant contribution to
curbing the excesses of his proposed legislation. Some retired law lords
speak more regularly in the Chamber and their views are never lightly
dismissed.

Law lords are respected for their intellects but are resented for
keeping aloof and having their own individual offices. Peers seldom meet
them, unless they happen to sit on the same committee or enquiry. Law
lords can hardly be blamed for this; they have a strenuous workload, busy

schedules and it is understandable that they prefer to eat quickly with their colleagues in the Commons' café, or grab a sandwich from the Bishops' Bar, rather than with other peers.

Law lords have a rigid hierarchy, a principle running through the whole judiciary, with the newest being the most junior. They almost never meet as a group to discuss the management of the judicial office or to reform the way they work, and such matters are decided by the most senior law lord in consultation with colleagues on an *ad hoc* basis. After a case has been heard, the five law lords deliberating in a committee room each give their statement in turn – starting with the most junior, and ending with the most senior. Although this means that the junior law lords are not pressurised into following the opinions of the more senior ones, the individualism in this ritual also means that a single-statement judgement is rare. Law lords were a tight-knit collegiate group until the Pinochet case (1998),[3] which provoked intense disagreement. Many of those involved with the case have retired, and they are slowly regaining collective harmony, but they remain split about whether it is wise to abolish the Lord Chancellor and establish a supreme court outside the House of Lords.

The relationship between the bishops, known as Lords Spiritual, and the temporal variety, is complicated. While bishops see themselves, very diffidently, as bringing a 'note of moral concern'[4] to debates, other peers – particularly other Christians, and most particularly Conservative Christians[5] – are sometimes disconcerted by their liberalism, and claim to find them maddeningly woolly; but this may just mean liberal by a ruder name. The Bishop of Lincoln revealed that two Tory whips have ticked him off for voting with Labour.[6] Others, non-believers especially, argue that bishops should not be in the Lords at all. On the whole, however, attitudes to bishops are respectful, as evidenced during discussions of reform when excluding the bishops along with the hereditaries had only limited support. It was frequently mentioned that they brought 'a spiritual dimension' to debate.

Whether or not peers value bishops tends to influence their behaviour towards them. According to one bishop, new peers scarcely return their greetings in the corridor, and he supposed it was because they feel bishops have no right to be there. On the other hand, many peers complain that courtesy has declined, so some peers mistakenly feel they are victims of pointed bad manners, of which this may be just another example.

The relationship between bishops is un-hierarchical, though precedence and seniority are significant: they dictate where they sit on the bishops' benches, how many weeks they are on duty to say prayers in the Lords, and in which locker they keep their episcopal robes. No one can tell them what to say in the House; if anything they are encouraged by Lambeth Palace to express a range of views. The twenty-six bishops form a group of elders, creating another mostly harmonious collegiate group.[7]

Class and region

The class attributes of peers as a whole have been transformed by the exclusion of most hereditary peers. The stereotype of the white male aristocrat now fits only a minority. On the other hand, before they left, the most privileged class laid down layers of the culture of the House and most of its amenities – the long tables in the Peers' Dining Room and the Barry Room, for instance, where members take the next seat available rather than sitting in groups of choice – which are perceived as quintessentially public school, gentlemen's club and upper class. They are consequently enjoyed by some, and heartily disliked by others.

Class has long been perceived as unimportant in the Lords. This assumption persists enduringly, even among insiders. In 1958 Bromhead observed: 'The atmosphere of the modern House of Lords is remarkable for its friendliness and lack of aristocratic exclusiveness.' That may have been true, as far as it goes, but he also observed that half the 116 men ennobled between 1945 and 1954 were upper class, and only twenty-three had working-class origins.[8] Lord Strabolgi claimed in 1998 to have known two classless communities during his life, Chelsea Art School and the House of Lords. And, just as class apparently goes unnoticed, life and hereditary peers are equally respected in the egalitarian rhetoric. A hereditary claimed: "After six months of being here, you do not notice the difference between life and hereditary peers. They become sensible. They are all the same, a senior bloke can be in awe of everybody. It is your experience and position that determines respect." Many peers would agree, both before the House of Lords Act 1999 and now. But is it really that simple? Some point out that when hereditary Conservatives referred to life peers as 'day boys', class snobbery was at work. Some can be disdainful towards those who are not independently wealthy. A tension between those some of those who do not need to work, and those who struggle to hold down jobs (especially difficult if working outside London), sometimes emerges.

In 1998 peers spanned every class background, from sons and daughters of the poorest backgrounds to descendants of countless silver spoons. Although irrelevant in the Chamber, such things were not forgotten in the eating rooms and bars. As in any situation in Britain, social class and its markers had a pervasive presence. I was advised, only half humorously, to put milk in tea first when sitting next to a lifer and second when beside a hereditary, to put them at their ease. One hereditary confided that when he looks at how other peers dress, "the wrong shoe or shirt and just too much polyester gives people away", and another recalled his horror at seeing, for the first time, brown suits in the House (when apparently such attire should be confined to country pursuits).

This kind of remark has become much more unusual. Among the hereditary peers who departed in 1999 was a large handful of unreconstructed snobs. Although only a tiny minority saw their position as ordained by the Divine Order of Things, some of them seriously felt that peerages were ranked according to their antiquity, so older peerages were more noble than newer ones (or, as Lloyd George put it: 'Aristocracy is like cheese – the older it is, the higher it becomes'[9]). Some believed in the wholesale class superiority of hereditary peers. A young one challenged me to account for what he believed to be the higher than average intelligence of hereditary peers and their greater success at Oxbridge exams. Apparently environmental factors were no explanation. "Perhaps," he blathered, "their honour attracts women with smart genes." I was also told that instability in society arises because the aristocracy have married out of their class, diluting their superior intelligence: "You don't get a racehorse out of a carthorse, people are not equal." Another, who thought the peerage should be kept pure, expressed horror at the socially inferior backgrounds of MPs: "Some of the members of the other place, one would not even have in one's house." He favoured a non-titled senate, so that "Joe Bloggs" up from the Commons could not contaminate the hereditary peerage. They were few and only occasional attenders, not much in evidence and of no influence, though there may have been regulars who had the sense to keep quiet about similar opinions. Some Conservative lifers complained that they were treated as lesser beings by hereditary colleagues, while others even went along with the idea of hereditaries as more "authentic". Baroness Trumpington is among the Conservative life peers who claimed that it is they who are impostors, inferior to hereditary peers with their history of public service. She held that 'being the son of your father and coming to the Lords is no worse than being a Prime Minister's favourite or failed politician', and she described hereditaries as her 'betters,' during a debate on reform.[10] Others more moderately portrayed peers by succession as more independent because, it was said, they owed nothing to anyone.

Some hereditaries and some lifers expressed their approval of a stratified society by saying that they saw no harm in class distinctions. Peerage raised individuals above these distinctions, in this view, so that their different backgrounds provided a useful range of professional expertise in the House but no longer formed their identity. This was seen as useful; exemplified by one who said that when he ran a large company and needed help negotiating with the unions, he would get excellent advice from former trade unionist peers. Those who took this position were at least inclusive as far as the House of Lords went, in the sense that they felt that once a person became a peer their working-class origins could be forgotten as they were transformed into a noble by the title. Whatever questionable opinions of themselves hereditary peers expressed in private, the House would not have countenanced their being rude, or even patronising, on the grounds of class, and no occasions of it were recounted to me.

While a few hereditaries revelled in the reflected glory of their ancestry, others were diffident, and a few seemed almost persecuted by it. Lifers usually have wider experience, and are often more used to media attention so tend to find the House less awe-inspiring than hereditaries, particularly young ones. Many of the latter are only too aware that lifers are there by merit, while they are not. One, taking the oath, heard someone ask, 'Who's that?' to the reply, 'Don't know, must be someone's son', and felt the full weight of how difficult his inheritance would make it for him to cut the mustard.

Labour hereditaries were patronised at times. Although a hereditary had been a Labour leader in the Lords in the 1970s,[11] by the time this research began most Labour peers held the hereditary principle in such derision that giving important office to one would have been unacceptable. They are seen by many as a constitutional idiocy, and know it. Although still sometimes taken seriously, in many walks of life mentioning a peerage can be disastrous, for instance, when applying for some jobs.[12] Lord Birdwood claims that hereditary peers are seen by the public as "senile, obstructive, reactionary retards, a mad assembly of Dornford Yates inbred simpletons", and another told me before 1999 that they were thought to be, "wicked layabouts, mediaeval relics or illegitimate sons of Charles II. Actually only six peers are descendants of Charles II and only one of those comes regularly." A younger Conservative peer conjured the mixture of mockery and reverence:

> "People forget that both life and hereditary peers are 'just human beings' ... If you grow up with a hereditary peerage and you are not a Hooray Henry, people assume you are Dim Tim. It is a millstone around your neck. People expect more from you ... The majority of hereditary peers are not rich, though many assume that they are ... The fact that others elevate you does not make you different but it makes others behave strangely. It can be isolating."

Such is the embarrassment of having a title for some that they conceal it outside the House, or play the role of joker and eccentric. But many of the diffident hereditaries left in 1999; the remainder have the confidence inspired by being elected by their colleagues, so this aspect has not survived.

Some peers tend to simplify the link between class origins and political parties. Upper-class Conservatives often refer to the natural alliance they feel they once had with working-class Labour colleagues. A Cross-bencher claimed that this had been shattered by New Labour and Liberal Democrats:

> "Morals are for the middle class. Working-class people can't afford them and upper-class people don't have any. In the past in the House you had working-class old Labour and upper-class Conservative and Cross-benchers getting along fine; the middle classes have now come along and spoilt everything."

The claim by upper-class peers that they have always got on fine with working-class colleagues is often heard, but only from the upper classes. Both groups, they hold, value tradition and the House of Lords, while middle-class peers are tricky. The alliance was said to be reflected in drinking habits: upper- and working-class peers tend to drink gin and tonic, beer or whisky, some from 11.30 in the morning. Middle-class peers, on the other hand, long for cappucino by day, and drink wine in the evening. This, at least, was the upper-class view: from the working-class peers' point of view, it was a good deal more complicated. While they were pleased that they were accepted and that their contributions were valued, they did not always perceive the upper class as allies. They were aware that their acceptance was conditional on their adapting to the lordly conventions of the House, which entailed far greater concessions than some upper-class colleagues guessed. It was partly an issue of style: there were outward signs of difference, such as accents and demeanour, that it was better to moderate. To walk and talk with an element of the urbane modesty expected of a lord meant they could achieve political ends more surely. These were adjustments that most could easily achieve, even if they did not always like it, but there were serious political compromises as well. Old Labour wanted the hereditaries out, root and branch. Heavily outnumbered, in the past they declined open battle. During the House of Lords Bill, however, class became a subject for debate, and Lord Davies of Oldham expressed the view of many in a mild form: 'Everyone loves an aristocratic Lord except when that Lord is exercising political power.'[13] Privately they were less polite. Now that most (upper-class) hereditary peers have gone, the process of going native – becoming a Lord irrespective of class background – has become more convincing.

Certain regions, particularly those furthest from the south-east, generate a strong sense of solidarity. Welsh, Scots, Irish and Northern peers are drawn together, both within and outside class. There is a

Yorkshire peers group, which meets with planners or councillors from the region every three months. The politics of some are formed in opposition to southern English peers. Whether it is the sound of Welsh in the Peers' Guest Room, Cumbrians worrying about foot and mouth, or Edinburgh lawyers bantering together, regionalism is very much alive in the Lords.

As soon as the House of Lords Bill was under discussion, differences were noticed and behaviour subtly changed. Tension, which had been absent, crept in and even life peers became interested in who was staying and who was not. New life peers, it was said, became abrupt, if not hostile, to hereditary peers. The lifers countered with old resentments that the older hereditary peers ticked them off and complained about their behaviour. Once the bill became law the dynamic changed again. The hereditary survivors enjoyed referring to their superior democratic legitimacy as elected peers.

Kinship and age

During debate peers refer to their relatives as 'My Noble Kinsman, Lord X'. They often have a number: aristocrats have tended to marry among themselves to beget yet more aristocrats. Between 1830–41, for instance, more than half the peers wed daughters, granddaughters, nieces or sisters of other peers.[14] The result is that the older peerages in particular are usually related to at least one other; and some in the old House had huge numbers of relations by blood or marriage among their colleagues.

Most peers had already accepted that nepotism is an arbitrary system that can perpetuate incompetent elites and deny equality of opportunity. Many were, therefore, reluctant to draw attention to kinship in the House, others do not admit to it, and some are just not interested. In a questionnaire in 1999[15] (just before the hereditaries were excluded) nearly all underestimated the number of their relatives in the House. Only eleven out of 176 peers admitted to five or more. One Cross-bencher named twenty-one noble relatives. Out of 176, 117 claimed that they had no relatives in the House, which, in some cases, must have meant only that they had none who interested them.

Despite voracious intermarriage for centuries, and popular expectation to the contrary, consanguinity was among the least significant connections between peers and has become irrelevant to the new House. A Conservative said that he occasionally managed to get Liberal cousins to vote with him, and a few votes in the hereditary peer elections were given to relatives, but these instances were exceptional. Outside the Chamber it remains a source of amusement and teasing, particularly between relatives belonging to different parties, and it applies to some lifers as well as hereditaries.

Presently, a number of peers enjoy connubial bliss together: Lord and Lady Howe (life peers) for instance, and Baroness Eccles of Moulton is married to an excluded viscount. Baroness Brigstocke and Lord Griffiths tied the knot since becoming life peers. Before the House of Lords Act, Baroness Masham of Ilton and the Earl of Swinton (life and hereditary respectively) both sat, and Lord Brabourne and Countess Mountbatten of Burma (hereditaries) were married and both entitled to sit in the House but rarely attended.

Age does not automatically accord respect. Peers – with an average age of sixty-eight in 2004 – marvel at someone of ninety-five who speaks well, but do not pay more attention on that account. The media love mocking elderly peers, usually with prejudice. When insiders joke about confused elders, on the other hand, they are talking of colleagues within the benign circle of the House, and tend to do so with affection. However, Lord Williams of Mostyn related that when sitting at the long table in the Peers' Dining Room, the venerable Lord Longford asked: 'Lord Williams is my very good friend, do you know him?' 'Yes,' Lord Williams of Mostyn replied. 'It's me.' Longford was referring to his close friend Lord Williams of Elvel, and was perhaps too polite to correct the minister, a reminder that assumption can reinforce prejudice.

Young peers are regarded ambivalently. They are under-represented (there were ten under thirty before 1999, none at present and 78 per cent of the peers were over sixty in 2001). They are, therefore, sometimes listened to with great attention. That some hereditaries are young was even used as an argument for the legitimacy of that group. If the subject is deemed to be associated with youth – such as information technology – older peers may defer to them, but on other subjects young peers can be patronised or marginalised. Some older peers see them as unreliable, particularly when they disagree with their views. Even when receiving enthusiastic support from other peers, they have to take care not to "get above themselves". When Lord Freyberg, at twenty-three years old, extracted financial support for war widows from the Conservative government it was considered a coup and outstandingly impressive; but along with the surprised congratulations, he was advised not to draw attention to himself again to avoid incurring their lordships' displeasure.

Young peers, and those who work closely with young people, too frequently find themselves forced to point out as forcefully as they are able the strengths of youthfulness because older peers are inclined to dwell on its vulnerabilities. Peers' ambivalence towards youth was most clearly expressed in debates about homosexuality. During the Sexual Offences (Amendment) Bill, Earl Russell suggested that young people's views were being ignored. Lord Elton replied: 'Does not age and experience count for something in the guidance of the young?'[16]

Gender

From what I had read of the House of Commons, I expected to find women peers patronised or overlooked. Sylvia Rodgers had written that women MPs were confined to feminised spaces, taking nurturing roles such as the education or social services briefs,[17] Helene Hayman (now Baroness) that, 'they either pat you on the head or pat you on the bottom', and another woman MP that, 'the House of Commons is a male institution with silly rules, secret conventions (not written down anywhere or justifiable), managed by men, for men'.[18] The Labour party is reputed to have a masculine ethos that tends to exclude women – 'women have a place and it ain't at the meetings that men attend', according to one MP – and many Conservative male MPs have little interest in equal opportunities for women.[19]

I could not have been more wrong: women thrive in the Lords. This cannot be attributed to any initial enthusiasm for the idea.[20] Even women visitors were only admitted to the galleries after the 1830s; before that they had to hide behind a red baize curtain or squeeze into the roof space out of their Lordships' sight. When Lord Simon introduced a bill in 1953 to create women peers, the fear of 'bossy political women disturbing the peace'[21] was expressed. The measure was defeated. In 1958 the Earl of Home, a Conservative government minister, argued for the introduction of women to update the House and bring it into line with the Commons. Rather optimistically, he said he expected widespread support even while acknowledging that many peers felt women talked too much and would contribute little.[22] Arguments against women had been led since the previous year – 'with a great skirl of pipes and swinging of his claymore'[23] – by the Earl of Airlie, who claimed that their place was in church, with the children and at the kitchen stove. Almost every speaker agreed and Earl Ferrers (who remains in the House) went further:

> I have the idea of your Lordships' House becoming a repository for over-exuberant female politicians, and unfortunately we are unable to elevate them further, for that prerogative rests with the Almighty. Frankly, I find women in politics highly distasteful. In general, they are organising, they are pushing and they are commanding. Some of them do not even know where loyalty to their country lies ... It is generally accepted, for better or worse, that a man's judgment is generally more logical and less tempestuous than that of a woman. Why then should we encourage women to eat their

way, like acid into metal, into positions of trust and responsibility which previously men have held? If we allow women in this House where will this emancipation end? ... I feel sure that nine out of ten noble Lords have in their heart ... that we like women; we admire them; sometimes we even grow fond of them; but we do not like them here.[24]

He failed to alter the course of events. Lord Airlie's amendment to exclude women from terms of the Life Peerages Act was defeated, and between 1958 and 2001 154 women[25] became life peers, in the early days many of them wives or widows of eminent men. Baroness Wootton of Abinger was the first to receive a life peerage, and Baroness Swanborough was the first woman peer to be introduced.[26] After the 1963 Peerage Act, another Conservative measure, female hereditaries (of whom there are few) were allowed to sit as well.

Initially, peers were displeased. The belief prevailed that politics was not an appropriate arena for women because they were unfit for rational debate. One peer said with disdain, "Fancy having to meet a woman in a library". Women, in addition, took up space. When I asked how they had changed the place, a hereditary who had been attending for half a century or so replied, "They pinched some lavatories". The ideal peer was male.

Over time women became accepted. Even those phobic of change admitted that women brought colour; some went even further and perceived a beneficial influence. For most, women made the social life in the House more enjoyable, though in the early years the women who gained most respect had to endure being 'one of the boys'. This was not exclusively however: one early woman peer was apparently boasting that she had slept with every member of the Labour front-bench. A soft voice piped up from the other end of the long table, 'Darling, what about me?' 'Oh God, I thought you were dead,' she replied.

Doubters remain. A male Conservative commented sadly that recent women peers were inferior to the earlier more masculine and robust sort. But on the whole women are now seen as equals as ministers, politicians, intellectuals and parliamentary performers. Women and men are treated as equals in the Chamber and committee rooms: they have the same opportunities to speak, are listened to with equal attention, influence proceedings to the same degree and receive the same respectful treatment from officers and staff. Lord Carter found that trouble among regulars always came from men; it was rare for women to complain, moan or be awkward.

I found the confidence of women peers striking. If anything, women seem to punch above their weight and make a larger impact than their numbers might justify. According to many, the gentle, courteous style of the Lords suits them well. Most have had to fight endless hard battles during their careers; many said that they had encountered far less sexism in the Lords than previous workplaces. Only during the tumultuous Question Time do women questioners appear to assert themselves less readily than men.

But at any time, there is usually a single woman peer who is the focus of male hostility. At the beginning of my research, it was a Liberal Democrat who attracted complaints because, to her critics (mainly Conservatives and Cross-benchers), she sounded shrill and spoke for too long. In due course she was replaced as the object of (especially) male censure by another woman peer from the same party who was considered hectoring and long-winded. Both were referred to as "fishwives". Most women are considered to be good performers but when they fail, unlike men, it is their gender that is blamed.

General acceptance makes women peers forgiving about the inequalities and irritants that remain. Only one woman peer pointed out that speeches are started with 'My lords', not 'My lords and ladies', and none seems to take exception at being addressed as 'Madam Chairman'. It seems likely that this will seem increasingly out of tune with the large number of institutions that use more neutral or specific terms. There are already signs of change: Lord Acton has already started referring to his step-cousin, Baroness Darcy de Knayth, as 'My Noble Kinswoman'; Baroness Hale (Britain's first woman law lord) has persuaded the door-keepers to announce 'Their lordships and her ladyship'; and Lord St John of Fawsley teased a Cross-bencher (when he used 'man' to mean 'man and woman') by saying, 'why not say that "she" should be taken to include "he"'.[27]

Outside the Chamber, the gentleman's club atmosphere can be excluding, and in the corridors and bars women can be demeaned. One said sadly that peers unknown to her frequently comment on her legs in a way only agreeable between lovers. A common complaint is that male peers appear happy when they are getting attention from their female counterparts but alarmed by women interested in each other. On seeing a group of women drinking coffee, male peers often assume conspiracy: the question, 'What are you plotting?' is annoyingly predictable. The comment of one hereditary peer, that a particular woman peer had slept her way to power, and of another that the same woman peer was "better horizontal than vertical", are typical of the attitude of a very small number of male peers. Such remarks, combining dismissiveness with envy, seem to be in the nature of debris of old-style sexism or even misogyny that has mostly gone with the hereditary peers, and even the makers of these remarks are able to conduct themselves towards women in the Chamber and in committees with courtesy and respect. What is left is misplaced gallantry. When a woman peer explained to a colleague that it is embarrassing when a more senior peer opens a door for her, although

Table 7.1 Ministerial posts held by women and men peers during their careers, 2002

House of Lords post	Male (all peers)	Male (regulars)	Female (all peers)	Female (regulars)
Leader of the Lords	9	5	2	2
Parliamentary under-secretary of state	17	10	6	5
Minister (excl. above)	29	20	9	7
Spokesperson	85	61	26	22
Whip	54	44	19	18
Total	194	140	62	54

Source: Crewe and Kruger, 2002, see p. 129, n. 28.

she is the one who should be paying respect to him, he did not seem to understand at all.

During this research the position of women peers changed as a result of the exclusion of hereditaries and the influx of new peers. The number of women peers increased from 83 to 110 while the number of men was roughly halved, so the proportion of women rose from 7 per cent to 16 per cent. Women have held many of the highest front-bench positions and won respect, and, in a few cases, adulation (see Table 7.1). The first woman Chief Whip was appointed in 1973 and Leader of the House in 1981 (the latter was the Conservative peer Baroness Young). Between 1998 and 2000 the Lords had a woman as Leader of the House; there were also women ministers of state in the Ministry of Defence (for the first time), the Europe, Foreign and Commonwealth Office, and the departments of Environment, Transport and the Regions, Scotland, Agriculture, Education and Employment, International Development, Social Security, and Women's Affairs. In 2003 a black woman peer, Baroness Amos, was appointed Secretary of State for International Development, and then Leader of the House, while Baroness Symons is Deputy Leader. Baroness Williams of Crosby has been Leader of the Liberal Democrat peers since 2001, all three parties have forceful front-bench women, Baroness Hale has been working as a law lord since January 2004, and many female Cross-benchers command huge respect.

Of women peers, 62 per cent attend regularly as opposed to 43 per cent of men. This means that 22 per cent of the regular peers were women in 2001–02.[28] A similar proportion of the frequent users of the Library are women peers.

The House now responds more rapidly to women's demands. For example, a woman peer was told off for wearing trousers in 1997, but by

1999 they had become perfectly acceptable. On the other hand, the furore caused by a woman visitor breast-feeding in the Peers' Guest Room in 2000 seemed hysterical. There is a way to go before womanhood in all its roles is accepted. This is also apparent in the way the work of the House is organised. Caring roles and family life become difficult, which still bears more heavily on women. Lord Strathclyde likes the hours because he is able to play with his babies of a morning, but Baronesses Ashton of Upholland, Buscombe and Northover, all with school-age children, can seldom see them in the evening because sittings start in the afternoon. Peers' outside obligations are ignored; their personal, family and work interests are deemed irrelevant.

Disability

The number of peers with physical disabilities is high partly because, with an average age of sixty-eight, conditions such as deafness and arthritis are common. It was higher before the exodus, partly because of age, and because there are more chronic conditions among hereditaries than among life peers (disability is a significant cause of discrimination, and life peers are high achievers). The number of hereditary peers with disabilities is close to the national average of around 15 per cent.

Disabled peers are patronised neither more nor less than anyone else. Although some claim that in debate peers give way to disabilities, most say a stick, a wheelchair or a hearing aid make no difference. Disabled peers are inclined to take part in debates concerning disability, but specialise in as many other topics as well as anyone else. Lord Carter pointed out that giving wheelchair-users a good spot in the Chamber during disability debates, but not on other occasions, was an example of classic stereotyping (in this case of their interests). He managed to secure agreement to a permanent central place for those in wheelchairs. One able-bodied peer complained that the "disabled lobby is too strong", but most appreciate this as one of the areas of House of Lords' expertise, under-represented in the Commons. The one story of outrageous disrespect that I was told was untypical. A woman peer in a wheelchair was collaring a minister in the Bishops' Bar about a particular bill and a third peer told her to stop, but she did not, so he wheeled her out of the bar. The story-teller was more shocked by someone irritating a minister during his lunch break than by a wheelchair user being pushed about like an object.

While I found no widespread discrimination towards disabilities, the building is unkind to wheelchair users. Inside the Chamber there are satisfactory areas to park, but:

"The only problem is that the physical layout of the palace is not good for wheelchairs. To get from A to B you have to go around. When getting to the Grand Committee Room you have to get an attendant to help you. You then have to go down the Commons, across the yard, up in a lift and finally you get to the Committee Room. You can't change your mind at the last minute, you have to plan everything. It is just the physical side of disability that is a bore. But there are always younger, fitter people around to help. It does not make much difference."

Mental illness is another matter. The *Standing Orders* do not disqualify the insane from taking part; but those with serious mental illness usually stay away. There is tolerance towards unfocused behaviour – whether caused by senility, drunkenness or illness – but it occurs less often than the media would like us to believe. Staff tactfully guide peers unable to cope with the Chamber to a taxi home, if necessary lending them the money to pay for it. It was usually only for three-line whips that very confused peers used to make their uncertain way to the division lobbies – then kept out of harm's way in the bars. Both madness and eccentricity have become rare since the departure of most hereditary peers.

Sexuality

It was a peer, Lord Arran, who first proposed the decriminalisation of homosexuality in 1967, but the Lords then stepped backwards in relation to the rest of the country, introducing an amendment (since then known as Clause or Section 28) to the Government Bill in 1988 that prohibited the promotion of homosexuality by local authorities. In November 2000 they voted against equalising the legal age for consensual sex for hetero-sexuals and homosexuals by 205 to 144.[29] Votes are not a clear indication of opinion on their own, even unwhipped ones such as this, but the contributions to debate reveal the disgust that many peers feel towards gay sex. Peers never seem so remote from the rest of society, and seldom so ill-informed, as when discussing this issue. That it is not yet accepted would be gross understatement. Like Queen Victoria, most peers refuse even to recognise that females also indulge. Earl Russell told the House: 'This issue has done more damage to the reputation of this House in the quarters within which I move than anything else since Irish home rule.'[30]

During debates about homosexuality some peers have given vent to a hostility towards gay men that they dare not direct to any other group. According to this faction, gay sex is abhorrent, and not only a serious danger to marriage but to the entire social fabric. It is one of the few areas in which the 'alliance' between Conservatives and a few old Labour

members holds true. In both, religion may form the backbone of the senti-
ment: many Conservatives are Church of England, and the influence of
Methodism on old Labour is strong. Argument, on the other hand, has
shifted since the 1950s from God to society: there are fewer references in
debate to mortal sin and corruption, and more about social consequences,
particularly the threat to the family.[31] Bishops (with a few exceptions)
tie themselves in complicated theological knots, one after another
standing in the Chamber to proclaim the absolute inclusiveness of the
Church, and then proceeding to relegate gays to the margins. Many peers
appear to see homosexuality almost as a kind of addiction, easily caught
by those with no previous inclination, after just one puff. In their eyes,
therefore, unless contained by legislation, it could spread like a cancer
through society, turning our proud manhood to degenerates. A more
moderate statement of the same principle is that boys are naturally
attracted to each other during late adolescence but will recover their
'natural' inclinations unless turned permanently astray by preying older
men. To protect society, therefore, legislation is needed, they say, against
the older men.

Only one peer, Lord Alli, has declared himself gay, and is described
by others, demonstrating the courtesy of peers even at their most bigoted,
as brave for having done so. Peers' descriptions of male gay sex are
usually graphic, detailed, biological and irrelevant to the argument, and
while some of the views expressed in debate seemed peculiar and
surprising, they get worse in private. I was told, for instance, that homosexual men wanted the age of consent lowered because younger boys were
less likely to infect them with HIV.

Most Conservatives, and the majority of Cross-benchers who voted,
oppose reform to legislation that discriminates against homosexuals,
while most Labour and Liberal Democrats, particularly women, are for
change. But there are exceptions. Conservative hereditary Lord Lucas
made a forceful plea in favour of acceptance: 'It is ridiculous to crimi-
nalise young people of 16 and 17 for engaging in homosexual activities
among themselves. If that law had been in force when I was at school,
Eton would have been decimated.'[32] Besides Lord Alli, there are also, of
course, discreet gays on all benches who support gay rights. There is a
Tory campaign for homosexual equality, and Conservatives and Cross-
benchers who clearly detest homophobia on the one hand, and, on the
other, anti-liberal Labour peers. (In 2000, fifteen Labour peers voted
against repealing Clause 28 – outlawing the 'promotion' of homosexuality – and seventeen against equalising the age of consent for homosexual
and heterosexual sex.)

Baroness Young was perhaps the doughtiest combatant against
homosexuality – she moved amendments, made press appearances, and

was responsible for an exhibition in the House warning of the dangers of pro-gay propaganda, but few believed that she was homophobic. Even her opponents say that while she had strong views about marriage and the protection of young people, she was not hostile to gay men. Unlike many male peers, she did not express revulsion for gay sex, but she made no secret of her feeling that homosexuality threatens individual happiness and society's stability. She derived this from a Christian belief in the sanctity of marriage; a position shared by the majority of her supporters. Evidence of her concern for children is clear in her speeches:

> I have argued consistently throughout the debate that what adults choose to do in private is a matter for them. It is certainly not a matter for me and not one on which I wish to comment. However, what we put in front of children is a matter for us all. I shall fight for the protection of children while I have breath in my body.[33]

Even peers of no particular faith tend to assume that happiness can be found only in the nuclear family, preferably within holy matrimony. Peers in regular contact with children, such as teachers and sociologists, point out in vain that such households have ceased to be the norm, and that even the Conservative party has ended its war against single parents. Evidence does nothing to deflect traditionalist peers from campaigning for a very particular ideal of family life with marriage as its foundation.

Leaders of the 'pro-marriage' lobby receive massive support from the public. Their postbags come mostly from people who are elderly and Christian, and who link homosexuality with other social changes that they find calamitous. The Bible is often cited. According to one correspondent, homosexuality is 'no more sinful in the eyes of God than perhaps theft or murder or even telling lies'. Another felt that if we push the boundaries of tolerance to allow homosexuality, then other deviant behaviour would follow such as bestiality and necrophilia. Concern about moral decline is expressed with gusto: 'It is extraordinary that Section 28 should be necessary in a Christian society; but that merely reflects the parlous state of morality today. To repeal it would be to continue on a course of destruction and chaos.' This support undoubtedly gives the anti-gay lobby confidence, and also provides manure and sunshine to a homophobic culture among Tory peers, among whom visceral dislike of gays can still be voiced without risk to reputation.

So prevalent has been animosity among many Conservative, Crossbench and old Labour peers toward male gays, and so unbridled its expression, that theories to explain it have proliferated. One clerk speculated that it may be seen to threaten the inheritance from father to son. This may be a rationalisation for a few hereditary peers, but homophobia affects also those without wealth or a hereditary title to pass on. Others attribute it to peers being forcibly sodomised at public school, but some homophobes did not attend a public school, and it is improbable that more than a tiny proportion even of public school boys have been raped. Less immoderately, it is suggested that peers are troubled by memories of gay sex or romance at public school, whether they found it pleasant or unpleasant, and wish to protect children from similar confusing experience. But, again, public schools cannot be held entirely responsible: alumni of other kinds of school, and women – notably the late Baroness Young and Baroness Blatch – are among the most vocal opponents of more a more liberal approach to homosexuality.

Some other explanation is needed to account for homophobia in the Lords. The emotional intensity engendered by the specific issue of homosexuality may be attributed to a much broader reaction to change. Traditionalists have numerous bitter defeats behind them, and some are not entirely reconciled to any of them. Britain's multi-ethnic society is an offence to them, but to grumble about it can lead to accusations of racism. Women taking their place in politics is also uncomfortable for some, but to voice discontent could insult female colleagues. They have a clutch of other old scores: loss of empire, Britain's declining world influence, and the other stored resentments of an all-powerful caste that has had pre-eminence knocked from under its feet in only a couple of generations. Homosexuality may be one of the few subjects on which it is it still, they feel, permissible for them to express their traditionalist views, and tolerance towards it has become symbolic of all societal change, so they give it all they've got.

Most see themselves not as 'anti-homosexual' but as 'pro-children', protecting young people from suffering. Their alarm for family and society are unfeigned, and feelings of disgust for the act of sodomy expressed by some peers are articulated as saving children from having to endure what they feel must be terrible experiences. Their position is therefore defined not so much by deep-seated malignity toward homosexuals, though that exists among a few. Rather, it has become part of the explosive wider moral debate about the character of British society; whether tolerance and liberalism has damaged what they hold dear. The combination of this with the equally inflammatory subject of sex creates an emotional heat found in few other debates.

It is an issue that both sides regard as central to the cosmic struggle for the soul of the nation. Apart from reform of the House, it has been *the* emotive issue in the conflict between traditionalists and modernisers. The latter value sexual tolerance and are not necessarily impressed by the family as a moral force. Traditionalists tend to believe in Christianity and the family as the founts of all virtue. Both sides are symbolically wrestling for the nation's identity and future.

The average age of the House is relevant. Attitudes towards sex have changed dramatically during the last half-century and can be more reliably predicted on the basis of age than any other issue that comes regularly before the House. However, since Baroness Young died in 2002, more liberal legislation on homosexuality has been allowed through: attempts to stop gay couples from adopting children were thwarted during the Adoption Bill in 2002, and Clause 28 was finally repealed in the Local Government Act 2003.

Race, ethnicity and religion

The ethnic and religious composition of the House of Lords cannot be exactly quantified as peers do not fill out an equal opportunities form; but it is obvious that the proportion of black, Asian and non-Christian peers in House of Lords has considerably increased over the last ten years. The first Lord Stanley of Alderley, taking his seat in the nineteenth century, has been described as the first Muslim peer, but we can be more certain of Baroness Uddin and Lord Ahmed who took the oath in 1998. The first Jewish peer, Nathan Rothschild, was ennobled in 1885, and in 1911 Lord Sinha was (reputedly) the first non-white peer. The number of black and Asian peers was roughly estimated as twenty-one in 1999 (see Table 7.2), and nineteen after the House of Lords Act when two Asian hereditaries left.

As Prime Minister Mrs Thatcher was, according to colleagues, reluctant to ennoble black or Asian people on the grounds that it could lead to demands from other minorities. Most black and Asian peers received peerages during the 1990s and a few more were selected by the Appointments Commission in 2001. As a result of the House of Lords Act and introduction of new peers the proportion of black, Asian, and mixed-race peers doubled from roughly 1.5 per cent to 3 per cent (the national figure is closer to 8 per cent).[34]

The number of peers with other religious or ethnic affiliations is uncertain. The questionnaire I sent to the House in 1999 presented a very incomplete picture: of the 170 peers who responded to a question about religion, 126 indicated that they had a religious faith of whom 123 identified themselves as Christian, two as Jewish, and one as Buddhist.[35] Of the forty-four with no faith, one was a humanist. No Muslim or Hindu responded, and neither did a scientologist I interviewed earlier that year (who was anyway excluded in 1999).

Lord Patel of Blackburn raised a few eyebrows by appearing in what a clerk described as 'Muslim dress' when he took his seat in 2000, but the House has got used to his attire without a fuss. When a *yarmulka* (the

Table 7.2   Black, Asian and mixed-race peers, 1999

Ethnic group	Women	Men	Hereditary	Life	Total
Afro-Caribbean	3	1	0	4	4
Asian	5	10	1	14	15
Mixed race	1	1	1	1	2
Total	9	12	2	19	21

skull-cap worn by many practising Jews) is seen in the Lords, it usually belongs to a visitor. No regularly attending peer wears one in the House. Peers estimate that there are at least twenty to thirty Jewish peers and probably many more (higher than the proportion nationally), but as one pointed out to me, they tend not to draw attention to their Jewishness. Why is this? "Anti-Semitism sleeps lightly in British society," he replied.

Anti-Semitism partly evaporated in Britain during the second half of the twentieth century, and in part it went underground. It is seldom visible, but a peer who disagreed with the War Crimes Bill nevertheless detected hints of it in some of the debate. Some old diehards remain ambivalent towards Jews, impressed but wary, regarding them as intelligent and high achievers, but given to protecting their own and not always to be trusted. Raising the subject of Jews during the research could make peers uneasy: some wished to criticise Israeli government atrocities but were reluctant to risk the accusations of anti-Semitism that such a view could provoke. Very few, and only those with experience of the Middle East, dared to draw attention to the occupation and human-rights abuses suffered by Palestinians.

Other forms of racism are no easier to pin down. White peers do not want to appear racist, even if they are; and non-whites may not always wish to see, or admit to, prejudice when it happens. As they become assimilated as peers, it becomes beneath their dignity to be victims, especially in the House. An Asian peer airily observed there was no trace of racism in the Lords, then added that a doorkeeper had been rude as though the peer were "a jumped up person who had no right to be here", and a hereditary in a bar had gone for the jugular:

> "He started talking about, 'These people, they have no right to be here', and I said 'How dare you speak to people like that, we came to help you'. I attacked him back. Nowadays peers would be far too gentlemanly to say such a thing. It is the human condition for people to be suspicious of people who are different."

The expression of this kind of hostility has been extremely uncommon for some years and since the exclusion of the more backward-looking hereditaries, it has become unthinkable. Prejudice against difference – whether on the basis of race, ethnicity or religion – is likely to be subtly conveyed if at all. One elderly Labour peer, for example, disapproved of a Deputy Speaker living in an ashram as if Eastern religion were insufficiently dignified. Old-fashioned peers can still flounder in conversation, unable to find common ground with conventional gambits such as 'which school did you go to?' or 'which regiment?', but they have the same problem with younger, non-public-school peers. Others, brought up under British colonialism, are often sincerely interested in the countries of origin of black or Asian peers, which is usually welcomed by those born elsewhere. Those born in Britain can find it misplaced and irritating.

Several black and Asian peers report that being accepted takes time, even now. When Lord Alli first showed up at the Peers' Entrance in 1998, police officers assumed he could not be a peer (perhaps partly also because he is thirty years younger than the average) and took him round to a visitors' entrance – and he has not been the only one. Pressure on black and Asian peers to prove that they can conform and perform in the Chamber is manifest. One reported peers walking out when he began to speak, as though he was unlikely to say anything of interest, when, in fact, his speech was later praised as one of the best in the debate. Black Baronesses Amos and Scotland, both ministers, are widely admired for their courtesy, competence and command of procedure. Scotland is on most peers' lists of top-performing peers, and was voted Peer of the Year in 2004,[36] while Amos was Britain's second black minister and has recently been made Leader of the House. The emphasis and frequency of the praise they draw betrays a hint of surprise, reflecting lower expectations and perhaps a desire to prove their anti-racist credentials. Other less dazzling black or Asian peers, who may not have integrated sufficiently in the eyes of other peers, are described as "chippy", when it is unlikely the same adjective would be used for white peers.

The ambivalence of those white peers fearful of cultural change is a pale shadow of the emotions black peers evoke among racist Britons outside the House. All black peers receive quantities of virulent hate mail, of which this is a typical example:

> We do not live in a multi-cultural society ... How dare you ... come here and tell me an indigenous white Englishman how we should behave and what we should do. If you people don't like it here then go home ... Nothing will ever make [you] British. In fact I resent people like you even sitting in my Parliament passing laws over me.

Death threats are taken seriously and the police try to find out who has sent them, but the recipients are invariably very quiet about it because, they say, they are reluctant to give publicity to maniacs. Consequently white peers have no idea what their black and Asian colleagues have to put up with.

There may also be a less conscious reason for their silence. In the social goldfish bowl of the House, peers' primary identity is lordly and it is important how well they are seen to measure up to such expectations. Characteristics like race and sex or class are supposed to be subordinate; if emphasised they may detract from an individual's lordliness. In this context, receiving hate mail, although involuntary and profoundly unwelcome, might well be seen by some peers to be well below the dignity of a peer. And the recipients, by admitting to it, might be drawing attention to something intrinsically unlordly about themselves, both in terms of ethnicity and vulnerability. It is not dissimilar to the silence of most Jewish and gay peers about respectively their ethnicity (or religion), and their sexuality, and suggests that, although many points of view are represented in the House, a social stereotype of a peer remains. Although women seem to have been easily absorbed into the category of peer, for some others the price of influence is a conformity that may be uncomfortable.

Notes

1 Even during the State Opening of Parliament peers are not placed in a seat prescribed by rank, though their wives are, and since the 1960s attendance and voting records have been in alphabetical order rather than rank (J. P. Morgan, 1975, *The House of Lords and the Labour Government 1964–70*, Oxford University Press, Oxford, p. 12).

2 A. Mitchell, 1999, *Farewell My Lords*, Politico's, London, p. 149.

3 In 1998 the former Argentinian dictator, General Pinochet, was arrested in Britain on a warrant from Spain requesting his extradition on murder charges. The law lords ruled that he could face an attempt to extradite him, but they were split 3:2. When one of the three was later criticised for failing to declare an interest – a connection to a human-rights organisation – the law lords disagreed about whether he had acted appropriately.

4 Bishop of Ripon, HL Deb., 23 February 1999, col. 967.

5 Christianity has also had a strong influence on the Labour party, but perhaps because much of it was nonconformist they seem less concerned about the role of the bishops (see Graham Dale, 2000, *God's Politicians: The Christian Contribution to 100 Years of Labour*, Harper Collins, London.)

6 Bishop of Lincoln as quoted by Mitchell, *ibid.*, p. 77.

7 There are also several other bishops who do not hold ex-officio posts but have been made life peers.

8 P. A. Bromhead, 1958, *The House of Lords and Contemporary Politics*, Routledge and Kegan Paul, London, pp. 22, 29.

9 Quoted by James Plaskitt MP, HC Deb, 1 February 1999, col. 662.

10 Baroness Trumpington, as quoted by Mitchell, *ibid.*, p. 146 and in the HL Deb., 14 October 1998, col. 980.

11 The late Lord Shepherd was Leader in 1974–6. He was referred to by another Labour Lord as the 'father of the Labour peers', a hugely influential figure in their group. Lord Shackleton was a hereditary peer and Leader before him, as was Lord Longford, a peer by birth and appointment.

12 Lord Ponsonby, HL Deb., 15 October 1998, col. 1072.

13 Lord Davies of Oldham, HL Deb., 30 March 1999, col. 305.

14 E. A. Smith, 1992, *The House of Lords in British Politics and Society 1815–1911*, Longman, London, p. 57.

15 See Appendix 2 for details.

16 Earl Russell and Lord Elton, HL Deb., 13 November 2000, cols 43–4.

17 S. Rodgers, 1993, 'Women's space in a men's house: the British House of Commons', in S. Ardener (ed.), *Women and Space: Ground Rules and Social Maps*, Berg, London.

18 L. McDougall, 1998, *Westminster Women*, Vintage, London, pp. 192–3.

19 Joni Lovenduski, 1996, 'Sex, gender and British politics', in J. Lovenduski and P. Norris (eds), *Women in Politics*, Oxford University Press, Oxford, p. 14; P. Norris, 'Women politicians: transforming Westminster?' in Lovenduski and Norris, *ibid.*, p. 96.

20 Smith, *ibid.*, p. 12.

21 As quoted by Baroness Gould of Potternewton, HL Deb., 29 March 1999, col. 142.

22 Earl of Home, HL Deb., 3 December 1957, col. 611.

23 Lord Chancellor (Viscount Kilmuir), HL Deb., 5 December 1957, vol. CCVI, col. 943.

24 Earl Ferrers, HL Deb., 3 December 1957, vol. CCVI, cols 709–10.

25 Source: House of Lords Information Office.

26 'Life peeresses take the oath, first in history of Parliament, Lords ceremony, from our Parliamentary Correspondent', *The Times*, 22 October 1958, p. 10. It has been claimed that the first woman life peer was the Countess of Norfolk, created in 1397, but she could not have been a member of the Lords as women did not sit in the House until 1958 (see http://www.baronage.co.uk/bphtm-01/const-03.html).

27 HL Deb., 12 January 2004, col. 404.

28 Regular attendance is defined as appearing on a hundred or more of the sitting days out of a total of 177. Seventy-two of the 117 women attended for a hundred days or more; 255 of the 597 men attended for a hundred or more days. E. Crewe and J. Kruger, 2002, *Database of Information about the Expertise of Members of the House of Lord in 2002*, UK Data Archive, University of Essex. The main source of information for this database was *Dod's Parliamentary Companion 2002*, Vacher Dod, London.

29 A government amendment to repeal the prohibition on promoting homosexuality by teaching or publishing material was also defeated on 7 February 2000 by 210 to 165.

30 Earl Russell, HL Deb., 13 November 2000, col. 45.

31 HL Deb., 4 December 1957, vol. CCVI, cols 733–832.

32 HL Deb., 13 November 1999, col. 749.

33 Baroness Young, HL Deb., 24 July 2000, col. 103.

34 2001 National Census, http://www.statistics.gov.uk, accessed 17 July 2003.

35 Of the Christians, eleven did not specify their denomination. The remainder were: Church of England 77, Catholic 15, Church of Scotland 8, Methodist 6, Church in Wales 1, Quaker 1, Church of Ireland 1, Welsh Presbyterian 1, Scottish Presbyterian 1, Non-conformist 1, United Reform Church 1.

36 Channel 4 television viewers voted Baroness Scotland Peer of the Year in February 2004, for details see http://www.channel4.com/news/2004/02/week_2/10_award.html.

8 Parties and Cross-benchers

Joining

Until about 1830 peers tended to identify their interests with the crown. Since the monarch chose governments, opposition to government in the upper Chamber was negligible. From then, however, 'the onset of a long period of mainly Whig and Liberal governments meant that they [peers] had to choose between government and resistance to reform, two principles not previously incompatible'.[1] Issues of reform rapidly polarised Whigs and Tories in the Lords and, in order to field adequate numbers for divisions, the machinery of party management was quite quickly brought into being. By 1880 all but thirteen lords described themselves as party peers: 280 Conservatives and 204 Liberals; and it had become usual, by that time, to ennoble a high proportion of former MPs. In the 2003 House of 668 peers, almost two-thirds belonged to the three main parties (209 Conservative, 185 Labour, 64 Liberal Democrat), while 179 were Cross-benchers.[2]

In 2001, well over half the life peers had been politicians; that is, former MPs or local councillors, usually awarded peerages for commitment to a party and to maintain its numbers in the Lords. Others were, and still are, elevated to the peerage so that the party could make use of specialist knowledge, such as Lord Carter speaking on agriculture for the Labour party. These are working peers, expected to bump up numbers during debate and present themselves to vote. Until recently, others were given peerages solely in recognition of their distinction, such as the architect Lord Foster of Thames Bank, the author Baroness James of Holland Park, the civil servant Lord Allen of Abbeydale, and all former Speakers in the Commons, Cabinet Secretaries and Chiefs of the Defence Staff. These were honours peers. They were free to sit with any party, or might prefer the cross-benches, if they cared to sit at all. Only a few honours peerages have been created since the Prime Minister established the Appointments Commission in May 2000.[3]

Party peers tend to be swept along by their party machine, attending meetings and 'taking the party whip'. This signifies active party membership: the whip is withdrawn from disloyal or delinquent party members rather than administered to them. (Losing the whip is temporary exclusion from the party, and is not the same as the permanent expulsion which befell Conservative Lords Nunburnholme for being too right-wing and Archer when imprisoned for perjury.) When it is withdrawn, peers no longer receive the papers (whips) produced by parties, outlining forthcoming business and instructing them how to vote, and they cannot attend party meetings. It may sound desirable to lose the whip but being treated as an outcast can be shameful and distressing. Regular peers will put up with huge inconvenience and political compromise to avoid the disapproval incurred by even temporary exile from the party.

A one-line whip indicates that peers should be there if possible; two lines means 'very important', and the message of three-line whips is 'drop everything and be there or else'. It has been claimed that the 1911 Parliament Bill had a four-line whip.[4] Whips are also the bottom rung, in each party, of the usual channels – party peers who make sure other members vote by phoning them at home, sending messages through their pagers, dragging them out of bars and sitting on the gate (fender) in the Prince's Chamber to prevent them skiving off early. They are the subject of a large number of bad jokes – 'I'd give a lot to be whipped by your lovely lady whip' and so on. When the whip is on, whips sit outside the Chamber; when it is taken off, they evaporate and word goes round that everyone can go home.

Clerks explain to new boys that they may sit anywhere in the Chamber, but in practice each party has its own benches and party segregation is not only unquestioned, the alternative is unthinkable. They are, after all, opposing teams. Propinquity is essential: it makes it possible to maintain competitive mettle in the Chamber through hours of debate, and over years and decades it feeds the sense of party unity. Colleagues become your social milieu, they share your moral code, protect you from the hostile groups in other parts of the Chamber – by rising to defend your argument against attack from members of another party – and occasionally make sacrifices for you. They might, for instance, cancel important engagements to get into the House to vote for your motion or amendment. They are your tribe.

The word 'tribe' is often abused, referring to a range of social entities that have little in common. I am not trying to classify political parties as tribes here, but suggesting by analogy that both are social as much as functional groups. Tribes in other parts of the world are usually bound together by shared territory, putative kinship and religion, which combine to create loyalty between members *vis-à-vis* other tribes. Political parties cannot be identified by religion, although many Conservatives are Church of England, and Methodism was formative in the Labour Party. But members of each party tend to share a moral worldview. They can be identified by their territory in the Chamber (the benches they sit upon), they are united by feelings of loyalty *vis-à-vis* other parties, and, although parties do not share a single ancestor or family tree, party members often share comparable class provenance, and admire common intellectual ancestors such as Burke, Tawney and so on.

Now, as in the past, social background is an important determinant in the individual's choice of party. Social class – the most significant part of social background in this context – is not always easy to pin down. It is linked to people's assets, occupation, education and lifestyle, but the mobility between classes makes categorising people often tricky. In spite of this, it is clear that in general the upper and upper-middle classes tend to go to the right, working-class peers tend to the left, and the middle class distributes itself promiscuously, tending more to the centre and 'new' left. When Labour peer Lord Bruce anathematised the Conservatives – 'social class determines very largely the composition of the Tory benches rather than political conviction'[5] – he might have also looked at the class composition of his own benches. A Conservative caricatured how peers join parties, relating a conversation he had had with his mother at age twelve or thirteen:

Boy:	Tell me about this election, does it matter who wins?
Mother:	Yes, it does.
Boy:	What am I, then?
Mother:	Your father is a Conservative.
Boy:	What will happen if Labour get in?
Mother:	They will take away all our land.
Boy:	All of it?
Mother:	Well, they might leave us the park.

Historically, there were grand Tory and Whig families whose scions had little choice about which to join. According to diverse informants, people still very commonly sit on the benches their ancestors sat on, and hereditary peers who defy Conservative family tradition are viewed by their relatives as 'class traitors'. Most peers, though, are drawn to the party that seems genial, familiar social territory, whether its welcoming aspect is derived from family or more recent social contacts. But the choice does not necessarily present itself in these terms. When Lord Stanley of Alderley, a farmer, decided which party to join, he relates:

I wasn't quite sure what Party I was a member of for, by tradition, my family had been radical Liberals but, remembering the reason that I had appeared at all was due to Madeline Middleton [Stanley's aunt]'s father's sword, I decided to take the Conservative Whip as Madeline's husband had been Conservative Minister of War in the Boer War, so it seemed logical to take the Tory whip.[6]

There are, of course, plenty of examples of peers choosing a party other than that of their ancestors: Conservative Lord Attlee is the grandson of a Labour Prime Minister (and his father sat with the Liberal Democrats) but, like many other political sons, he may have shifted party as his family moved to a new social position. Others told me that while not following in their father's footsteps, they were being true to the political tradition on their mother's side.

This mixture of influences is not confined to the propertied classes, nor to hereditary peers: Labour peers, both hereditary and life, acknowledged that they too had joined their party because of family precedents or other social determinants. "I was born and bred Labour", "My family has always been Labour", or "That is my background, it never occurred to me to sit anywhere else", peers told me. In whichever party, individual peers' politics are rarely shaped by simple individual self-interest nor by independent-minded conviction alone.

Most working peers chose their party years before they entered the House. Many have already been party politicians, but some (especially honours peers) choose only after they have accepted a peerage. In either case, some choose parties for social reasons rather than purely ideological ones. Some, for instance, make the choice by attending political meetings of each, and joining the party of whichever group of people they feel most comfortable with. Accident played a part with others, at least initially: in the 1960s a (future) Liberal Democrat was approached in a pub by a young man who explained that the Liberal party was trying to have a meeting but not enough members had turned up for a quorum, could he join them? He did, and never looked back.

When asked specifically, peers often also attribute their choice of party to political calculations of various sorts, including commitment to their beliefs, and ambitions for their careers. Some review the party manifestos and pick the party whose principles seem to resonate with their own. One chose the Liberal Democrats – although his father was a Conservative – because they are under-represented relative to votes cast at elections. For the career minded, it can make sense to join the weaker of the two main parties; then, when the party has recovered strength the individual may be established within it and have access to power. Others, by similar calculation, choose the party in government. But even then, some do not stick with parties over time unless they develop a feeling of belonging to the tribe.

There are some who join a party but find that their convictions gradually diverge from it, or that their party's policies change while theirs do not. Some come to find the policies of the party of their life's work deeply unattractive or even unacceptable, or become more interested in another party as its ideology shifts. Several moved to the Labour party from the Cross-benches once it had dropped Clause 4.[7] Another changed to the party that he thought would most improve his chances of being elected as a hereditary peer after the House of Lords Act 1999. But while a few swap parties once they have entered Parliament, it is significantly rare. For social reasons changing parties can be just too difficult for most; it involves letting down colleagues, and can mean creating completely new social networks in a new tribe. Although the Cross-benches are an option it is usually easier to stay away from the House altogether. When such peers come to speak on issues of importance to them, they sit with their old colleagues.

Until the seventeenth century, the seating in the Lords was arranged in two opposing banks along the sides of the Chamber. Then the cross-benches, running across one end, were installed to accommodate viscounts, and some overflow barons. They have since been taken over by peers who do not take the party whips, whose name is often shortened to XBs. The first regular mention of lords of the 'crossbench' appears to be the 1830s, but they did not become a substantial group until the 1960s. It was Baroness Swanborough, with Lords Iddesleigh and Strange, who began to convene meetings of the Cross-benchers; Lord Strange then became the first Convenor.[8] Since then their numbers have grown so much that they have overflowed, and now also sit on some of the government benches beside.

Until fairly recently, peers who sat on the cross-benches did so because they wanted to appear apolitical, or did not want to be harassed by whips, or wanted to participate only minimally. In the 1950s only one peer among the sixty-eight regular speakers in the House was non-party.[9] Since then, Cross-benchers have multiplied and in 1997–98 constituted over 20 per cent of the most active peers in the House (see Table 8.1).

As the ferocity of party whips intensifies, the Cross-benches – allowing independent thought, speech and voting – become increasingly appealing and their expansion reflects a corresponding disillusionment with party politics in society. They attract those who do not want to be told what to do. Some Cross-benchers wish to be seen as neutral; usually because they have been in Crown service as judges or civil servants, or in the armed services. Even party members may opt for the appearance of neutrality while sitting on quangos, charity boards or international committees. For some it is a negative decision: there is no political party that has policies or attitudes they respect. One leftish hereditary Cross-

Table 8.1   Party and peerage of the top 400 peers by attendance
(1997–98 session)

	Hereditary	Life	Sub-total	% of total in the group
Conservative	97	75	172	36
Labour	14	97	113	64
Cross-bench	45	25	72	22
Liberal Democrat	14	29	43	62
Total	172	228	400	34

Source: Original data from the House of Lords Information Office.

bencher who dislikes the class hatred in the Labour party and cannot relate to the Liberal Democrats has nowhere else to go. Others may be inclined ideologically toward a party, but not toward socialising in it. One thought of joining his father's party but did not feel they were his type – they had attended different kinds of schools, had different jobs and different styles – so he became a Tory-voting Cross-bencher. Others agree with Conservative policy but find their formality tiring, and some on the left find the power-suited spin of New Labour hard to stomach.

Before 1999, diffidence drove some hereditary peers to the Cross-benchers. Some felt embarrassed at being in the House and wanted to attend only occasionally and in the lowest possible key; others were shy and wished to avoid the sociability of the political parties. Life peers can also choose the Cross-benches on these grounds, but are less likely to be shrinking violets and tend to appreciate the lack of pressure for different reasons. It suits those with demanding careers, little interest in the less powerful upper House, or too many other commitments. Most Cross-benchers seldom stay after dinner time (or around 8 p.m.). There is no one to tick them off if they disappear indefinitely, although the Cross-bench regulars will encourage them to vote as much as possible because they worry that their irregular voting habits may be used as an excuse for abolishing the Cross-benches entirely when the House is reformed. They receive far less information and have to work harder to participate seriously. Some feel ill-informed on most topics, which makes them reluctant to participate, and others feel lonely in the un-clubby Cross-bench milieu. Any bill, however, will attract a small group of determined Cross-benchers working through the detail of legislation on their specialist topic, and lobbying ministers and other peers, with considerable conscientiousness. Cross-benchers may not vote as often, but their participation and influence on committees and commissions is probably greater than most party peers.

Party loyalty

Many doubters, dissenters and discontents lurk in the main parties. The Cross-benches would probably have many more immigrants, but it is not easy to leave the tribe and 'cross the floor'.[10] It is a personal and a public gesture. It incurs the disappointment and lasting wrath of friends, and sometimes the sense of having let down those who gave the peerage. The taint of the turncoat is never shed. It takes courage, and many are simply too modest to make a gesture that would be regarded by their friends and colleagues as self-important, as well as a betrayal. In the words of one former minister who scarcely agrees with a single policy of his party: "It would be pretentious and mean that I thought I was more important than I really am." These are expressions of a tribal loyalty whose binding power can be mysterious to outsiders.

It is assumed that parties are less significant in the Lords than in the Commons, because the ethos of individual independence creates greater room for manoeuvre. This is true, but party loyalty nevertheless exerts extraordinary pressure on the individual peer, as Earl Russell explains:

> My loyalty to my party is one of the strongest emotions that I possess. It is a greater loyalty to a collective group of people than I ever believed myself capable of. I agree – we all do – that all political effort is and must be a team effort. In my actions so far I have tried to give effect to that principle. I had been here 10 years before I voted against the party Whip.[11]

The relationship between the individual and his party is not a one-sided contract with an abstract ideology, in which the party member gives his all out of selfless political conviction, and receives little in return besides perhaps a self-affirming moral glow. It is a network of relations with other party members. A political party is a moral community of individuals giving and taking (support, votes, information, jobs) and governed by the (universal) rule identified by the French anthropologist Marcel Mauss, that what is given must be repaid and that all social relationships are based on the principle of reciprocity.[12] The political fervour backbenchers sometimes demonstrate is often derived more from reciprocal obligations and ties to their friends and colleagues than from weighing up the merits of the policy or anticipating the impact of political compromises. Whether travelling hundreds of miles to vote in the middle of the night, or making passionate speeches in the Chamber, peers are normally moved by their loyalty to each other and to the leadership at least as much as to any commitment to the issues they are championing. A party leader described part of the contract between front- and back-benchers:

> "Controlling the troops involves a cocktail of different tactics because peers come from different backgrounds. There is an inherent contract – as a peer

you get access to a minister; you get information from the party. In return, party and personal loyalty is what you give. I had to understand the motivation of particular individuals and develop a good working relationship with them."

It is relationships between individuals that drive party loyalty rather than commitments to abstract principles. It is important that party members share a certain moral perspective about how society should be ordered, but relationships generate another dimension to party membership. Combat soldiers, it has been observed, are seldom inspired in battle by political goals, or any other abstract concepts, even patriotism, but much more by group cohesion and the personal ties that bind them to their 'buddies', to their officers if they respect them, and their combat unit.[13] In this most extreme form of conflict, it is loyalty to members of the immediate group that 'makes possible the seemingly incomprehensible willingness for self-sacrifice' and it is the feeling of 'spiritual unity' with comrades whose shoulders they jostle that keeps men going despite dangers and appalling adversity.[14] Strangers do not fight together effectively. It is clear from conversation with peers that, similarly, most of them, most of the time, are animated more by loyalty to their colleagues than by devotion to indefinables such as their party, the issues, or the benefits to the nation of the position they are taking. Earl Russell found it so difficult to vote against the party whip he could only justify it by claiming (in the Chamber) that his disobedience was loyalty to a different section of the party, that is, the activists in the country outside:

> Loyalty can also be a loyalty to a person or to a group. When I think of my loyalty to my party, I think of the people with whom I ran up steps in Oldham in a heat wave or who held the torch for me when I looked for numbers in Winchester Cathedral Close in the rain and in the dark. If I were to vote with this Whip, they would not understand me.[15]

He may have been disobeying the leaders, but, he argued, he was keeping faith with the majority in his tribe.

Politics is a team activity. Team loyalty is prized as a moral virtue, and to question the decisions of the majority, or the leadership, is seen as venturing into dubious moral territory. This is rationalised morally by peers idealising their own parties as forces for good in an uncertain moral world. To question leadership decisions can be seen as diminishing their power for achieving good, and awkward questions can be simply answered: the party enshrines a higher moral purpose, and it is enough that the foot-soldiers have been told what to do. Although it is seldom precisely spelt out in these terms, the logic of this is that the individual's moral contribution to the general good is not paid in thinking out the implications of policy for themselves, but in simple party loyalty. And from back-benchers' point of view, viewing themselves and their party colleagues as faithful combatants in the battalion of moral rectitude avoids seeing themselves as slaves to party managers.

In parallel with this there is a pragmatic rationalisation: "I don't always like everything I vote for," one peer told me, "but I am only one person and I owe it to the party to support the general consensus, just as others support me even when they are not 100 per cent happy."

In comparison with the Commons, the whips in the Lords are not powerful. MPs are easily cajoled or threatened. About ninety are on the government payroll as ministers, and still more as parliamentary private secretaries, for whom to step out of line would jeopardise their positions and futures (these things are not forgotten by those who count); and all MPs are dependent on party not only for office space, secretarial and research help, social life and future preferment, but, above all, for re-election. In the Lords, in contrast, there are limited ministerial posts on offer, most peers no longer care for position anyway, and re-election is irrelevant. Lords whips have to work personal relationships almost to death. They may say, 'as a favour to me' or 'I'll get into trouble if you vote against us', and peers usually respond. As former Government Chief Whip Lord Carter puts it: "its all about charm and goodwill." (The necessary qualities for a successful chief whip were revealed to him when he discovered that he shares his birthday with Lloyd George, Mohammed Ali and Al Capone.) Humour keeps them sweet: mocking the opponents, telling your troops it is "precision whipping" when you win by only one vote, and so on. More powerful still is the appeal to party loyalty, as former Deputy Chief Whip Lord Strabolgi explains: 'You can't bring any pressure to bear. You can't do anything through the constituency party. They know they're here for life. So you have to appeal to their sense of loyalty.'[16] There is a great fund of loyalty to draw on. From the point of view of a back-bencher, Lord Dahrendorf:

> the only sanction is shame. But shame is rather an effective instrument in the House of Lords, and so one does think twice before one defies the whips ... Shame is often more effective if you are a member of a club in which there is an assumption of common membership. Then you don't particularly want others to feel that you've been a bad man.[17]

Since their administration of 1945, Labour governments have demanded tight discipline among their supporters in the Lords: with so few, it was hardly surprising. (Several had to be dissuaded from renouncing their titles; their support was needed in the House and principled rejection of the right to sit and vote was a luxury the party could not afford.) The Conservatives on the other hand were so over-represented they have been allowed great latitude, and Conservative legislation was regularly defeated by its own peers during their most recent administrations. Although Labour peers now almost match the Conservative numbers in the Lords, they maintain discipline more easily. They attribute their years in the wilderness between 1979 and 1997 to disunity, and members remain peculiarly susceptible, and obedient, to calls for party unity. (As Conservatives get to grips with their new need for coherence, their members too are becoming more obedient.) Some Liberal Democrats take an independent line and defy the whip, but not too often, because, as one puts it, "we are conscious as a united group that we are capable of holding the balance between the two main parties, and don't want to jeopardise that position".

Whether information is summarised in party meetings by the whips, or back-benchers obtain it from each other, asking 'What's this amendment all about old boy?', they almost invariably get the low-down from their own side, and it tends to be one-sided. Party managers try to control members' understanding of issues carefully. They justify the care spent putting the right spin on information given to back-benchers by invoking the necessity of maintaining party unity. Before important votes party managers try to whip up disdain for the other side and its supposedly pathetic positions and arguments. With a near-monopoly on information, the other side can be made to appear misguided or morally deficient, and the whips spread gossip about their dubious tactics. Sometimes this excitement is heightened by combative exchanges between parties in the Chamber so that by the time the division is called, both sides bristle with moral fervour.

Voting against your own party is seen as arrogance, and in the context of emotional tribal loyalties, party managers are able to elevate this misdemeanour into a crime, not just against the party, but against democracy itself. To put your own principles above those of the party with its democratic roots in the country is, according to them, to bypass the democratic process. Being a party member, they say, requires a team effort. The majority of those who occasionally disagree with their own party on a particular issue will find good reasons for being elsewhere when the vote takes place, in effect quietly abstaining without causing embarrassment to their party, often with the tacit agreement of their party whips. The exasperation with those who break ranks by voting against the party is all the greater because all are tempted to do it sometimes, or often, but are held back by tribal ties. With a combination of irritation and sanctimoniousness typical in this context, one Labour peer said, "Lots in the party feel, why should someone else get away with defying the whip? We are considering disciplinary procedures for those who put themselves above the party."

Once a peer rebels a few times, it becomes increasingly easy to develop a habit, particularly if not a regular attender.[18] They can be admired by outsiders – such as Labour peer Baroness Kennedy of the Shaws who voted eighteen times with the government and twenty-three times against, in one session – but those who rebel too often tend not to be taken seriously within their party; they cease in fact to be entirely one of the party. They can no longer gain the ear of ministers or colleagues, they may not be kept fully in the information loop, and their hopes of gaining influence end. In voting against their party, they are breaking their contract, and as Mauss tells us, 'failure to give or receive, like failure to make return gifts, means a loss of dignity'.[19]

Now the two main parties are more evenly balanced than they were, the votes of individual peers are becoming more important to their parties. Perhaps because of the consequent more strenuous whipping, attitudes to other parties are changing. This is affecting the social life of peers. They used to chat, drink and eat with those with whom they had rapport, common interests or roots. Even as late as 1998, one asserted:

> You don't get anything like the tea room divisions that you get in the Commons where we're shoved at one end and the rest go down to the other part. They all mix together quite freely and I normally have coffee in the morning with a Liberal, a Tory whip and an independent. Sometimes even with my own side.[20]

Since the influx of new peers, they more often sit in single-party huddles. Mixing still goes on, particularly between Labour and Liberal Democrat and between Conservatives and Cross-benchers, but the tendency to socialise exclusively within tribes is increasing in parallel with the greater pressure on peers to toe the party line.

Tribal tensions

Very substantial differences within parties constantly threaten tribal unity. All contain competing clans and alliances (described in the next section) as well as fissures such as that between the front- and back-benches. To deal with these potential conflicts, and to create a sense of unity, party managers are indefatigable in trying to drum up tensions, even animosity, between tribes and to encourage a perception of 'us' against 'them'.

Whether ethnic, sporting, geographical, organisational, economic or whatever, people in groups show a distinct tendency to praise their own and disparage others. Peers are no exception, and, increasingly, since the House of Lords Act 1999, they savour differences between themselves and those in other parts of the Chamber. They flatter their own by moaning about the dreadful lack of respect for procedure of other parties, and their slipping standards of courtesy. Peers are seldom happier than when rubbishing other parties in conversation, cataloguing their failures with relish. A dream world of moral and intellectual superiority created in the bars and restaurants is fortified with gossip and jokes. With a variety of intonations, peers from different parties will lament that none of the other parties have an ounce of sense between them. They all respect certain individuals in other parties tremendously, and loathe some of their own, but this tends to be forgotten when denouncing the collective others.

Members of the same party tend to see other parties through the same spectacles, or roughly so. The grain of truth in most accusations gives them myth-making potency in constructing the tribal sense of superiority; and this applies equally to all parties. Liberal Democrats are mistrusted by both Labour and Conservatives, but for different reasons. Labour see Lib Dems as unreliable, and cannot understand why they exist: they share so many principles they should be in the Labour party. Old Labour peers, in particular, can explode with anger when Lib Dems fail to support their party in the lobby. If they cannot be persuaded to join, they should at least vote with them. Since they have not the sense even to do this reliably, they are regarded as hopelessly unsound. They are also seen as failing to take account of public opinion, and as naïve on law and order. On the other hand, while I was there, many Liberal Democrats were once Labour members themselves – including the Leader and the Chief Whip – and continued to have Labour friends. Deals between them were frequently made and rarely broken.

Conservatives also see Liberal Democrats as unreliable, and tend to disagree with all their policies. They see them as naïve, idealistic and shrill, and so lacking in practical or moral sense as to be almost destabilising, incomprehensible and not to be trusted. Of course there are exceptions: at least one Conservative agrees with virtually every Lib Dem policy. Furthermore, since they are often co-operating in their opposition to government legislation, relations between front-bench Tories and Lib Dems tend to be friendly.

Conservatives' view of Labour is more complicated. They respect them as serious politicians with their eye on the opinion polls, and redoubtable adversaries, but they feel outrage at what they perceive as Labour hypocrisy. Labour members, they say, typically spout egalitarian principles while sending their children to private schools, espouse class-war while enjoying the benefits of wealth and title, and make noises about modernising Parliament but rely on patronage in making 'Tony's cronies' peers.[21]

Politically, New Labour and old Tories are perceived by the latter to occupy similar ground, but there is no love lost between them. Most

Conservatives feel closer and warmer towards old Labour. One reason may be New Labour's success: it was they who ended the Conservatives' eighteen-year run in government. Some Conservatives cling to the romantic idea that they understood and got along perfectly with working-class old Labour – the socialists, as they refer to them – but that it is middle-class New Labour peers who spoil the fun. The most extreme resent Liberal Democrat co-operation with New Labour as a distasteful alliance of the slippery members of the middle class with the hypocritical ones.

Tories see Labour as incompetent, narrow-minded and motivated by class hatred. They also complain about Labour loyalty and discipline, in contrast with their own (principled, they feel) opposition to government even when they were in office. Cross-benchers do not take a whip at all, but Conservatives nevertheless see themselves as the party of independent thought. The point of being a back-bench peer, they say, is to put ministers on the spot, whichever party they belong to, but Labour members avoid censure of their own. Labour peers counter that government defeats during Conservative administrations were far lower than current levels.[22] Tories are only less disciplined because they were able to afford to be with their large majority, and are merely piqued at being in opposition. As (Labour) Lord Desai claimed: 'Noble Lords opposite assume that what they do is always in the national interest and what we do is in the party political interest. When they have a majority, they look after the nation's interests. When we have a majority, it is an elective dictatorship.'[23]

The Labour view of Conservative peers is that they are bigoted, arrogant, backward looking and often dim. They accuse the Tories of protecting class interests, failing to move with the times, and lacking the brains or motivation to understand those outside their social circle. They see them as intolerant to vulnerable groups such as homosexuals, single mothers, minorities and low-income families. Women Labour peers assume that the worst misogyny can be found on the Tory benches, while trade unionists see them as enemies of workers' rights. The more extreme believe that Tories are selfish, uncaring and ruthless. Labour peers remain bitter about their long years as a small group in the Lords. They point out that Prime Minister Margaret Thatcher deliberately created many more Tory peers than Labour (or Liberal Democrat) ones; Tories retort that Labour leaders were so left-wing they sometimes put forward no candidates.

Some Liberal Democrats, especially excluded hereditaries, have relatives on the Tory benches; some were close socially, but politically very distant. They share the Labour view of Tories as the moral enemy, but with added passion: Conservatives, they feel, are narrow-minded xenophobes, illiberal, prejudiced and incapable of learning. They do not like women, gays, lesbians, blacks, offenders, Europeans, refugees or liberals; in fact, anybody worth defending in Liberal Democrat eyes. They also accuse Labour of being illiberal: many find what they see as Labour's class hatred ridiculous; they detect sexism and homophobia among the trade unionists and more currently fashionable prejudices among some New labour politicians, such as intolerance of refugees and offenders.

Differences between Cross-benchers and members of parties are huge. Cross-benchers see themselves as the only independent thinkers and, at their harshest, see the rest as lazy, unthinking lobby-fodder. One Cross-bencher commented: "Party loyalty is quasi-religious, this side of it is under-estimated." Some reserve their bile for one party rather than another, but many tar all with the same brush. A former member of the House, the Earl of Clancarty, spoke reflectively about Labour, with implications for all:

> Like most other political parties, it has developed over a long period its own strong family atmosphere, with all the attendant problems that that brings; its own professionalism and its sense of professionalism; its party politicians as a body of professionals, like doctors or lawyers; its own protective shell, which also constitutes a barrier; and its own self-interests. All of these are aspects of party politics, to which I believe, over a period perhaps dating from around 1945, the public have become more sensitive or even sensitised. This is in no way an indictment of individual politicians; it is a problem of the system that has evolved.[24]

Cross-benchers and their Convenors are almost permanently furious at not being taken more seriously by the usual channels. Because the Cross-benchers take pride in their disorganisation, they have no group power. They are regularly sidelined on issues such as the allocation of rooms and desks, places on committees, forthcoming business and the management of the House. Until a few years ago, their most frequent and bitter complaint was how few desks they were allocated: approximately one per 3.8 Cross-benchers. Liberal Democrats had one each; there were 1.8 Conservatives, and 3.2 Labour peers to a desk. Party managers defended their desk-greed by saying that Cross-benchers attended irregularly and that some Cross-bench desks were not used, and that anyway Cross-benchers cannot be party to deals because they cannot deliver bloc votes. (Until recently desks were a scarce resource, more valuable to the party managers than to anyone else because they were almost the only bribe available to them in inveigling back-benchers. However even this bribe has been lost since plentiful desks have become available in outbuildings.)

Some Conservatives view Cross-benchers as too lazy or uncommitted to take the whip, but most tend to appreciate their specialist knowledge, independence of mind and historical tendency to vote with them. Labour peers are less forgiving, seeing Cross-benchers as closet Tories, incapable of decision, commitment or loyalty, and democratically unaccountable to boot. One complained: "You should not have politics decided on the whim of an individual". Their vehemence may be related to their perception that Cross-benchers vote with the Tories about 90 per cent of the time. (The true figure, at least during recent sessions, is about two-thirds, and even that is partly because Cross-benchers tend to vote against whichever party is in government.[25]) In any case, with the departure of hereditary peers, and the recent introduction of more politically diverse Cross-benchers, they have become a more heterogeneous group.

Labour irritation with Cross-benchers has a particularly illogical side. Because of Cross-bench voting habits, their (democratically unaccountable) votes very seldom determine outcomes, but their enormous value lies not in their votes but in their contributions: their thoughtful speeches, introducing Wednesday debates on topics neglected by parties, probing questions and useful amendments unfettered by party polarisation.

If the Cross-benchers were reliable, the Conservatives could, with their help, win most votes, but their voting is too unpredictable and infrequent. In the 2001–02 session, for instance, Cross-benchers comprised nearly a third of the peers, but accounted for only 8.6 per cent of the votes. The Liberal Democrats are few, but they are organised and can deliver votes, so now hold the balance of power. They are likely to be courted more often by the two other parties, particularly for tactical alliances over particular amendments.

The 'them and us' attitudes that fuel party tribalism are often roughly based on reality, but involve exaggeration, absurd generalisation and obliviousness to exceptions. Filtered through an ideological lens, an occasional tendency appears to be the norm. In the way of prejudice everywhere, myths are given vitality and longevity by gossip and anecdote so that accusations become self-evident in the eyes of accusers. The ideological lens tends, in particular, to colour opponents' motives, turning them very unattractive shades. When the issue of which defendants should be tried by jury, and which by magistrates, was the subject of party confrontation, Conservatives and Lib Dems saw themselves as protecting traditional British liberties against Labour's dangerous and irresponsible zeal for modernisation. Most Labour MPs, on the other hand, saw them as obstructionist backward-looking fuddy-duddies and, with the self-righteousness of the party that has the mandate, were outraged by what they saw as Conservative arrogance in obstructing government policy. Lib Dems are shocked and horrified by what they feel to be the narrow-minded nationalism influencing Eurosceptics, while Eurosceptics feel Europhiles are contemptibly unpatriotic and naïve to boot.

Divisions between parties, though great, are not straightforward; they are fraught by other factors. Prejudices are not held evenly within parties, others cut across parties, and different interest groups – women and men, old and young, varying professions – view each other quite dissimilarly. Most of all, there are professional and interest groups that are not confined within a party, but distributed over all. Academics, lawyers or those interested in health from all parties can often be heard talking shop in the corridors and bars. Consequently, alliances between back-benchers from different parties are always being made and run alongside the tribal warfare. Cross-party alliances are forged between people sitting on the same committee, attending the same overseas trips, meeting at all-party parliamentary groups, or finding common ground during debate.[26] There are also ideological divisions within each party.

Clan rivalries

Each party contains at least two major subdivisions, each revealing a great deal about tribal history. The Conservatives have one-nation[27] Tories disagreeing with Thatcherites; old Labour and New Labour are not happy about each other; and Liberals and Social Democrats favour different strategies and ends. These divisions present party managers with problems.

Old and new Tories

The word 'tory' originally signified Catholic Irish outlaws. It was applied disparagingly to supporters of the Catholic James II in the seventeenth century, and stuck as a name for one of the parliamentary parties. In the twentieth century the Conservative party is said to have changed with the 'new class of 1964', when an old Tory was overheard saying about a new Tory MP, 'they've even got my tailor in the House now'.[28] The new intake gained control after Mrs Thatcher became Prime Minister in 1979 and gradually became known as new Tories. Most Conservative hereditary peers and older life peers tend towards the old Tory faction, while the more ambitious hereditary peers and more recent lifers are inclined to be new. Exceptions include not-so-old old Tories 'kicked upstairs' to get them out of the Commons.

The old Tories were patrician, moderate and paternalist. Many who had shaped the policies of their party during the third quarter of the twentieth century were animated by, among other things, a respect for the 'lower' classes forged during conflict in the world wars.[29] New Tories rejected both their tolerance and their condescension.

According to Lord Tebbit (Thatcher's close aide) they were "out of touch because their drives were too long to walk down to meet the postman". New Tories see themselves as close to public opinion, meritocrats, leaders in a dynamic new wealth-creating class. Old Tories see them as 'nineteenth-century individualism dressed up in twentieth-century clothes'.[30] Aristocratic resentment of these upstarts was stifled by their ability to win elections, but though they took control of the party, they did not on the whole win the hearts or minds of the old Tories, who still occasionally grandly dismiss them as ill-educated, badly behaved and ill-bred. Most of the time, however, they rub along quite well together and one new Tory who had been doubtful about the grandees when he first came to the Lords admitted, "some of my best friends are earls now".

Thatcher and her cohorts were ideologues who prided themselves on their 'radicalism'. New Labour sabotaged that conceit by purloining some of their policies, and what new Tories stand for now seems less certain: loosley it is a fluctuating rightist agenda including patriotism, minimal government, a free market, a forceful attitude to law breakers and misgivings about foreigners interfering with British culture or government.

The old Tories, known as moderates, wets, or one-nation Tories, regard Thatcher's revolution with ambivalence. While they recognise that her trade union reform was necessary and they supported privatisation, they saw her style as authoritarian, ruthless, even fanatical, and they disliked her Malthusian attitude to poverty and unemployment. Their politics occupy similar ground to New Labour: they are anti-ideology, pro-common sense, and dislike great inequality either of wealth or of opportunity.

Old and New Labour

Understanding the present Labour party requires seeing its wilderness years, 1979 to 1997, through Labour eyes. In the 1960s, the domestic policies of the two main parties were so similar that their shared agenda became known as 'Butskellism'.[31] This pragmatic confluence disguised ideological differences. Labour, in theory, was socialist, and Clause 4 of its constitution committed it to Marxist economics: 'the most equitable distribution [of wealth] that may be possible upon the basis of the common ownership of the means of production, distribution, and exchange, and the best obtainable system of popular administration and control of each industry or service.' In the 1970s, some members began to feel Butskellism was failing, and at the same time extreme Marxists turned *en masse* to the Labour Party as a vehicle for entry into parliamentary politics. Concerted efforts were made at grassroots level, and above, to alter party policies, resulting in painful ideological convulsions. The election in 1979 of the charismatic, forceful and anti-socialist Conservative Margaret Thatcher made Labour look marginal, as well as divided. Three years later Labour was moving so far to the left that some of its leaders quit to form the Social Democratic party. When, in 1983 Thatcher was re-elected by a landslide, it seemed to some that the decline of the Labour party could be terminal.

Even then, instead of pursuing power, Labour devoted its energies to internal feuding, and it was said – with only moderate hyperbole – that the principal opposition to the Conservative government came from old Tories (then the largest group) in the House of Lords. The moderate socialists in the party held their ground against those on extreme left and expelled many, but were then muscled out of the key positions by those further right. Old Labour are the moderate socialist survivors. Incorporating these veterans, but under now substantially middle-class management, the party reinvented itself as 'New Labour', and its leaders concentrated on presenting themselves and the party in the most electable way, symbolically dropping Clause 4, and adopting a soft version of neo-liberal economics (the Third Way), thus trying to define themselves as neither socialist nor free marketeers.[32] New Labour, like the new Tories, clinched their hold on their party by winning elections – but without winning over all old Labour members. They remain further to the left, and view Blair's ideas and followers as lacking substance, emphasising presentation over content and betraying the party's ideals. To old Labour, Blair is too close to the Tories: hard on the unions, cosy with business interests, and neglectful of the most vulnerable in society. Legislation that gives greater freedom to the corporate sector is unpopular with them, as are proposals for House of Lords reform with no democratic element. They despair that some New Labour peers – and even some ministers – were not party members when ennobled.

New Labour peers have respect for their older colleagues, but also see them as unrealistic, ideological, out of date and tradition-bound, not to say obstructive. Much of what old Labour stands for is seen by New Labour to break its cardinal rule – if adopted it would make re-election more difficult. 'Modernisation' is the central plank of the New Labour Third Way, and is applied to party, Parliament, public sector and everything else the government touches; its pragmatic advantage as a doctrine is that no-one ever knows precisely what it will entail until the leadership defines its meaning in each context. In reaction to the ideological warfare that split the party in the recent past, it is the antithesis of an ideology.

In contrast to the party in the Commons, Labour has traditionally been a coherent group in the Lords and divisions between old and New

Labour peers rarely surface in public.[33] The eighteen fractious years out of office are recalled with gloom so sombre they seem not yet past. Behaviour that might make the party less electable is unacceptable, and party discipline has become a ruling passion. Despite the wide range of opinions held by Labour peers on almost every subject, disagreements seem still usually to be fairly easily managed.

Liberals and Social Democrats

Liberal Democrats dislike authority and authoritarianism and the party has a less hierarchical structure than the others. Since 1999 the names they have put forward to become peers have been elected by rank-and-file party members. Lib Dem leadership in the Commons does not dictate party policy to peers too rigidly, and spouting official policy in the Chamber is seen as preachy. Latitude in interpretation of policy is accepted. One former spokesman did not keep himself *au fait* with official party policy because, he claimed, he always got it right by guessing. When I asked one about his party, he asked, "What does party mean? Is it the party leaders, the activists, those in the Commons, the Lords?"

As party leader, Paddy Ashdown appointed a liaison MP to create greater coherence between Lords and Commons Lib Dems and since they have held the balance of power in the upper House, the two Houses have communicated even more regularly. In addition to teams created to respond to particular bills, there are policy teams of Lib Dem peers and MPs that meet at least weekly. Peers also spend more time than they did maintaining links with constituencies.

Even so, when there are disagreements within the party, it is not always easy to pin down the actual policy issues that are causing disharmony. There is, however, a fundamental difference of approach dating from the fusion of the Social Democratic party (SDP) with the Liberal party[34] in 1988, and their joint re-branding as Liberal Democrats. The SDP were a Labour splinter group who tended to believe in party discipline more than old Liberals, and found alliance with Labour fairly natural, while the Liberals emphasised the need to remain distinctive: "Get too close to Labour and why should voters chose Liberal Democrats at all?", they ask.

Those with an SDP inclination tended toward the old Labour tradition, favouring a strong state and considerable economic control, but that tendency has gradually weakened over the early years of the twenty-first century. Old Liberals had a larger proportion of hereditary and eccentric peers than their ex-SDP colleagues, and tend to be champions of social liberalism and democracy almost *a l'outrance*. The environment is particularly an issue for Liberals, and Lib Dems have greener policies than other parties, getting greener all the time. (Despite this, a former Chairman of the Liberal Party, Lord Beaumont of Whitley, found the environmental position of the Lib Dems too tame and set up a one-man-band as the representative of the Green party in Parliament.)

Leadership contests in the Lib Dems tend to divide along SDP versus Liberal lines, with the former presently preponderant. SDP founding members Baroness Williams of Crosby, Lord Rodgers of Quarry Bank and Lord Jenkins of Hillhead are the present leader and her predecessors respectively. Both clans view themselves as more liberal and progressive than the other, and light years ahead of the other parties.

Cross-benchers and independents

The parties are held together by shared ideology (in theory) and in practice by social ties and obligations of reciprocity. The Cross-benchers are not a party, and the only ideology they share is determination not to organise on a common political line. Most of the time this ethos is sufficient to hold them together as a loose group, but the contradictions in their position – their political lack of organisation, on the one hand, and the need to ensure they are adequately resourced and well-represented (for example, on committees), on the other – present them with constant challenges.[35] In the Chamber, they are not unlike a tribe whose quietist religion proscribes militaristic organisation, even down to so much as a boy scout or brownie troop, but whose neighbours all believe in militaristic organisation and warfare as a way of life. It seems probable that no comparable phenomenon exists anywhere in the world, at least at present.

The reasons individuals choose the Cross-benches are various and mentioned elsewhere.[36] As well as those with no party sympathies, there are others with party inclinations or even, in the past at least, party membership (mostly Conservative), but who are disinclined to be whipped. Being a party peer is a slavish existence, while no-one can tell Cross-benchers what to do or say. There are also high-profile ex-party politicians who may not take the whip by reason of offices they hold; for instance, until recently, Lord Robertson (former Secretary-General of NATO), and other ex-ministers such as Lord Marsh, who no longer feel at home in the parties they served, and quantities of distinguished ex-servants of the Crown who feel obliged to appear neutral, as well as a number of honours peers. In fact, the Cross-benchers have among their varied membership a cross-section of the most distinguished peers. In addition, small parties – such as the Ulster Unionists or, some years ago, the member of the Communist party – sit there too. In the 1950s most Cross-benchers sympathised and voted with the Conservatives and the majority still tend to vote against Labour, but the group increasingly contains more diverse views.[37]

Parties have hierarchies and public funding; the Cross-benchers have only £35,000 to cover all parliamentary needs, and a single elected officer, known as the Cross-bench Convenor, who sits in a small but well-placed office on the main corridor of the Principal Floor. He acts as intermediary on behalf of the Cross-benchers as a group, in dealings with officials and parties, and keeps them informed. He is never included in the usual channels' political discussions, is usually kept in the dark by party managers, but takes part in meetings about desks or membership of committees. With assistance from a few other Cross-bench peers, the Convenor organises weekly meetings and occasional functions, sends out the agenda for forthcoming business, and advises new Cross-bench peers on how to find their way around.

The purpose of the weekly meetings is to exchange information. Discussion contains no secrets. Unlike the political parties, who, by arrangement and in strictest confidence, let me into a few whips', front-bench, or back-bench meetings each, the Cross-benchers gave me freedom to observe all the meetings I wanted so long as any quotes used were unattributed. The first time I attended I was asked, without warning, to explain my project. I stood before former heads of the civil service, ambassadors, governors of the BBC, judges, field marshals, newspaper owners, and other pinnacle-surmounters, and nearly died of shock. Red in the face, I tremblingly joked about studying the natives of Westminster. A few Cross-benchers whom I had already interviewed, including a highly respected law lord, had spoken up for me, and they let me stay. For two years I had the pleasure of joining them in their resplendent committee room, to joke and gossip with some of these urbane, intellectual heavy-weights before the meetings began. Gradually my sense of awe shifted; I still hold many individual Cross-benchers in highest esteem, but appreciate them as people rather than venerable, distant and altogether excessively important. Once I was seen as a near insider, they shed formality and became positively cosy:

> "I believe we are meeting later today?" I would say to a prospective interviewee.
> "Lucky you," a peer from behind would remark politely.
> "Me or him?" I ask.
> "Do you mind," my interviewee complains to his friend behind. "I got her first, you can arrange your own interview." And so on.

The weekly meetings were usually attended by around fifty or sixty peers. One of the Convenor's assistant peers handed out photocopied sheets of information and, once everyone was settled, the Convenor would make announcements. These might typically include the imminent funerals of recently deceased peers, the need to comply with procedures, which bishop was on duty, and who had won the ballot to lead the Wednesday policy debate. Then, for most, the substance of the meeting was discussion of forthcoming business in the Chamber.

Such is their ethos of independence that the Convenor is debarred from even hinting at how he thinks Cross-benchers might vote, and even among themselves it is bad form to be seen to try to influence others. Individuals still encourage others to attend particular debates they may be introducing, 'to hear the arguments'. They frequently preface remarks about business with, 'of course I am not suggesting that your Lordships should follow me in the lobby, but I would like to encourage you to come to listen to the argument', then put the argument, as they see it. They may also subtly try to persuade each other of the merits of amendments they have tabled, or make a pitch for a campaign they are interested in. If discussion of one topic rambles on for too long, or strays into party-style tactics, the Convenor mildly suggests it is continued after the meeting. When Lord Weatherill was in charge, Miss Sally Beely, in twin-set and pearls (posher than the peers), took minutes. Lord Craig of Radley (Marshal of the Royal Air Force, ex-Chief of the Defence Staff, and Convenor from 1999 to 2004) spent the money on a researcher and typed his own armed-services style agenda and minutes, which is fairly typical of the lack of self-importance among Cross-benchers.[38]

Modest though they are as individuals, as a group Cross-benchers tend to feel they are vastly superior to party politics with its compromises and unthinking loyalties. As public disillusion with party discipline grows, many peers are reinventing themselves as an independent force in politics.[39] Wherever they sit in the Chamber, many hereditaries justify their presence in the legislature by reference to their being 'beholden to no-one' and consequently independent; but the Cross-benchers see themselves as embodying this virtue. In the Chamber, and in committees, the perception that they are independent gives weight to what they say and they can have considerable influence as a consequence, particularly if they can claim politically neutral expertise.

Although the tides of political passion flow calmly among Cross-benchers compared with the stir of party politics, their recent history has had a ripple or two. The prospect of reform of the House created tensions everywhere, but peculiarly on the Cross-benches because a wholly elected House would spell destruction for them. To their great delight, the Royal Commission on reform, and then the white paper, both suggested there was wide support for independent members. Some Labour party members, however, voiced doubt about this, dismissing independents as whimsical, right-wing and absent. Lord Lipsey made the discussion public in a newspaper article about crypto-Tory Cross-benchers.[40] Despite his admission that Cross-benchers were becoming more heterogeneous, and the factual error in his argument that they held the balance of power (when clearly the Liberal Democrats have since 1999[41] in practice), it put Cross-benchers on the defensive. They were, like other peers, obsessed with survival, and became convinced that the key to life after reform lay only in independence. 'Closet Tories' and other crypto-party members among them were seen as a threat to the survival of the others. Tensions that had always been present flared into life between those who felt they were the real independents, and those whose party associations were seen as compromising the purity of immaculate Cross-bench lack of ideology. Even those who favoured just a little more organisation to increase Cross-bench impact were seen as heretics, recklessly jeopardising the future of all Cross-bench peers. These tensions flickered restlessly throughout the passage of the House of Lords Bill.

During the passage, Lord Weatherill, the respected former Speaker of the Commons, was Convenor. When he was asked by the Lord Chancellor to front their deal to retain ninety-two hereditaries during the first stage of reform, he agreed in order to save a proportion of active hereditaries who had, by common consent, performed a valuable service. He was joined by Lords Carnarvon, Tenby and Marsh. They always made it clear that, as Cross-benchers, they could only deliver their own four votes. At a weekly meeting, however, colleagues asked about the deal, and one of the four volunteered that although he knew he should not lobby, he felt that he should explain. He did, the Cross-benchers present approved, and most supported the amendment; which made them, for the occasion, uncommonly like a party.

Subsequently, in the matter of the election of hereditary peers, the Cross-benchers went even further. What had been proposed in the Cranborne/Irvine deal was that only hereditary peers should be entitled to vote in the elections for the surviving hereditary peers, but the majority of Cross-benchers wanted the electorate to include lifers, on the grounds that better decisions with greater legitimacy would be made. At the weekly meeting, consensus was assumed to the extent that one said, "I don't want to use the language of a three line whip but it would be great if Cross-benchers listened to the argument and voted the right way". Most laughed, but some expressed their displeasure at this breach of the most sacred Cross-bench taboo. In the Chamber a Cross-bencher even referred to his colleagues almost as though they too were a tribe, using the party political phrase 'my noble friends':

> a substantial number of my noble friends on the Cross Benches believe the
> same thing – it seems that the only way in which we, the independent element

in the House and in any future House, can avoid being bulldozed by the major parties and bring about the system that we want to see, is to support the Motion tabled by my noble friend Lord Bledisloe.[42]

In an unusually high turnout, only five out of seventy-two Cross-bench votes rejected the amendment. Like Buddhist monks resorting to violence only when Buddhism itself is threatened, Cross-benchers exerted pressure on each other in order to save their political existence. When asked how they felt about strategising during the House of Lords Bill, the regulars say it was necessary to defend the independent element in the House while some irregulars complain it was merely assisting the government.

Cross-benchers go quasi-tribal over one other topic: homosexuality. When the government suggested making the age of consent between homosexuals the same as that for everybody else, and repealing Clause 28, many Cross-benchers joined the campaign against these changes. Some even got carried away and began discussing tactics at one of the weekly meetings: would an alternative Cross-bench pro-marriage amendment split the anti vote, they fretted, and should they press it to a division only if the first amendment failed? Finally a baroness piped up that she did not agree with the campaign. This abruptly halted discussion, which had to be recommenced at a separate meeting. In the division, three-quarters of Cross-bench votes opposed a more relaxed attitude towards homosexuals.[43]

The faltering tendencies towards tribal unanimity they had displayed during the House of Lords bill rattled the Cross-benchers. It was a threat to the one thing that bound them together. When Lord Weatherill retired as Convenor, they had to choose between Lord Craig of Radley, standing for neutrality, independence and lack of organisation, and Lord Marsh, a Labour ex-minister, clever, politically astute and well-connected with the tribes. Marsh would have fought harder for a fairer share of information, facilities and committee places, but it was felt that even this might impel the Cross-benchers toward the occasional modest show of organisation and it made them nervous. The second stage of reform might do for them if they looked like a party. The majority voted for Craig.

In a bid to refashion the Cross-bench as the independent peers, Viscount Bledisloe then initiated discussion about distinguishing between 'Cross-benchers' (who could sit on the cross-benches in the Chamber) and 'Independents' (who claimed non-party status, attended their meetings, and elected the Convenor). The definition of 'independence' was debated lengthily, but with no conclusion as none would agree to a decision that excluded them. Those with party affiliations (some even had two) would not stand for being classed as non-independent and the Ulster Unionists refused to be ejected. So they decided that the category 'Independent' would automatically apply to all current Cross-benchers, even those with recent party membership, and those in the future if they had no party membership. Even this diplomatic decision does not appear to have been implemented; all Cross-benchers are still known by that name.[44]

Moral conflict

Those who assume that political parties are ideological groups of rational individuals, and no more, should think again. Parties are the product of political ideology together with its social context. Self-interest (personal ambition, or class or sectional interests) does exert influence, but people remain in parties, and respond to their demands, partly for social reasons. They are moral communities: members feel moral obligations of loyalty and obedience, and perceive themselves as morally superior to those in other parties. Loyalty to party is kept alight not so much by ideology as by the sense of belonging, and competition with enemy tribes fans the flames. Even when differences within parties seem irreconcilable, hostilities with other parties nearly always create accord and unity.

In this, as in some other ways, parties distinctly resemble some African tribal communities, despite numerous differences. A comparison with Evans-Pritchard's description of the tribal politics of the Nuer, a nation of Nilotic pastoral semi-nomads of the southern Sudan, studied during the 1930s, is revealing. Like peers, they had an ethos of egalitarianism, and (mostly because of disagreements about cattle, women or land) differences and confrontation formed the background to daily life.

The Nuer nation was composed of a number of tribes, each of which had its own territory, its own economic resources and 'a name which is the symbol of its distinction. The tribesmen have a sense of patriotism: they are proud to be members of their tribe and consider it superior to other tribes.'[45] Each tribe consisted of a number of clans whose members were all descended (at least putatively) from a common ancestor whose name was known to all. (In each tribe there was a dominant clan, regarded as more aristocratic than the rest.) Each clan, in turn, was composed of a number of lineages made up of people who knew their exact genealogical relationship to each other in terms of their descent from another common (but more recent) ancestor. In spite of this, if an individual moved to live permanently in the territory of a different tribe, he became a new member.

In normal times, a man's strongest identification was with the smallest unit, his lineage. Quarrels between members of different lineages or clans within the same tribe were settled by arbitration or duels between individuals: violence was prevented from escalating by means of mediation by a ritual specialist called the Leopard Skin Chief. If conflict between clans within the same tribe could not be resolved, then the tribe was likely to split into two. Disputes between tribes, on the other hand, tended to be resolved by warfare, and when this happened all of a tribe's quarrelling clans would unite. And again, when the Nuer nation of many tribes was threatened by another, usually the neighbouring Dinka, all its component segments came together against the common enemy.

Evans-Pritchard named this process 'fission and fusion', and the political equilibrium he claims that it gives rise to, 'segmentary opposition'. It has relevance to our political system (in both Houses, but particularly in the rather more loosely disciplined Lords), in the sense that conflict is restlessly endemic within, as well as between, political parties, but has to be resolved peacefully. If it is not, tribal unity is drastically impaired, and the party's potential for the ritual combat of party politics is depleted. Differences between parties, on the other hand, invariably result in confrontation, using words not weapons, on the floor of the House (the ritual battleground). When unity is sufficiently damaged, a party's ability to fight the symbolic conflict of debate can become almost negligible. Each party has at least two recognisable clans,[46] even if their membership is less clearly defined than among the Nuer. Informal factions also arise because each party espouses the policies agreed by the majority, of which most individual members find a proportion unpalatable. Factionalism, therefore, is always rife, but in the face of threat from other parties, or in the war of words in the Chamber, factions nearly always unite to form an undivided party front. Occasionally, irreconcilable internal differences cause parties to split into two.

Thus, like the tribes of the southern Sudan, the politicians of Westminster comprise numerous shifting alliances between factions who always have much to quarrel about. Members of the same party try to resolve disputes in private, and when faced with common enemies in other political parties, unite to do battle against the traditional adversaries in the Chamber and the press. When disputes within tribes become so serious that they might threaten party unity, they are settled by arbitration, involving, not leopard skin chiefs, but the also quaintly named chief whips. In both cases, the tribe invests much collective authority in its ritual specialist mediators to achieve reconciliation; its survival depends on their success. At least in theory, when all the parties are confronted by a common foreign enemy, they rally, like the Nuer, to the national cause, and support the party in government (or even join forces in a coalition) as soon as Parliament approves war. By organising membership of groups along segmentary lines, with different mechanisms for settling disputes according to context, both systems are about managing conflict.

To work effectively, both systems rely on the flexibility of people's identity, which allows clans within the tribes to express dissent in one context, but rally wholeheartedly to their party in another. As with all social classification, the group an individual feels he belongs to depends upon where he is, what he is doing and who he is with. In the Chamber, and especially during voting, the party is the identity that matters; but during a party meeting, or an informal plotting session in one of the bars, it might be the clans within a party, or the alliances across parties, that claim an individual's loyalty. Of which group an individual peer feels a member depends mostly on context because, as Evans-Pritchard puts it:

> the process consists of complementary tendencies towards fission and fusion which, operating alike in all political groups by a series of inclusions and exclusions that are controlled by the changing social situation, enable us to speak of a system and to say that this system is characteristically defined by the relativity and opposition of its segments.[47]

A fluid and changeable sense of identity can be found within all communities and organisations. Among House of Lords' staff, the doorkeepers and the attendants are rivals until they are in conflict with other departments and then it may become an issue between the Parliament Office and Black Rod's Department; and they too will join forces and make common cause against, for instance, civil servants from elsewhere or, even worse, journalists. It is only where differences are structurally endemic within the community (as is the case among both peers and the Nuer) that it becomes so pronounced and recognisable a feature of organisation that we may speak of it as a system.

Of course, the analogy between the party political tribalism of the Lords and African tribal politics has limits, but some of the dissimilarities are revealing too. For a start, unlike the Nuer, party members in the Lords usually identify more closely with their party (tribe) than with their faction (clan or lineage), and it is members of parties, not clans, whose party identity is augmented by the claim to shared ancestors, albeit ideological ones rather than supposedly genetic: Burke and Adam Smith versus Paine, Keynes and Tawney. Common intellectual ancestors are sometimes also used as a badge of clan membership (for example, Disraeli by one-nation Tories), but only when they are quarrelling with other factions.

Related to this, according to Evans-Pritchard at least, the tribes within nomadic African nations tend to have no permanent organisation or specialised holders of political or judicial authority (the Leopard Skin Chief does not rule or judge; his authority is confined to mediation). A consequence is that the constant fission and fusion within Nuer tribes works automatically to maintain a balance of power (segmentary opposition) between competing units: by combining and recombining, political units are always mobilised against others of the same order – lineage against lineage, clan against clan, tribe against tribe and nation against nation.[48] Contrastingly in Parliament, parties have hierarchies, political leaders and long histories of organisation. In spite of this difference, balance of power is also achieved through segmentary opposition, but in a different way; when all the factions in one of the main parties give a significantly more convincing appearance of unity (in both Houses) than the other parties, they tend to get elected to government, and hold control for as long as unity is maintained in public. Once the splits between segments again become overwhelming, the other party gets elected. Clearly segmentation within the parties is relevant to the balance of power in the British political system.

That it maintains a balance of power does not imply that the system is static (a common criticism of Evan-Pritchard's analysis) because segmentary opposition in the British political system in its present form can have existed only since the advent of political parties and could evolve into something different as the political system changes.

Tribalism, in the sense of a common identity, is a concept to which members of the House of Lords are as susceptible as Nuer herdsmen-warriors, and helps explain why so very few disaffected peers leave their parties. It constitutes some of the extra glue to keep members on board in spite of their discontents, and to preserve the minimum of unity necessary for credibility as a political force. Shore describes, as part of the cultural process of 'inventing Europe', how European Union officials have designed symbols – anthem, emblem, flag and passport – to promote a sense of European identity; and that they aspire to rewrite history to emphasise the greatness of European civilisation, rather than dwelling too much on the competitive nationalism that has hitherto been the staple of history teaching.[49] Similarly, political parties have their symbols – colours and logos – and regularly rewrite their past to shed a more flattering light on the present, to accentuate what they perceive as their differences from other parties, to brush under the carpet murky deals done by party managers, and to recall their victories. Victories matter: as in combat, nothing succeeds like success and it is as if winning itself proves the moral superiority of one's own side.[50] Thus, when party leaders, whether in Parliament or the media, draw attention to the failures, defeats and short-comings of the other parties they are not only endeavouring to point these grievous inadequacies out to the electors, they are also inspiring their own troops with loyalty, discipline and a proper fighting spirit. Morale and political unity among the rank and file in the House of Lords are kept up, not so much by ideology and still less by appealing to self-interest, but by forging the sense of moral community.

Notes

1 E. A. Smith, 1992, *The House of Lords in British Politics and Society 1815–1911*, Longman, London, p. 94. Also see pp. 93–6, 157.

2 There were also twenty-four archbishops/bishops, and seven categorised as 'other', according to the official parliament website, http://www.publications.parliament.uk/pa/ld/ldinfo/ldanal.htm, accessed 1 December 2003.

3 They have been awarded to a Speaker, a Chief of the Defence Staff, a Cabinet Secretary and a former Governor of the Bank of England.

4 J. P. Morgan, 1975, *The House of Lords and the Labour Government 1964–70*, Oxford University Press, Oxford, p. 121.

5 Lord Bruce, as quoted by A. Mitchell, 1999, *Farewell My Lords*, Politico's London, p. 145.

6 Lord Stanley of Alderley, Unpublished diaries 1971–1999, p. 10.

7 See section on 'Old and New Labour' later in this chapter for details.

8 A subsequent Convenor, Baroness Hilton-Foster, has recently deposited all her papers in the Parliamentary Archives.

9 P. A. Bromhead, 1958, *The House of Lords and Contemporary Politics 1911–1957*, Routledge and Kegan Paul, London, p. 38.

10 This means change parties because it entails walking across the floor of the Chamber to sit on the benches of another political party or group.

11 Earl Russell, HL Deb., 13 October 1998, col. 1324.

12 M. Mauss, 1969, *The Gift: Forms and Functions of Exchange in Archaic Societies*, Routledge and Kegan Paul, London. (Original French edition, 1925.)

13 M. Janowitz and R. Little, 1965, *Sociology and the Military Establishment*, Russell Sage Foundation, New York, pp. 82, 112.

14 E. Carlton, 2001, *Militarism: Rule with Law*, Ashgate, Aldershot, p. 194, and S. L. A. Marshall, 1947, *Men against Fire*, William Morrow and Company, New York, p. 42.

15 Earl Russell, HL Deb., 13 October 1998, col. 1324.

16 Lord Strabolgi, as quoted by Mitchell, *ibid.*, p. 133.

17 Lord Dahrendorf, as quoted by Mitchell, *ibid.*, p. 114.

18 Cowley found in the Commons that once MPs had rebelled once, they became far more likely to rebel again the next time they disagreed with their own party (P. Cowley, 2001, *Revolts and Rebellions: Parliamentary Voting Under Blair*, Politico's, London).

19 Mauss was writing about the Kwakiutl of the American North West, but extrapolating to the rest of the world, *ibid.*, p. 40.

20 Lord Bruce, as quoted by Mitchell, *ibid.*, p. 34.

21 The claim was that Prime Minister Blair appointed his friends and close colleagues to the Lords to do his bidding.

22 See Table 4.1.

23 Lord Desai, HL Deb., 29 March 1999, col. 135.

24 Earl of Clancarty, HL Deb., 30 March 1999, col. 253.

25 Between 1998 and 2001, of the 2330 votes cast by Cross-benchers about two-thirds were against the Labour government. Source: House of Lords Information Office statistics on divisions.

26 See Chapter 9 for cross-party alliances.

27 After the novel by Conservative Prime Minister Disraeli in which he postulated that Britain was divided between two nations, the rich and poor (1845, *Sybil; or the Two Nations*, Henry Colburn, London).

28 They were referring to Bernard Weatherill – later Speaker of the Commons and Lord Weatherill – who was a director of one of Saville Row's finest tailors.

29 Timothy Raison, 1990, *Tories and the Welfare State: A History of Conservative Social Policy since the Second World War*, Macmillan, Basingstoke.

30 Lord Gilmour, 1992, *Dancing with Dogma: Britain under Thatcherism*, Simon and Schuster, London, p. 12.

31 After Labour Leader Hugh Gaitskell and Conservative Home Secretary R. A. Butler.

32 For a discussion of the critique of old Labour by Blair and his allies, see D. Kavanagh 2004, 'Forgetting history: how New Labour sees old Labour', in A. Seldon and K. Hickson (eds), *New Labour and Old Labour, The Wilson and Callaghan Governments, 1974–79*, Routledge, London and New York, p. 322). The similarity between New Labour and Old Tory philosophy, at least in its rhetoric, is clearly illustrated by Harold Macmillan's book, *Middle Way* (1938, Macmillan, London), with its talk of rights, obligations, reconciling private ownership with the public good, a minimum wage and social justice.

33 As Bromhead pointed out in the 1950s, *ibid.*, p. 44.

34 The historical precursors to the Liberals were the Whigs, from the word 'whiggamor' or cattle driver.

35 See Chapter 9 on negotiating with the usual channels.

36 See the section on 'Joining' earlier in this chapter.

37 Bromhead, *ibid.*, pp. 45, 51; and statistics on divisions 1998–2001, House of Lords Information Office.

38 In July 2004 Lord Williamson of Horton took over as Cross-bench Convenor.

39 Mitchell claims that the 'House of Lords has reinvented itself as the defender of the people and changed its image from the Chamber of privilege to the house of independent judgement' (*ibid.*, p. 119). This may be especially true of the Cross-benchers.

40 Lord Lipsey, 2001, 'The crown jewel of the Lords loses its lustre', Comment, *The Times*, 2 January 2001, p. 18.

41 Lord Craig of Radley makes this point in his response to Lord Lipsey's article ('Crossbenchers make better bills', Letters, *The Times*, 13 January 2001, p. 25).

42 Lord Chalfont, HL Deb., 22 July 1999, col. 1165.

43 On 7 February 2000 forty-three Cross-benchers voted against, and fourteen for, an amendment to repeal Clause 28. On 13 November 2000 thirty-five voted against and thirteen for lowering the age of consent for gay sex. Source: House of Lords Journal Office statistics on divisions.

44 This excludes a handful of party members who are classified as 'other' because they do not receive the whip, whether permanently or temporarily, but choose to sit with former party colleagues (currently seven, including the Green party member, an Independent Conservative, an Independent Socialist, an Independent Labour and three unaffiliated).

45 E. E. Evans-Pritchard, 1940, 'The Nuer of the southern Sudan', in M. Fortes and E. E. Evans-Pritchard (eds), *African Political Systems*, Oxford University Press, Oxford, p. 278. See also Evans-Pritchard, 1940, *The Nuer*, Oxford University Press, Oxford.

46 See the section on 'Clan rivalries' earlier in this chapter.

47 Evans-Pritchard, 'The Nuer of the southern Sudan', p. 296.

48 J. Middleton and D. Tait, 1967, *Tribes Without Rulers: Studies in African Segmentary Systems*, Routledge, London, p. 6.

49 Chris Shore, 2000, *Building Europe: The Cultural Politics of European Integration*, Routledge, London and New York.

50 Marshall, *ibid.*

9 The usual channels

The 'usual channels' in the Lords are secretive. Agreements between them are verbal and their meetings not minuted. Seasoned members of the House, accountable to only party leaders and working behind closed doors, they wield power in an aura of mystery. They have played a significant role since the mid-nineteenth century, though official recognition in print was not until 1946,[1] in the fourteenth edition of *Erskine May*. For smooth operation they depend on concealment, trust, restraint and flexibility. A Commons ex-whip who broke the code of secrecy in print described it as an act of betrayal, but decided it was in the public interest to 'let daylight upon magic'.[2] The Hansard Society recently published a pithy booklet on the subject,[3] but no detailed analysis of the usual channels exists.

So who are the usual channels? The *Companion to the Standing Orders* has this, and little else, to say:

> The smooth running of the House depends largely on the Whips. They agree the arrangement of business through 'the usual channels'. The usual channels consist of the Leaders and Whips of the main political parties. For certain purposes the usual channels include the Convenor of the Crossbench peers.[4]

The 'business' referred to is principally the 'parliamentary business' of legislation; that is, what peers will debate in the Chamber and in committee. To achieve this, frequent, usually private, negotiations are held over the most precious of parliamentary resources: time. The government needs time to get its business through the Chamber. In the Commons, government has hijacked time: procedural reforms since the 1880s – guillotines, timed debates and the Standing Order giving precedence to government business[5] – have given government formal control over parliamentary time. While none of these has been formally adopted by the Lords, time is allocated by agreement within the usual channels:

numbers of days are allowed for particular bills, and limits on the number of hours for particular debates or motions are agreed. Self-regulation means that in theory back-bench peers can bring the government's legislative programme to a standstill. Without agreements between the government and the opposition about time, opposition peers could submerge bills in amendments, and keep talking until time ran out. The Lords' usual channels have the critical job of preventing this, and in this sense are, therefore, more important on their own patch than the Commons' on theirs.

Without the overall majority that the party in government has in the Commons, the usual channels' negotiations are infinitely more tactful than those in the lower House. There is far more give and take. But there is also agreement that the government must get its way. Because 'today's government knows that it could be tomorrow's opposition, and today's opposition hopes to become tomorrow's government',[6] there is recognition by the two main parties that the government has a paramount right to achieve its legislation, and the usual channels of both sides scheme with each other closely to this end. Even in the Lords, such fixing between party managers is deemed acceptable, and the usual channels are seen as working extremely successfully: according to one Labour peer, the opposition failed to deliver a bill in the number of days agreed only twice in the last Parliament. Bearing in mind that back-benchers can be unpredictable and are free in theory to savage legislation for as long as they like, it is no mean feat.

This success is achieved partly through chicanery. From the whips' viewpoint, peers' most important duty in the Lords is to do as they are told in the division lobbies, and they are persuaded into regarding this as a privilege by a range of inducements, some of which have in them an element of deception. Mere obedience might not accord with their grand status were it not for the dignity conferred on peers by the work done by the House. Few doubt it does an excellent job and it is sometimes justifiably seen as an exemplar of how a chamber of revision should work. It often gives more days to scrutinising bills than the Commons and passed 2993 amendments to legislation in 2002–03 alone (even if the vast majority of those were introduced by the government). But peers are not, as most would suppose, really much of a bulwark to protect the body politic from the excesses of the over-excited demagogues at the other end of the palace, as it is those same demagogues in the Commons who give the Lords' Leader and the Lords' Government Chief Whip many of their instructions. These grandees – key players in the upper House – are quite lowly in the democratic hierarchy, often ignored by ministers from the Commons where the unelected Chamber itself is often regarded as a tiresome and obstructive sideshow. In the eyes of government, it is the job of the Lords to do its bidding, and it is the job of the Government Chief Whip in the Lords to see the government's bidding is done. If time and public opinion allow, the government usually reverses its defeats in the Lords when the bill reaches the Commons. Because it is agreed that the government is entitled to get its way, and questions about the legitimacy of the upper Chamber remain unresolved, the independence of the Lords is in part a mirage. At the same time, a belief in their freedom and independence is part of the enduring ethos of the House, and even works as an incentive that keeps some of them motivated.

This usual channels' cooperation on timing rarely fails. A former Government Chief Whip revealed that between the General Elections of 1997 and 2001, only one bill was not negotiated through the usual channels.[7] As one whip put it: "People don't realise how much the whips run this place, and nor should they." Notification of some kind is always given by any peer or party before proposing a motion or amendment and it is usually possible to guess when a party has a whip on a particular piece of business by who is present in the House. The main opposition party only rarely reveals the strength of its whip or that it expects to lose, but each side tries to warn the other if timing agreements may break down.

Achieving the government's main business by means of agreement between the chief whips is only one aspect of the usual channels. Within their parties, it is the whips' responsibility to keep members in order and on side and to deliver their votes. They re-tell the well-worn joke: 'The whips are to the Parliamentary system as a sewerage system is to a big city. If you don't have them, the whole system gets fouled up.' Most backbenchers can be persuaded, as a former Leader tried to convince me, that whips' business is solely to ensure that peers can get on with debating the issues of substance instead of getting bogged down on procedure and timing. They argue with some justice that if they were not there, there would be stalemate (or according to one, mob rule), and that since an aspect of their job is to keep the leaders in touch with party opinion, they are agents of democracy. And they add, slightly contradictorily, that since peers' perceived illegitimacy makes them democratically inferior to the elected representatives in the Commons, the control by the usual channels ensures that the more democratic Chamber dominates decision making. Before returning to that, the membership of the usual channels deserves a closer look.

The oligarchs

The Government Chief Whip meets the chief whips of the other two main parties at least weekly, but at their fullest, the usual channels comprise all three party chief whips, all three party leaders, private secretaries, advisers, or whips' co-ordinators, and the Cross-bench Convenor.[8] Within parties, the leader and whips are referred to as party or business managers, depending upon the context.

Who is present at a meeting depends on what is being planned. The chief whips of the two largest parties negotiate the legislative timetable in private, followed by a meeting between the Government Chief Whip and the Liberal Democrat one. When the latter suggested tripartite meetings to Lord Carter in 1997, his Private Secretary advised wisely, 'Don't do it, they'll gang up on you'. Three-way meetings between the chief whips are rare. What is said to one is not necessarily said to the other; a deal with the Tories may be concealed from the Lib Dems. The only recent exception to this took place when the government was in a hurry to get the Anti-terrorism, Crime and Security Bill through Parliament in 2001. The three chief whips sat down and together went through the amendments, with the opposition whips warning which would not be allowed by their back-benchers. The Government Chief Whip then suggested to the Home Secretary the changes that had to be conceded. Because time was so important to the government, the Lords' power to delay gave the opposition unusual leverage. Even so, there was a fierce tussle when the bill was debated in the Lords, where the opposition parties forced some further important concessions.

The role of the Liberal Democrats in the usual channels has changed since the exclusion of most hereditary peers. It is now they who hold the balance of power, rather than the larger Cross-bench group that never whips its members. When the Conservatives oppose the government, it tends to be the Liberal Democrats who decide which side will win.

The key office of Private Secretary to the Lords' Chief Whip has, since the 1960s, been filled by a clerk seconded from the House of Lords Parliament Office.[9] They are usually transferred back within three years, before they become too partial or acquire too much influence. He or she receives a 'hand-over note' from the previous incumbent explaining how to do the job. This was considered too sensitive for me to read by one Private Secretary (although other clerks thought that ridiculous), no doubt because it would have revealed some of the government's tactics for manipulation.

"The job of the PS is to stop anarchy breaking out, keep it all going", said a peer who knew the ropes. Although that is the job of the usual channels as a whole, the Private Secretary, with party political neutrality, can deflect some of the more hostile tribal tensions that emerge in negotiation. She/he guides government as to where it has room for manoeuvre and, more importantly, finds procedural devices whereby the two (or sometimes three) sides can find accommodation. The Private Secretary has a calming influence on the battling factions.

The political advisers and managers of Whips' Offices are entirely partisan.[10] They are subtle: discretion is part of their make-up, and they are alert to distinguish between categories of information – what has to be kept within the usual channels, what can be shared with a wider circle, and what is in the *Daily Mail* and can be discussed with anyone. Some dodged my questions – particularly about deals struck by their bosses – more deftly and elegantly than any other group.

At the chief whips' weekly meetings, key decisions are made by the principals but it is the Private Secretary who drafts the detailed timetable, negotiating with the advisers as and when necessary. The chief whips get involved in detail only when problems arise. On controversial or partisan issues the leaders get consulted, even across the two Houses with particularly difficult bills, but this is usually avoided by the advisers' careful work. As each bill progresses through the House, front-benchers and advisers constantly confer and bargain. The more complex the bill, the more need for detailed negotiation during debate.

The unexpected has to be accommodated:

> "When a loony peer asks you to put down a ridiculous unstarred question you cannot say, 'Forget it', you have to say, 'Yes, what about Thursday?', because you have to recognise their right … You can get rogue campaigns … and if they put down a private members bill it can take up a few hours' time. You have to allow the flexibility for this otherwise you could face terrible disruption to the programme. It is a question of managing their expectations, they expect to get a piece of the pie …"

Government pre-eminence is recognised in various ways, all of which augment its power. Government party managers perform cross-party roles that would otherwise fall to the Speaker or chair (if there were one):[11] the Leader of the House chooses which private notice questions to allow; the Government's Whips Office draws up the speakers' lists (in consultation with the usual channels) before debate; the Leader steps in if there is disorder during debate and if the Leader is absent, this then falls to the Government Chief Whip, or any government whip. If none of those can be found, only then do the opposition party managers have that duty.

Technically the maintenance of order is the responsibility of the House as whole[12] and the Leader should only have to draw attention to violations and advise on procedure. In practice, the Leader will be viewed as deficient if she or he does not reflect the 'will of the House' by keeping order when rules are transgressed. Even though a government minister, the reputation of the Leader depends on his or her ability to interpret this 'will' in a non-partisan way. Baroness Jay's pro-Labour bias, and disdain towards Conservatives, was seen as a betrayal of the House by many opposition peers; the late Lord Williams of Mostyn was even-handed and universally respected for it; Baroness Amos is reputedly still learning the ropes.

The chief whips are in the compact to get the government's legislation through, but the Cross-bench Convenor is never included in political negotiation. When Convenor Lord Craig of Radley regularly approached the then Government Chief Whip, Lord Carter and asked to be involved in important discussions, Carter would reply: 'You can't deliver more than one vote, so you can't be in the political usual channels.' When he wanted to see the terms of reference for the Joint Committee on Lords Reform, for example, Lord Carter said he could be the first to see it, as an individual, but only after it had been agreed by the three political parties.

Members of the the usual channels and the Cross-bench Convenor sit on the main domestic committees (i.e. those relating to the management of the House) as well as the Committee of Selection (to decide who sits on all the other committees). The domestic committees are all chaired by the Chairman of Committees, a peer selected by the usual channels (with the automatic approval of the House to date), and paid a salary to carry out a range of managerial duties. As far as the business or management of the House and membership of committees are concerned, the dominance of the usual channels is almost unassailable.

Besides this macro- and micro-management, questions or problems that are too delicate to be generally known, or for which there are no existing formal procedures, are referred to the usual channels. (Even the question of whether an anthropologist should be given privileged access goes first to them.)

Managing the troops

Once the timetable has been agreed, the parties have to muster support in the Chamber at the right moments. Peers are difficult to manage. The party managers rely on the whip (a letter instructing party members when to vote) and the whips (peers who persuade, cajole and emotionally black-mail fellow party members to be there and vote). Before the House of Lords Act, Conservative peers were quite relaxed and Lord Stanley of Alderley's approach was typical for the early 1990s:

> Every week that Parliament was sitting, I got a missive by special delivery telling me that our presence was required. To which I paid no attention whatsoever, though, very occasionally indeed, Bertie[13] would be made to send out a three line Whip, which insisted on an appearance, in which case one had to think of an excuse such as a previous engagement, which probably meant hunting, fishing or shooting. I got the impression that, taking a cue from the 18th Century French aristocracy, having to work was not an acceptable excuse for missing a three line whip.[14]

Lord Swinfen claimed with pride that he had voted against all Conservative three-line whips during twenty-two years in the House.[15] This is changing. Labour back-benchers have had a reputation for tight discipline for a long time and have been subjected to three-line whips continually since they came into office in 1997. They are expected to vote in at least three-quarters of the divisions. But some do not worry unduly about obedience. Lord Shore of Stepney, for instance, felt his status as a former cabinet minister made whipping inapplicable to him:

> Why should I? I have no ambitions. I have a good relationship with them. Those of us who take a Whip do it because we broadly agree with our party's policies. But when we do not agree, what can be done? We are as free as the Cross-Benchers in terms of how we vote and speak.[16]

The perception that Conservatives are less disciplined than Labour may reflect their ethos more than their behaviour; and is more than counterbalanced by the tendency of back-benchers in all parties to vote against their own party more when in government, so that during the 1999–2000 session Labour cast 120 votes against their own side and the Tories only 21 against theirs.[17] The difference in ethos is expressed in their explanations too. Conservatives follow Burke's idea that individuals can represent the interests of 'the people' when they vote against their own side, so they are seen as 'independent-minded' even by their whips; whereas Labour and Liberal Democrats tend to say that representation can only be expressed through election and see those who break ranks as arrogant traitors. Many Tories feel free to vote according to conscience while Labour peers are inclined to defer more readily to elected representatives in the Commons. Furthermore, Conservatives use three-line whips far less often than the other two parties, partly because their party was so large until 1999 that they had less need to. Lib Dems, as a small but politically important party, display high turnouts and better discipline than either of the other two.

To mobilise party loyalty, chief whips make their whips build social networks, largely by hanging around and gossiping in the bars, corridors, libraries and restaurants. Alcohol is more freely given by Conservative whips, but even they drink less than they once did, and only one Labour whip works the bars. With little practical leverage, emotional appeals (usually to party for Labour and to friendship for Conservatives) are the whips' most effective weapon. Though sometimes whips try to be menacing, their generally genial approach contrasts with the Commons and contributes to the Lords' agreeable atmosphere.

Parties have their own cultures and whips and leaders have their own styles. According to Lib Dems, Lord Rodgers relied on patronage to get things done, while Lord Jenkins (a miner's son) ran the party in a 'lordly' way with little open debate.[18] A former Conservative Chief Whip used emotional blackmail, giving those who voted against three-line whips a glass of whisky in his office and complaining: 'You are so selfish. I have to go down to the other place and explain this to Mrs T.' Lord Cranborne felt his key trick was to try and make voting entertaining.[19] Baroness Jay, with practical and democratic efficiency, paid attention to links between party managers, ministers and back-benchers and created liaison peers for each department, including her own, to ensure back-bench opinion could be canvassed and expressed.

Tangible rewards for obedience are few. The minority with political ambitions behave themselves – vote the right way – because rebel status makes the front-benches unattainable, but there are only a few posts available as inducements. Under the present government it is made clear that the Prime Minister is informed about all Labour peers' voting records, but not everyone cares. The opposition has even less to offer; except for the top two, their front-bench posts have no tangible rewards and no salary. Some peers behave in the hope of securing places on select committees or being recommended for overseas parliamentary jaunts. For the majority, rooms close to the Chamber are the most desirable commodities. Grandees are often given whole offices in the palace to keep them sweet, where the headed paper may get dusty and curled, but a few are distributed as rewards to good attenders.

Until recently, rooms were the most delicate issue handled by the usual channels. The bishops gracefully gave up one of theirs for conversion to a family room, but other changes have been bitterly contested. The allocation of two small offices exclusively to women peers in 1959 upset some male peers who saw injustice in there being no male-only rooms (with only a handful of women it was almost an all-male institution). A Muslim peer was given access to another room, used mainly by Labour women peers, for his prayers (it was quiet and had washing facilities nearby) and they were highly displeased when he made some telephone calls from it.

Having your own desk was once a rare privilege. Many of the recent intake of peers, often young, and not interested in whiling away time in the bars, were frenzied by the inadequate work facilities in the House.

Desk-allocation discussions in 2000 became so tense that I was barred (one of only two meetings that I requested to attend, but was not allowed).[20] They tend to be charged with as much, or more, tribal emotion as empiricism. But desks are not particularly effective as bribes; once given, they cease to motivate. In any case, they have become even less significant because of the departure of hereditary peers and the availability of desks in newly rented nearby buildings.

In government or in opposition, back-benchers enjoy their unique status and membership of an exclusive club. Many feel they owe something, which helps draw them into the voting lobbies. Indebtedness is also perpetuated by the parties. At the Labour Back-bench Group meetings, the Chief Whip reports on plans and developments, ministers from the Commons provide explanations of bills, and perhaps even the opportunity to influence them, and discussion gives the impression of consultation. The Association of Conservative Peers and the Liberal Democrat peers' meetings perform the same function. Party leaders and their deputies talk to these meetings once a year or more.

Back-benchers are encouraged to believe in their own importance because occasionally, and often at quite critical moments, they are. The usual channels promote and perhaps exaggerate this belief, repeating the mantra: 'In the Lords the opposition and even the government are much more open to individual initiatives and cross-party alliances.' Back-benchers can influence ministers, for example at all-peer meetings held by ministers for any peers interested in a forthcoming bill; even in the Chamber, as Earl Russell put it, once in a blue moon the speeches of back-benchers can be seminal.[21] But while impressive debates take place, vital scrutiny is achieved and numerous amendments passed, their contribution is undermined by the Commons continually reversing government defeats and, almost invariably, policy making, legislative priorities and the key principles underlying legislation are determined by the leadership in the Commons.[22]

Most peers are content. Although they can stay away, join the Cross-benches or ignore the missives sent by their party, most regularly attending working peers are co-operative for the majority of the time. Without the record of improving legislation, the camaraderie of party loyalty, and a seductive place to work, the usual channels might confront more resistance.

Subterfuge with restraint

The usual channels' strategies change according to which party is in government. The last Conservative administration could easily muster a majority in the Lords, so, while they played the game, arranging the agenda by agreement, they relied on compliance and deals far less than Labour now does. Labour and Lib Dems, on the other hand, to get results with their few troops had to resort to 'ambushing' the government, usually late at night, stowing away members in offices, to vote when a division was called. On occasion votes were planned for a particular time, irrespective of the amendment under consideration, just to annoy the government. Ambushes are partly a form of theatre to maintain the virile competitiveness of back-benchers and make them feel they are doing something to oppose. Labour allowed themselves to do this about three to five times a year, and were allowed to get away with it because the government could reverse such victories in the Commons. Now that numbers are more evenly matched such underhand tactics would cause terrible strains within the usual channels.

There are other theatrical displays among the tricks available to the usual channels, usually to avoid back-bench demoralisation, which is often a threat. Peers may be hauled in to vote, but in the meantime a deal with the opposition has been made. On other occasions, deals often cannot be made until party managers know how many members are likely to vote. The more successfully government peers have been brought in, the less likely it is that the opposition will call a division. Whipping, in this respect, is least straightforward for the government side, as a Conservative explains:

> "... one of the frustrating things when you're in government ... you could have three days on a big bill on Committee with no votes, the result of which is the government back-benchers, who had been shipped in to vote, would feel extremely frustrated that they had been here for three days on the trot and they had given up sitting on the bench in Yorkshire, doing all the things that grandees do for no votes. But if, of course ... we hadn't whipped the party and they weren't there, the opposition would have said, 'Well, I'm afraid that's very unsatisfactory and although the Minister says he's going to look at it again, I think we have to register our strength of feeling on this issue by calling a division', knowing perfectly well they're going to win because you haven't got the troops. So it's very hard to get that right. If you have the troops there won't be a vote. If you don't have the troops there will be a vote."

When the troops are dragged in for days or kept late, whips may have to force a division to prevent their back-benchers feeling cheated.

In an incident mystifying to outsiders, but typical of the quandaries whips occasionally find themselves in, during one debate the Government Chief Whip could see that if there were a vote he would win it, but that the opposition were not going press the matter to a division. They had got cold feet about supporting a motion against peers having to sign up to a register of interests, in case it looked as if they had something to hide. But the Government Chief Whip could not let his troops feel they had struggled in for nothing. So, having made sure the Deputy Speaker was alert to the likelihood of a division, he persuaded the Liberal Democrats to shout 'not-content', though in fact they were perfectly 'content' (meaning in agreement with the motion). Reluctantly, they murmured rather than shouted, but the Deputy Speaker heard this feeble sound where another might have ignored it, and called a division. Then a vigilant clerk pointed out that since the government had created only an illusion of opposition to the motion, it was possible no opposition tellers would be appointed, so the Chief Whip sent a whip to ask a Liberal Democrat to act as a second teller (the first being a Labour peer), to count the vote of three.[23]

A chief whip can have to make terrifyingly important decisions on the hoof. Lord Carter was just about to leave the palace when he caught sight of Lord Cranborne on the TV monitor and heard him say that he was minded to call a division. Carter grabbed a colleague who was just getting into a taxi to go home and rushed back to the Chamber knowing that if Cranborne won the vote, he would kill the bill. He did a quick count and realised that he would lose the division. He decided to send a few peers home, so there was no longer a quorum, and thus force the House to adjourn. Cranborne said at the very last minute that he was not intending to defeat the government, but merely to make a point. By that time it was too late for Carter to retrieve his colleagues. The House had to stop for the evening, but from the government's viewpoint at least the bill was saved. Carter paged his troops in the middle of night asking them to attend the deferred second reading at 11 a.m. the following morning and eighty Labour peers appeared.[24]

The usual channels at least once even conspired to arrange a government defeat. During the European Elections Bill the Conservatives and Liberal Democrats had repeatedly won votes against 'closed lists'.[25] It was agreed by the usual channels of the two main parties that, to get the bill through in time to prepare for elections to the European Parliament, the opposition should win a vote that would allow the government to use the Parliament Act. (The opposition's normal tactic would have been to let the bill through at second reading and then amend it at committee stage; had they done so, the use of the Parliament Act would have been delayed and the bill would have been too late for the elections.) While Conservative whips acted conventionally, chivvying peers into the Chamber, the government deployed theirs to get their back-benchers back into the bars and the Liberal Democrats agreed to abstain unless needed to make sure that Labour peers were outnumbered. Lord Carter needed to know exact numbers. For the first and only time, he stationed two whips at the beginning of the division lobbies counting voters and told them to say to each Labour peer going through 'Tell Denis the number is 42' and so on. As planned, Labour lost the division but won the bill.[26] This degree of management was exceptional. Strategies like this cannot be used often because some back-benchers would become disgruntled. Moderation with subterfuge is necessary to keep relations cordial both in your own party and with the opposition.

Problems too lengthy to resolve in the Chamber or committee are referred to the usual channels. They are ideal too for issues that need to be hidden. This applies even to deals about bills, both because of their far-ranging extent, and because at least some in each party would disapprove of the details of the trade-offs. Even in the Chamber secret negotiations continue by notes carried by doorkeepers, who obscure who is communicating with whom by leaving the Chamber and giving the note to another doorkeeper to deliver. Of the negotiations, and the discussions beforehand, nothing is written and all that remains are rumours and myths.[27] This consolidates the aura of power.

When the usual channels are working well, their deals are sacred. Genuine mistakes, like miscalculation of support, are generally forgiven, though even then irritation and wariness may set in for a spell. Those who rat on a deal even once would not be trusted again. Good personal relationships between opposing party managers are the key to smooth business. The combination of honourable brokers – Irvine and Cranborne – and honest delivery-men – Weatherill, Carter and Strathclyde – was important in securing the Weatherill Amendment during the House of Lords Bill.

But judging honour in the give and take between the usual channels is not necessarily a matter of sticking to the rules. Back-benchers can be unpredictable, and sometimes refuse to support their parties' line, so both sides need leeway. Although it is unusual for the usual channels to get into a muddle, there was an occasion during the last Conservative administration when the House reached a certain amendment and Labour whips called 'not moved' (i.e., cancelled), forgetting it was the one they had been planning an ambush for. Two or three further amendments were not moved – to the Tories' amazement – before the opposition woke up to their mistake. The Conservatives could have forged ahead, but accommodation has to take place or business grinds to a halt. The House was adjourned for a few minutes while Labour peers tore about bumping into each other in total confusion. Then they wrote a 'manuscript' amendment, which the government accepted with good grace, so that Labour could make their point, if not the ambush.

Resisting the whips

It is the job of the usual channels to work behind the scenes with invisible reliability. Occasionally they have a public row. The House of Lords Bill unsettled the Conservative back-benchers who felt that their front-bench was giving up the fight too quickly. After one ambush by the opposition, the usual channels found themselves bickering publicly on the floor of the House. On other occasions the government forcing bills through quickly at the end of a session sometimes gives rise to complaints that they have not been agreed.[28] According to Lord Carter, however, breakdowns in the usual channels were rare while he was Government Chief Whip between 1997 and 2002, the biggest being when the Conservative Chief Whip let him know that his side were likely to lose but was wrong: more Conservatives turned up than expected. Business was lost for that day, and the government in addition had a hole later in the week where a second committee day had been scheduled. As a rare example of the Government Chief Whip being completely taken by surprise, it shows how effectively the usual channels normally operate.

In private, peers complain about the usual channels. Until recently their main gripes were that they not only dominated the House committees, but even chose the other members as well. The usual channels recommended appointments to the Committee of Selection, which consisted of the usual channels and two Cross-benchers. A back-bench move to make the committee more inclusive was thwarted by the chief whips merely by adding the deputy chief whips to it. In June 2001 the committee invited back-benchers from the two main parties, but many loyal party members still feel that if the usual channels do not further increase back-bench representation on committees, the House may demand elections for committee membership. Even some clerks find it worrying that the usual channels resolve so many decisions before the committees actually meet, so that back-bench members do not get a chance even to express a view. To circumvent this, some clerks make suggestions to committee members without mentioning them to the usual channels in advance; but such proposals often get short shrift when the committee deliberates.

The usual channels' role in law making is rarely challenged. Back- or Cross-bench victories against the party managers are unusual, but celebrated, not so much because the usual channels' political role is resented as because of the distinction such victories confer on the individual back-benchers responsible. In 1995 Cross-bencher Lord Freyberg miraculously squeezed £45 million out of the government. The twenty-three-year-old sculptor (grandson of one of Churchill's generals) was nobbled by the War Widows Society before he made his maiden speech; and he made a good one. It led to a campaign – supported by the army former top brass (or their descendents which was almost as good), such as Field Marshals Lords Carver and Bramall – which culminated in a vote 190 to 145 in his favour. It reached the Commons three days before the anniversary of VE day. The date, the historical resonances, the vocal support of Winston Churchill's grandson (a Conservative MP), and much of their rank and file, made it impossible for the Conservative government to reject.

Another case of successful back-bench pressure was the Countess of Mar's campaign to show that organophosphates used in agriculture were damaging to human health. At first she was considered a bore. After a sustained effort over many years, she built a coalition between the two Houses in an all-party group and gathered enough support to force the government to take note. Organophosphates were banned, and now peers can be heard saying 'wasn't she marvellous!' Cross-benchers have also managed to get six private members bills onto the statute book since May 1997, and have chaired fourteen influential committees since 2000 alone[29] (that is, that have produced reports that have provided frameworks for legislation or have influenced public policy). Lord Laming's inquiry into the death of Victoria Climbié in 2002–03, for example, has led to a shake-up of the social services and the introduction of government legislation.

Freyburg, Mar and the others are Cross-benchers. It is harder for back-bench party peers to initiate campaigns, especially if defying party policy, but some succeed. They have to make alliances in other parties, as Labour Baroness Hollis explains:

> On the women's pensions issue I worked very hard. I chose some Tory women who count in the Tory Party and coaxed them to come into an alliance with me; I worked the Cross-benchers to get them, and the Lib Dems. So I put together an alliance. Several of them were women. I ended up in some cases having to draft their speeches but you had to do it in a way that made it possible to talk about the good sense of the House. The moment you start doing ding-dongs or 'Labour's good, Tory is bad', you've lost the House. You've wasted your time. Cross-benchers don't want to know.[30]

This is not just a question of securing votes in the division lobbies; having visible supporters from all four blocs is considered important when building a legitimate campaign. Wily operators also watch the relevant debates from the Commons' gallery so that they can quote the arguments by those MPs that support their cause when the bill returns to the Lords.

The government may react ruthlessly even against members of their own party. When a Conservative baroness tried to get an amendment through against the last Tory administration, first the Leader of the House spread a false rumour that a former services chief was against it, and then the Commons party managers told *The Times* newspaper that her amendment had been withdrawn. Even so, she won a division against a three-line whip with the help of Labour, Liberal Democrats and ten of her own.

The extent of the influence of individuals is unknowable. Labour peer Baroness Kennedy of the Shaws is said to have played an important part in defeating her own party during debate on the Mode of Trial Bill. But the Conservatives and Lib Dems had already chosen the bill as an issue on which to defeat the government and it was their votes that counted.

Cross- or back-bench-led initiatives do not interfere with the principle of usual channels' control. In fact, despite some resentment, it is publicly questioned only seldom, and almost always over the way the House is run. For example, back-benchers successfully resisted government attempts to move the day for debates from Wednesday to Thursday, despite support from the opposition, on the grounds that they would attract less attendance. But this is unusual.

'Domestic' decisions are made by a number of sub-committees that report to the House Committee (known as the Offices Committee until 2002), which then makes proposals to the whole House for approval. But since the usual channels control this committee, proposals about the management of the House are either suggested by them or have their backing. If the usual channels do not support it, it cannot get past the House Committee.

The management of the House was neglected during the 1990s. The usual channels were not much interested: Labour managers had enough on their plate; Conservatives did not see much wrong with it; and when Lib Dems complained about inefficiency, they were ignored. Aware of a gradual slither, the Clerk of the Parliaments suggested an external review by a consultant. This, with other suggestions, was agreed by the then Offices Committee, expecting the House to pass their report on the nod. Instead, it precipitated revolt.[31] The idea of an outsider meddling in their affairs upset some, the proposed fee irritated others, but more were enraged by the arrogance shown by the usual channels in the way they presented it. Furious peers demanded that it be withdrawn and reasons for it given. A month later it came back in the form of a fuller set of proposals but without much more explanation, as the usual channels, demonstrating rather vividly that they are not always as closely in touch with back-bench opinion as they like to claim, still assumed back-benchers would prefer not to get tangled up in administrative detail. The reaction was outrage. Lord Tomlinson expressed their feelings with delicacy: 'too many noble Lords have so far participated in the debate in private. Some back-benchers want to say something in public, because this is the only time we shall have the opportunity to give any expression of view.'[32] Others were blunter – whether or not to recruit a consultant was not a matter for the usual channels, who often ignored back-benchers; it should be decided by the House. Peers were not to be soothed. Lord Peston railed:

> We cannot carry on in this gentle mode of saying, 'Really, we want a few changes but we don't want to criticise anyone. We don't want to hurt anyone's feelings.' It is all nice and cosy, as your Lordships love to be. But there is something wrong about what has been going on in your Lordships' House.[33]

This was unresolved when the Chairman of Committees unfortunately died.[34] Two months later another Chairman of Committees was appointed: the Liberal Democrat Lord Tordoff, who set up a new working group, side-stepping the Offices Committee on the grounds that it would obstruct reform. His committee proposed to the Offices Committee that it should be abolished and replaced with a smaller group who would feel more responsibility for the decisions they made.[35] This the usual channels welcomed, but the suggestion that members of the new committee should be elected rather than chosen by them was rejected and dropped before it got to the House. Lord Tordoff broadcast the proposals for the new House Committee, as well as a staff management board, around the House, making sure that there could be no accusations of secrecy, and got them through quite easily.

So what had started out as a rebellion against the usual channels dissolved. In fact, the original suggestion of the consultant, and most of the proposals in subsequent reports, were the work of the clerks. Back-benchers had wrongly assumed that the usual channels were trespassing on their territory.

The only other rebellion I witnessed against usual channels' control also concerned the working practices of the House. When the late Lord Williams of Mostyn became Leader of the House in 2001 he initiated a review and emulated Tordoff by setting up an independent cross-party working group to side-step the unwieldy committees. When their proposals got to the Procedure Committee (with a majority of back-benchers but controlled by the usual channels) in July 2002, all hell broke lose. Several Tories assumed the mantle of back-benchers' champion in the struggle against the usual channels. They dismissed the proposals on the grounds that they would increase the power of government at the expense of back-benchers.[36] When they came before the House, Lord Trefgarne complained:

> These proposals have emerged from a Leader's Group and the Procedure Committee. In truth it is the so-called 'usual channels' that bring the proposals before the Chamber. Even the Procedure Committee consists

principally of distinguished citizens of the usual channels. When noble Lords such as myself seek to offer a different view, we are very soon seen off.[37]

Lord Lucas pointed out that the usual channels work well but, 'they have their own agenda. On two or three occasions this week alone, their judgment of what should be done with a particular motion or amendment has clearly not been the same as that of back-benchers.'[38] From the viewpoint of the majority of back-benchers, however, these opponents had chosen the wrong issue to do battle on. There was merit in the proposals, and the report was passed unamended.

In recent years back-benchers have only shown resistance to the usual channels over these two issues. Why did back-benchers take a stand on these? The answer lies in the Commons. The usual channels derive their control over the Lords' legislative processes by virtue of their link to the Commons' democratic legitimacy, but the Commons has no right to interfere with the administration of the Lords. Where domestic issues are concerned, the usual channels are hamstrung and back-bench peers can occasionally express their corporate will. The two stories also demonstrate that rebellion can only go so far. The usual channels – with their control of time and committees – always win in the end.

The desert and the jungle[39]

Government control in the Commons is domineering, especially with a large majority. Crucial to it is the little-known office of the Private Secretary to the Chief Whip.[40] The Lords equivalent (the Private Secretary to the Chief Whip and Leader of the House) is important but rotates every two to three years; of the more permanent Commons Private Secretary, it was said only half-jokingly that the previous incumbent, Sir Murdo McClean, was the third most important person in British politics, after Tony Blair and Alastair Campbell. During a period of particular hostility between the two main parties in the first half of the twentieth century, this official was sometimes the only person talking to both sides. Allegedly, part of the Private Secretary's power derives from decades of gathering knowledge about MPs' secrets so that no one ever dares sack him or her. But, also, when someone performs so delicate and demanding a job for decades, no government wants to snarl up a working system by replacing them with a novice. If the Lords Private Secretary was in post for as long, that person would also accrue enormous influence; as it is, she or he is a key member of the usual channels.

The Commons is confrontational and the usual channels there are a different species. Peers who have been Commons whips report that they have had to be nannies to MPs, and psychiatrists, confessors, detectives, pastors and, as the intelligence-gathering arm of government, friends. They are also fixers: the men and women who keep the show on the road, using subtle threats and rewards to 'accumulate reserves of informal authority that are based upon indebtedness and gratitude'.[41] Former MPs in the Lords remember only their ferocity.

Power lies mainly in the Commons, where the potential for anger is far greater. Whips work in the heart of the political whirlwind and spend time soothing frayed tempers, usually but not always of their own side, openly in bars, covertly in their offices, and sometimes in secrecy. Of their three principal functions – as fixers, spies and sheep-dogs – it is in shepherding techniques that they differ most from the Lords. MPs are far more tightly controlled, mostly because they can be. Their dependence on party for re-election and the satisfaction of their ambitions makes them easily coercible. Some MPs feel beholden – whips put the needy in touch with richer MPs to bail them out, or help find them consultancies (such as the job found for one Conservative MP as 'parliamentary adviser' to some East End demolition contractors who were taking up upper-class pursuits and wanted advice about when to tip game-keepers and so on). Incredible inconveniences are sometimes inflicted on rebels; calling them in when they are at the end of a 120-mile drive home, for example. It can get nastier; there are credible rumours of whips blackmailing MPs.[42]

MPs are ambitious. Wounded feelings from not being given the job they coveted, or jealousy that a leader looks with a kinder eye at a rival MP can cause disappointed MPs to vote against the party out of spite. But medicine is often at hand: "If I learnt one thing when I was Chief Whip in the Commons about politicians, that is a politician has, by and large, an infinite capacity to absorb flattery." When an MP is wobbly, whips can organise a meeting with the most senior members of the government. He may even get the chance to speak to the Secretary of State; but more likely it will be arranged at a time when the whips know the MP cannot make it. Then they can say: 'Surely you are not going to vote against the party when the Chief Whip offered you a meeting with the Secretary of State?'

They are far more intrusive than Lords' whips; it is not possible to imagine the (probably apocryphal) Commons story at the other end of the palace:

Whip: Is Bloggins there, because we need him back here to vote?
Wife: No, I'm afraid he's not.
Whip: Well, would you ask the bloke you're sleeping with to come back then?

It is often argued that intense whipping stifles democracy. In the eyes of whips and true party loyalists, a system that gave back-benchers more freedom would only increase the powers of cranky or whimsical individuals or groups at the expense of the majority. In fact, the House of Lords has such a system and in practice back-bench minorities very rarely abuse it.

Deciding policy is the job of the cabinet (or, increasingly, the Prime Minister, according to many MPs). Achieving it is the job of the whips. By dealing with timetabling, procedures and personnel, the whips deliver policies and bills to the Prime Minister. Lord Wakeham saw his job as trying to control the anarchy of political confrontation so that MPs could get on with discussing issues, not waste time debating modalities. Only when the government has a narrow majority do negotiations between chief whips in the Commons share the delicacy of those in the Lords, as a story about the fall of the Callaghan government illustrates. In March 1979, the Labour government faced a motion of no confidence but hoped to win the vote by one. Lord Weatherill, then the Conservative Deputy Chief Whip in the Commons, knew that the Labour government had two jokers: one was too sick to come to the House and the other was terminally unreliable. He noticed that the latter's wife had managed to take him back to Ireland. He told a government whip: 'You are going to lose.' The whip reminded Weatherill that they had always had a gentleman's agreement that sick members from their respective parties would be paired. Weatherill replied that as it was a motion of no confidence it was of no relevance, but that he would nevertheless honour the agreement by standing out himself. This, he knew, would have got him into the very deepest trouble. His opposite, knowing his own position was still more dire and that if the government lost, he would be finished, said: 'Jack, I am not going to put you in that position.' The Labour party lost by one vote, the government fell, and the government whip's successful political career came to an abrupt end.

With a respectable majority the government demands its own way in the Commons, merely informing the opposition of the timetable; the Speaker controls debate which limits delay; and MPs, for reasons given above, are usually obedient. So what can the opposition do? The more brilliantly the Opposition Chief Whip anticipates the government's next move, the more he or she will be respected by his own side. So the Government Chief Whip sometimes outlines salient bits of the legislative timetable to his counterpart in strictest secrecy well in advance, and adjustments are made – trading a day or two of debate on one bill for the late-night, easy passage of another, and so on. "The business of the House is settled by the Government Chief Whip with the Opposition Chief Whip secretly and privately before it ever goes to the cabinet. They fix it up between them." Then, at cabinet or shadow cabinet meetings, when chief whips speculate about how the other side will react, they know their 'guesses' are accurate because they have been negotiated. They may even suggest making fierce demands, knowing they will be conceded because they too have already been traded for something else. Close collusion benefits both. It forms a virtuous circle. On the whole government concessions are procedural: more time to debate issues, for instance, not policy. Policy is not the business of the whips and has to be referred back to the minister, whole cabinet or the Prime Minister.

MPs, with their eyes on the next election, have to make sure they are seen to be fighting their corner. They assume, rightly or wrongly, that journalists and public are impressed by partisan heat and relentless claims to the 'moral high-ground'. But lords have no constituents and have, therefore, more time to concentrate on scrutiny. Their House is a revising chamber; its business is to consult with the public, review drafts of legislation and edit texts. Rows serve no useful purpose. The government does not have a majority, and co-operates with other parties. The Leader of the House is responsible for the smooth running of the whole House, and the government party managers take care to be seen as restrained. It forms a stark contrast to the Commons:

> "In the House of Lords, you say to people, 'We're going to take this bill on Tuesday next week'. They say, 'Well, that's not really very convenient. Do you think you could have a look and see if you can change it?' And so the debates behind the scenes in the House of Lords are much more gentle ... Whereas in the Commons there is a tendency to say, 'Well, fine, that gives us a good opportunity to have a row. So let's get ready for the row.' In the House of Lords they don't do that. The other parties expect the government to take a bit of notice."

Adjusting to the co-operative usual channels of the Lords causes some consternation for former Commons' whips: "I can't believe I have to postpone the committee stage of a bill because Baroness X has a hospital appointment that day", said one. In each House the usual channels are a power elite, but have evolved under different conditions. Commons whips do not conceal their control. The usual channels' interests are served by promoting respect, even fear, of the power of the whips and dread of their disapproval.

These differences between the usual channels in the two Houses reveal much about power in Parliament. MPs as a whole, and ministers in particular, do not rate the unelected Chamber. The Commons party managers treat ministers from the Lords as decidedly junior. The elected representatives claim legitimacy, create policy and ultimately control the agenda of both Houses of Parliament. But the relationship between them is more subtle and changeable than it at first appears. Where there is a large government majority in the Commons, some back-bench peers can have more influence over both law making and policy debates than some back-bench MPs.

In the Lords, the usual channels rely on gentle persuasion, loyalty and chicanery – smoke and mirrors – never letting on how much or little they deal with the enemy. Back-benchers attend only if they feel a sense of their individual importance and their freedom to act according to conscience, at least some of the time. But their obedience is required in order to fulfil party commitments. Rituals of debate – the subject of the next chapter – help to ensure their compliance.

Notes

1 They were mentioned in Parliament by an MP in 1905.

2 Gyles Brandreth, 2000, *Breaking the Code: Westminster Diaries*, Phoenix, London. Bagehot as quoted by Brandreth, *ibid.*, p. xi.

3 Michael Rush and Clare Ettinghausen, 2002, *Opening Up the Usual Channels*, Hansard Society, London.

4 The House of Lords, 2000, *Companion to the Standing Orders and Guide to the Proceedings of the House of Lords*, 28th edn, The Stationary Office, London, Para. 1.47.

5 Standing Order 14 gives government business precedence for a substantial proportion of Commons time.

6 Rush and Ettinghausen, *ibid.*, p. 6.

7 Lord Carter, HL Deb., 17 May 1999, col. 137.

8 The posts included in the full usual channels are as follows: Leader of the House, Government Chief Whip, Private Secretary to the Chief Whip and and Leader of the House, Special Adviser to the Chief Whip, Opposition Leader, Opposition Chief Whip, Director of the Opposition Whip's Office, Leader of the Liberal Democrats, Chief Whip of the Liberal Democrats, Head of the Liberal Democrat Whip's Office and Convenor of the Cross-benchers.

9 Recently this post has been opened up to competition so that external candidates can apply.

10 During the eighteenth century managers were appointed by the two Houses to try to reach agreement at conferences, as they do in American congressional conference committees today, but these were unsuccessful (P. A. Bromhead, 1958, *The House of Lords and Contemporary Politics 1911–1957*, Routledge and Kegan Paul, London, p. 133).

11 A Lords committee, chaired by Lord Lloyd of Berwick, has recently suggested that some of the Leaders' duties should be transferred to a 'light-touch' speaker; their report was debated in the House on 12 January 2004. However, the legislation to abolish the post of Lord Chancellor has been referred to a committee for further scrutiny, so this change could not be made until the 2004–05 session at the earliest.

12 House of Lords, *ibid.*, p. 14.

13 Lord Denham (Conservative), then Government Chief Whip.

14 Lord Stanley of Alderley, Unpublished diaries 1971–1999, p. 6.

15 Lord Swinfen, Official Report, 30 March 1999, col. 316.

16 Lord Shore of Stepney, HL Deb., 30 March 1999, col. 269.

17 Based on information supplied by the House of Lords Registry.

18 Lord Wallace of Saltaire as quoted by A. Mitchell, 1999, *Farewell My Lords*, Politico's, London, p. 107.

19 As quoted by Mitchell, *ibid.*, p. 135.

20 It was decided during these negotiations that twenty desks should go to Conservatives, twenty to Labour, ten to the Liberal Democrats, and five to the Cross-benchers. The last were enraged. As they always do, they argued that they are three times larger than the Liberal Democrats and should have appropriate perks. The Lib Dems maintained that Cross-benchers attended rarely, left early, and barely used the rooms they already had. Labour, forgetting that they will be in opposition again one day, begrudged Conservative demands because government peers, they said, make better use of working space.

21 Quoted by Mitchell, *ibid.*, p. 45. For example see the section on 'Resisting the whips' later in this chapter.

22 The Leader of the Commons, Labour MP Peter Hain, recently complained that government decision-making is too centralised and even government MPs are not sufficiently consulted about legislative proposals before decisions are made ('Reclaim the party', *Guardian*, 10 March 2004).

23 The three voting against the amendment were the Labour teller, the Liberal Democrat teller and one Cross-bencher, HL Deb., 16 May 2000, col. 1714.

24 HL Deb., 27 July 2000, col. 723.

25 This system of voting names the party, rather than the individual candidate, which many saw as anti-democratic.

26 When Celia Thomas, in the Liberal Democrats' Whips Office, prematurely sent a message to the Lib Dem party leader by pager, 'Tell Paddy bill is dead' the pager service asked, 'Will the person receiving this message be terribly upset?'

27 A record does exist of one deal struck by a Lords Chief Whip, because a Secretary of State in the Commons would only accept a promise from the Liberal Democrats in writing. Since the deal was potentially embarrassing, the document was handed over on condition that only the Chief Whip would see it; the Secretary of State accepted his word and the deal worked. Contrariwise, on another occasion, an opposition party leader wrote a memo of what had been agreed, and, as a result, the government promptly called the deal off.

28 For the ambushed adjournment, see the 'Four horsemen' in Chapter 4 and for complaints about the government being in a rush, see HL Deb., 22 March 1999.

29 The bills were: Road Traffic Reduction (National Targets) Act 1998, Sponsor: Lord Elis-Thomas; Criminal Cases Review (Insanity) Act 1999, Sponsor: Lord Ackner; Protection of Children Act 1999, Sponsor: Lord Laming; Census Amendment Act 2000, Sponsor: Lord Weatherill; National Lottery (Funding of Endowments) Act 2003, Sponsor: Lord Walpole; Ragwort Control Act 2003, Sponsor: Baroness Masham of Ilton (see http://www.crossbenchpeers.org.uk/, legislation and reports, accessed 14 July 2004).

30 Baroness Hollis, as quoted by Mitchell, *ibid.*, p. 128.

31 HL Deb., 21 June 2000.

32 Lord Tomlinson, HL Deb., 27 July 2000, col. 621.

33 Lord Peston, HL Deb., 27 July 2000, cols 623–4.

34 The Chairman of Committees, Lord Boston of Faversham, had promised that a committee of back-benchers should decide whether or not to recruit the consultant. This back-bench committee carried out a review of management and committees and dropped the idea of a consultant. Lord Boston was replaced by Lord Mackay of Ardbrecknish, who died and was replaced by Lord Tordoff.

35 House of Lords, 12 February 2002, Fourth Report From the Select Committee on the House of Lords' Offices, Session 2001–02, HL Paper 79.

36 These included family-friendly hours, more scrutiny of bills before they reach Parliament, and 'carry-over' (that is, allowing bills to be carried over from one session to the next). Although carry-over may be necessary to allow for pre-legislative scrutiny, it will be the usual channels that decide which bills are treated in this way, so it is arguable that the usual channels will gain control. See Chapter 10 for details.

37 Lore Trefgarne, HL Deb., 24 July 2002, col. 380.

38 Lord Lucas, HL Deb., 24 July 2002, col. 421.

39 See Chapter 5, note 1, for an explanation of this phrase.

40 Only four have held the post: Sir Charles Harris, Sir Freddy Warren, the recently retired Sir Murdo MacLean and the current incumbent, Roy Stone. Murdo McClean, to emphasise the point that no agreements in the usual channels are written down, was said to carry a pen only very rarely.

41 Donald Searing, 1995, 'Backbench and leadership roles in the House of Commons', *Parliamentary Affairs, A Journal of Comparative Politics*, vol. 48, no. 3, July, p. 430.

42 J. Paxman, 2003, *The Political Animal*, Penguin, London, pp. 165–6.

10 Rules and rituals

'Parliamentary occasions' are high drama, and can be like going to a first night at the opera. The Chamber thrills with expectation as seats fill up in the evening (though the show has probably been going since mid-afternoon) and more come in for good performers. The cast tend to be charged on adrenalin. Some prepare for speaking by downing a few in the bar. Afterwards, peers often recall such events wistfully. On one occasion a whip, a clerk and a party leader, standing around in Principal Corridor, regaled me for half an hour or more with stories about past bills, positively sighing with the pleasurable recollection of bygone histrionics – 'ahhh, the Education Bill …' – relishing the memories.

Even everyday debates are theatrical: their ritualisation is not unlike the studied unfolding of a play, and each season has a new programme with slightly different principal actors. But debate is more than theatre. Even if debates tend to be in part stage managed by the usual channels, they have no script, no director, and are a lot more than just performance. Kertzer says of ritual that it:

> helps societies deal with many kinds of interpersonal conflicts that threaten to poison social life and tear the community apart. Indeed judicial procedures, from the simplest societies to modern nation-states, are highly ritualised. Rites of the law court are not that different from rites of the royal court. In both cases the image of sacrality, of legitimacy, is fostered through ritual, while aggressive behaviour is sharply contained and lines of authority bolstered.[1]

Legislation is reformed on the anvil of debate, and each debate is not only a (modestly) creative workshop, it is also a contest and negotiation over the meaning and moral value of a text. While there is a theatrical quality to the rituals of debate, more importantly they constitute a web of cautionary principles conceived to ensure that in the endless series of collisions between different moral outlooks, each skirmish has an outcome (usually a victory for the government) that is accepted by the losers. Ultimately, debate in Parliament is a verbal war that exists to ensure that moral and political differences within the nation can be expressed without, on the whole, leading to violence, and the rituals of debate rely on rules and symbols of engagement to ensure that the discussion of explosive issues in the Chamber is always seemly.

So what is meant exactly by ritual in the context of the modern state? The behaviour of peers in the Chamber is ritualised in the sense that whatever they are doing or saying, they have to do so in a prescribed and structured way and by symbolic means. It is symbols – secular or sacred – rather than the supernatural that give rituals their potency. Symbolism communicates the relationships between people through behaviour, words or objects. When peers address each other as 'My Lords', it is a symbol rather than a mere signifier because of the layers of meaning its users take for granted. They are expressing a shared nobility and membership of the House, and distinguish themselves from MPs and commoners.

The ritualisation of debate is only a part of the plethora of rituals and ceremonies, encrusted with symbols and decorated by splendid performances, that either constitute or punctuate business. While the rituals of debate are precautionary, in the sense of preventing any undesirable behaviour, and define peers' relationships with each other, the ceremonies do something different. From the State Opening of Parliament, which takes place annually in the autumn,[2] to the Lord Chancellor's daily procession into the Chamber, ceremonies define peers in their relationships to MPs, the monarch and the public. Ceremonies and symbols are the subject of the next chapter. This one is more concerned with certain theatrical aspects of politics. But the Chamber is not exactly a theatre – it is more an arena where the outcomes of real moral conflict are decided, not entirely by the actors (or gladiators) themselves, but more by the unseen hand of the usual channels, who are themselves among the gladiators' champions.

Seasons, seats and scripts

Most parliamentary time is taken up with debates on legislation. These comprise a series of battles over amendments to draft bills that will become law, unless thrown out, by the end of the session (see Table 10.1).

The atmosphere of the Chamber changes according to the season and the time of day. State Opening by the Queen in November is a day of dignity. Afterwards, peers disrobe, eat a leisurely lunch while the

Table 10.1   Parliamentary seasons, sessions and sittings

A parliament
The period of time between elections – up to five years – when, usually, one party holds a majority in the Commons and is, therefore, in government. It is broken up into 'sessions'.

A session
A session is usually a year. Each starts with the State Opening of Parliament, usually in November/December (unless a general election takes place), and runs to July (or sometimes August). It has three main terms, with recesses at Christmas, Easter and in the summer, roughly coinciding with school breaks. In addition to the terms, there is 'spillover' usually from October to mid-November, when the last session's business is completed in time to get Royal Assent. The government decides the exact dates.

   The legislative programme allows at least five stages for each bill in the Lords. To get Royal Assent, which turns the bills into acts, all stages have to be complete before the end of the session (unless an agreement is made for 'carrying-over' a bill). Sessions end with 'Prorogation'.

A sitting day
The Lords usually debates bills on Mondays, Tuesdays and Thursdays. Wednesdays tend to be reserved for more general policy debates and the House occasionally sits on Fridays mornings. The day usually starts with prayers at 2.30 p.m. (11 a.m. on Thursdays and Fridays), followed by Question Time for forty minutes, often followed by a few 'motions' (that is, proposals, for example to approve a committee report, to dispense with a Standing Order on a particular occasion, to pass a government scheme, or to 'pray' that it might be annulled). The most time-consuming work of the day is then a stage of one (or more) bill(s). Motions are sometimes passed without debate, whereas bills are always discussed. When the day ends (usually in the evening or night but earlier on Thursdays), the House 'adjourns'. The number of sitting days was 228 in 1997–98 (a long session due to the election), 145 in 1998–99, and 177 in 1999–2000.

Chamber is rearranged, and return to debate the Queen's Speech. This, written for her by the government, introduces their programme of new bills. It and the debate following are the government's public announcement of their plans for the year. Senior ministers, who tend to be in the Commons, often insist on introducing new bills in their own House, although less than in the past because it means that their Lordships have nothing to do at the start of the season. Then December is packed with festive occasions, a social whirl of staff parties and drinks with colleagues.

   The spring term drags as bills are chewed over during their early stages. The pace quickens in the summer until 'July madness', when the government realises that, because so many bills started in the Commons, not enough days remain to get through the backlog in the Lords. Sittings go on until the small hours, the opposition is accused of wasting time, people are so driven they barely greet each other as they walk in agitation from one meeting or debate to the next; but time has to be found also for parties: the picnic in Black Rod's garden, the tug of war between Commons and Lords, the Cross-bench summer party, and cocktails to celebrate the end of term.

After the summer recess, there is the 'spillover'. The usual channels and senior clerks become wholly unapproachable in the race to get bills wrapped up by the end of the session, back-bench muttering about late nights becomes ceaseless, bags grow under people's eyes, tempers snap. Abruptly, and after a 'ping-pong' of contentious bills between the two Houses, disagreements are resolved and Royal Assent cuts the flow of debate.[4] The corporate sigh of relief is audible. The government front-bench has a party to celebrate bills passed, the opposition drink in sorrow, and the majority quietly slip away to rest. A week later, the next session begins with the calm solemnity of State Opening again.

The daily cycle is also ritualised. In the morning of each sitting day the Chamber is cleaned and searched for bombs by dogs, and the fringe on the Throne is brushed. Sittings begin with a doorkeeper in the Peers' Lobby allocating seats to peers' guests and distinguished visitors. The atmosphere has considerable glitz, with peers and their guests – well-dressed, confident and occasionally flushed after a good lunch – happily anticipating an afternoon of entertainment. Other peers rush from their work elsewhere: at universities, public relations companies, inns of court or wherever. Mere members of the public, referred to as 'strangers' by both Houses, are kept waiting in the corridor outside the Chamber, and tend to appear out of place and usually slightly nervous. As doorkeepers usher visitors to their appropriate corners and peers scurry into the Chamber, the Principal Doorkeeper, an ex-non-commissioned officer of prodigious dignity and lungs, cries 'Make way for the Lord Chancellor'. In black gown and full-bottomed wig, this austere figure – and his Pursebearer and Trainbearer – are led through the lobby and into the Chamber by the Yeoman Usher[5] bearing the Mace, with Black Rod taking the rear. The Mace is placed on the Woolsack and the massive brass doors of the Chamber close behind them.

Only peers and clerks can attend prayers, which are said by one of the bishops. All except the bishop and the Lord Chancellor kneel on their benches with their faces to the wall. The bishop recites one of fifteen psalms, the Lord's prayer, and a seventeenth century prayer for Parliament which begins with words for the monarch, asking God to 'endue her plenteously with heavenly gifts', and continues:

... Almighty God, by whom alone Kings reign, and Princes decree justice; and from whom alone cometh all counsel, wisdom, and understanding; we thine unworthy servants, here gathered together in thy Name, do most humbly beseech thee to send down thy Heavenly Wisdom from above, to direct and guide us in all our consultations ...

The only change permitted is the replacement of a monarch's name with the next when she or he dies. One bishop said a prayer for peace during the Falklands War and was roundly told off: 'the prayers have been the same since the seventeenth century and should not be changed even during war', an outraged peer protested.

Meanwhile, doorkeepers escort guests, visitors and strangers along the corridors, to admit them to the galleries when prayers are over. As they wait, the doorkeepers give a short speech:

"The bishop is just saying prayers. It usually takes between three and five minutes. It's the Bishop of X today, he likes to take four and he's about half way through. If you could please turn your mobile phones off now: if you're caught with one going off, you're liable to get thrown in the dungeon or hanged depending what mood the boss is in. When you get in there, after questions they will be discussing the House of Lords Bill but it will be interrupted by a statement on Northern Ireland which will come down from the Commons. You can leave whenever you wish but please do so quietly. Any questions? Oh hello Emma, you've heard all this before. Haven't you finished your book yet? I've got a good joke for you later."

Question Time begins. Questions are submitted in advance so the minister can obtain information for a proper response. After the minister replies, the questioner asks a 'supplementary' to probe for further information, especially if the minister has been evasive, and then others pitch in with their questions on the subject. Once the time-slot for each question is up, the clerk at the Table (the Clerk of the Parliaments for the first hour of the day), rises slowly and smoothly, as if practicing T'ai Chi, and announces the next. On popular subjects several peers rise, and all but one should sink down again, graciously giving way because it is another party's turn, or because an expert has also risen, or because they are particularly polite, creating the impression of a lively Quaker meeting. However, the number of people trying to intervene has increased over the last few years, and often several refuse to give way until peers shout out the name of the speaker they would prefer to hear or the Leader suggests who should go next.

After forty minutes the Clerk of the Parliaments calls the next business: usually a few motions followed by legislation.[6] Bills of little interest provoke a mass exodus, sometimes almost emptying the Chamber except for the front-benchers responsible for the bill, but contentious ones have peers filling the benches, the steps between them and the entrances.

Each stage of a bill constitutes a ritual with its own formalised procedures:[7]

1. first reading (formal introduction of the bill);
2. second reading (discussion of the principles);
3. committee stage (going over the bill clause by clause in 'committee' mode – from this point amendments may be made);
4. report stage (more detailed discussion as 'the House' rather than as a 'committee', so that no speaker may speak more than once to a particular amendment unless they moved it);
5. third reading (followed by a motion that the 'bill do now pass', which may also be debated).

At all stages debate is regulated by all peers. The occupant of the Woolsack (the Lord Speaker[8] or a Deputy Speaker) may not intervene in debate; he presides only in announcing the next amendment and calling divisions. At committee stage, a small number of bills are discussed in a committee room outside the Chamber, but the majority are debated by the whole House 'in committee' in the Chamber. This entails the Lord Speaker or Deputy Speaker handing over his functions to the Chairman of Committees (or his deputy) who sits at the Table. This formality and apparently pointless handover is meaningful to insiders – most importantly it signifies that the rules are less restrictive– but mystifies strangers.

When Lords and Commons disagree over bills, they take longer as they bounce between Houses. When both Houses are satisfied, messages in quaint Norman French are written on the bill, such as '*a ceste Bill les Seigneurs sont assentus*' ('The Lords assent to this bill'). When Royal Assent is given at the end of the session, the Clerk of the Parliaments tells peers, and MPs standing at the bar, for each other bill or measure, '*La Reine le veult*' ('The Queen so wishes').[9]

From committee stage onwards, each amendment is moved by a peer, replied to by another from the opposing side, and then debated by all peers who wish to. Most of the amendments passed are introduced by the government, and it uses the House of Lords to clean up the detail of legislation for which there is no time in the Commons. Some issues are dealt with in minutes by negotiation, for example with the minister responsible conceding that she or he will consider the matter again, at which the mover of the amendment withdraws it. On big issues – such as the preservation of ninety-two hereditary peers – a debate taking several hours can fail to achieve a resolution. A vote has to follow.[10]

Votes are the most dramatic rituals. Anticipation builds during the closing speeches. The mover triggers a division with the words: 'I wish to test the opinion of the House' or 'I beg to move amendment x'. The Speaker on the Woolsack then 'puts' the question to the House and 'collects the voices', to find out whether peers are 'content' (agree) or 'not-content'. If the ensuing shouting does not reveal which side has the majority a division is called, with the phrase 'Clear the bar'. Rather than an injunction to abstain from intoxicating liquor, it is an order to remove strangers from the division lobbies. Guests sitting behind the bar in the Chamber, separated only by fat red ropes from peers walking into the not-content lobby, are greeted by those who know them with a smile or a joke, despite the gravity of such occasions. Once one saw me and asked:

> "Are you finding this tribal behaviour anthropologically interesting? What do you make of it?"

> "Well, I can't understand what the Lib Dems are up to. Why are they voting with you?"

> "They're annoyed because no one warned them about the vote. But why are you still here? How's the book coming along? You should hurry up and publish it before we're all dead."

Peers delight in the breaks divisions offer: while a few maintain a portentous grimness, most chatter like starlings as they queue to be counted – speculating on the result, gossiping, complaining, trying to nobble a minister or checking what it is all about and how they are supposed to vote. Peers in the bars, the Library, working in offices or in meetings upstairs, are summoned by the division bell, and have only eight minutes to get there, after which the doors are locked and the question put again. When all have been through the lobbies and returned to the Chamber, the four 'tellers' – one from each side in each lobby – walk, holding their counting wands like rifles, to the clerks' Table to recite their tallies. The clerk adds any votes from peers still in the Chamber (for instance, those in wheelchairs). All eyes are on the clerk as she or he hands the result to the senior Teller from the winning side. Sighs and groans arise. The Teller takes it to the peer on the Woolsack, who reads out the numbers.

By late afternoon speculation about ERT (estimated rising time) begins. Instead of comments on the weather, in the House people greet each other with 'Looks like we'll be finished by midnight', and so on. Debates beyond midnight are rare; the average day in the House of Lords lasts till about 10 p.m., when ministers 'wind-up' and the House adjourns.

Rules of debate

In theory, peers may speak on any subject whenever the House allows them and for as long as they like. In practice, they allow the usual channels to determine the agenda and timetable. If a motion is put down without the usual channels' agreement, or at least forewarning them, the mover is liable to be reprimanded. When Lord Cranborne did so, the Government Chief Whip's censure contained an unveiled, though typically polite, threat:

> The noble Viscount, Lord Cranborne, is well known for his courtesy and commitment to the traditions of the house. He well knows that it is his right, as it is the right of any Peer, to table a Motion at any time he pleases. However, he also knows that this House works only by a system of self-regulation and self-restraint. Clearly, if even a small number of Peers table Motions for debate without consultation or regard for other business, this House would quickly grind to a halt ... If your Lordships decide that it is in order for Peers to table Motions without consultation or consideration for other business, we would swiftly find ourselves having to tighten our rules and having to spell out more clearly what Members can and cannot do. Such a process would only result in an erosion of the rights of Back-Bench peers, and is not one which I should like to see commence.[11]

Peers have to abide by dizzying number of rules and conventions.[12] Time is everything. The government needs it, it is the opposition's weapon, and through judicious use of it parliamentarians build their reputations. Its use and abuse are under incessant scrutiny. It provokes passion among peers and, consequently, jokes.

> Lord Carew: I made [my maiden speech] some 'three and half years ago. In my opening remarks I advised the House of a quotation from a famous 17th century French duke, who said: 'No man should speak longer than the period for which he can sustain the act of love.' The successor speaker, the right reverend Prelate the Bishop of Oxford, kindly congratulated me on being able to speak for six minutes. With the ageing process, my speech today is destined to be shorter ...

> Lord Ewing of Kirkford: My Lords, I apologise for interrupting the noble Lord. The actual quotation is that 'No man should speak longer in public than he could make love in private'. I suspect that the noble Lord is way beyond his time.[13]

Nothing makes lords madder than long speeches. It is an insolent violation of essential lordly traits: courtesy, modesty and restraint.

Politics is a passionate business, so the rules to control anger are many and effective. Within certain bounds peers may be as rude as they choose about others' opinions, but imputations about character are off-limits. On such occasions the speaker is usually compelled to withdraw his words by angry shouts of 'Order, order' from all around. When this fails, a peer who feels he has been injured may ask for the 1626 Standing Order on Asperity of Speech to be read. Three did so during the twentieth century, including Earl Russell in 1998 when he felt that Lord Whitty had accused several peers of hypocrisy. He first pointed this out and gave Whitty the opportunity to withdraw. When he would not, Russell proposed that the Order should be read.[14] It was voted on, a majority consented to this ticking-off, and the clerk at the Table did so:

> To prevent misunderstanding, and for avoiding of offensive speeches, when matters are debating either in the House or at Committees, it is for honour sake thought fit, and so ordered, That all personal, sharp, or taxing speeches be forborn, and whosoever answereth another man's speech shall apply his answer to the matter without wrong to the person: and as nothing offensive is spoken, so nothing is to be ill taken, if the party that speaks it shall presently make a fair exposition or clear denial of the words that might bear any ill construction; and if any offence be given in that kind, as the House itself will be very sensible thereof, so it will sharply censure the offender, and give the party offended a fit reparation and full satisfaction.[15]

It satisfied and amused many. Lords Whitty and Russell went for a drink and have been friends since.

When an individual takes another to task it is done gently, partly because the intervener knows that he or she may offend in the future. If unseemly behaviour is not admonished in the Chamber, peers may sometimes approach the malfeasant outside it to suggest that perhaps the point might have been better put another way. When offences are persistent, peers complain to the usual channels who raise it privately with individuals or at party meetings if there are many offenders.

Questions and amendments have to be approved beforehand by the clerks, who remove or do not allow anything that sounds (as they put it) 'controversial' or 'polemic', which reins in the behaviour of peers in the Chamber. Different clerks' interpretations of these strictures may vary slightly. All improve illiterate questions and block those that cast aspersions on the royal family or judges, but deciding what is controversial and what is the legitimate expression of opinion partly depends on the boldness of the clerk concerned.

To help make consistent decisions, clerks have their knowledge of the sacred texts and also a body of conventions and precedents that are not in the scriptures. Precedents are noted down by clerks and stored in the most chaotic filing system: the Registry. This treasure trove of procedural history contains, among other things: notes on unparliamentary language, such as 'to hell with it' and 'cock-up'; Vivian Leigh's protest at the closing of a London theatre; Lord Pakenham[16] producing coshes and knives in the Chamber to make a point; and which peers have been 'taken ill' in the Palace of Westminster (it is not permitted to die on the premises). Most are pretty dull – excruciating detail on hybridity or powers, and Hansard debates on procedure revealing that peers have believed for a very long time that the quality of speeches and observance of procedures are in decline.

Even after debate, the Official Report (Hansard, see Figure 10.1) evens out peers' speeches, putting nonsensical non-sequiturs into calm, grammatical 1950s English and making measured, polite sentences of remarks that may in fact have been not much more than the expression of bad temper. Hansard editors massage what is said so it appears in print in a lordly tone. In Hansard, peers always address each other with fastidious correctness – 'My noble friend, Lord X' for a peer in one's own party, 'The noble and gallant ...' for senior or decorated members of the armed services, 'The noble and learned ...' for senior judges, and so on – though they often fail to in the Chamber. A completely inadmissible outburst – such as lesbians abseiling onto Black Rod's lap into the Chamber in 1988, or the Earl of Burford jumping on the Woolsack and accusing the government of treason in 1999 – merely becomes 'an interruption'. "Hansard makes it homogeneous. It works against the spirit of independence. The ragged edges get smoothed over, which is also achieved by the dress code", according to a Cross-bencher.

Inappropriate dress is no laughing matter. When some bishops left dinner without enough time to get their episcopal robes on before voting and so did so in ordinary clothes, peers were appalled and instructed the Clerk of the Parliaments to notify the Archbishop of Canterbury that bishops had entered the Chamber improperly dressed. Peers nearly always wear suits, except the bishops of course.

Parliaments are about talking. This might lead the naïve to suppose that the regulation of speech would be the only important section in the rulebook. Procedure buffs, however, mind as much about behaviour towards the parliamentary symbols – Mace, Cloth of Estate, and Woolsack – and the officers of state, principally the Lord Chancellor. According to one who takes these things seriously, the most inflexible rules are those regarding movement in the Chamber – that you should not cross between the Woolsack and the Table, move when the Lord Chancellor or his deputy are on their feet, nor walk between the Wool-sack and the speaker. Peers are quick to insist on the practical reasons for such rules: the Lord Chancellor must be able to see whether anyone wants to speak. But since he never intervenes in debate, the restrictions on movement appear to be courtesies that emphasise the personal nature of these public conversations, rather than functional rules for greater efficiency. Just as it would be rude to walk between a speaker and listener in a drawing room, so it is in the Chamber. They also inspire awe in newcomers who hardly dare twitch once seated in case they infringe the rules.

Standing Orders state that 'every Lord is to make obeisance to the Cloth of Estate on entering the House'.[17] This is thought to date from at least the fourteenth century. The canopied throne is 'of the highest symbolic importance, commanding the same respect as that due to the monarch in person' and has had a central role in royal ceremonial and protocol since at least the sixteenth century.[18] But what is this cloth? Some

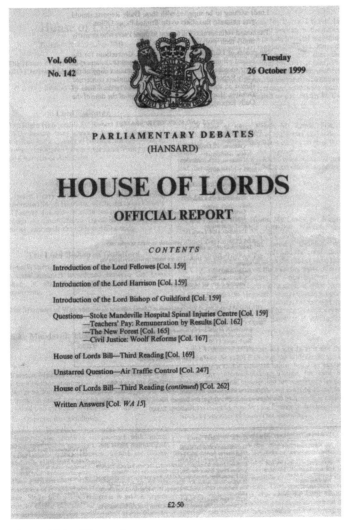

Figure 10.1 Hansard

peers have told me it is a carpet behind the Throne, but most peers and all clerks hotly deny this. Most claim that it was a velvet canopy embroidered in gold, once suspended above the Throne, but that it no longer exists. It apparently hovers ethereally to mark the spot where the Queen would sit on the Throne. So, it is an idea rather than an object. According to one clerk, it is only activated as a symbol of the monarch by the presence of the Mace.

Some peers assume they are bowing to the Throne and still more say that they bow to the Mace, 'the symbol of the authority of the sovereign', even though it is not a written rule or one recognised by the clerks or procedural experts. The Mace does merit a bow when carried in procession but it has captured the imagination of peers even when it is sedentary upon the Woolsack, and has somehow stolen their attention from the Cloth of Estate. The monarch's power and lustre have less significance to many peers so the Cloth may be a less potent symbol than it once was. The Mace is a symbol of the authority of the sovereign in Parliament and reminds them that the monarch's political powers have been handed over to Parliament. Thus, peers can nod to the monarchy, if they revere it, or, if they do not, to what also has become in part a symbol of parliamentary democracy.

Black Rod, the Yeoman Usher and the doorkeepers are responsible for ensuring that respect is shown for the Chamber, its peers and their symbols. They are also responsible for enforcing the rules of access: who is allowed in, when, and upon what seat they may sit. They deal with disturbances such as abseiling lesbians or the Earl of Burford, and Black Rod has discretion to deal with malfeasants as he pleases. He can lock people up in two cells provided for the purpose but he is seldom so draconian, and usually lets them off with a word of caution.[21] When a woman dropped condoms into the Chamber to protest against abortion he instructed the doorkeepers to give her a cup of tea and send her on her way. Even Burford, and the lesbians before him, were merely told in no uncertain terms not to return.

Such picturesque dramas are embroidered by the doorkeepers – always on the lookout for good stories – but in fact they emphasise the extent to which both peers and public are obedient to the rules. Even minor solecisms grate on the nerves. As I spent day after day watching proceedings, I developed intolerance for the disregard of certain conventions, particularly if the disobedience appeared to arise from arrogance. Peers walking out during a maiden speech, or dodging from front-bench to back-bench so as to speak more often, as I witnessed once, could ruin my day. The noise of modern technology in the Chamber is peculiarly distressing: when a mobile phone or pager rings everyone cringes.[22]

The House sometimes descends into confusion, and when a deputy speaker on the Woolsack does not know the proper procedure for a situation he or she cannot reach one of the clerks at the Table to ask. Although the clerks do not usually venture to the Woolsack, I have seen one stride over three times in succession to explain that a question had been put the wrong way round. Usually front-benchers, procedurally minded peers and those moving amendments try to clarify, with the help of the Table clerk (often repeatedly pointing to a passage in the *Companion* or nodding vigorously when a peer gives a correct assessment). The language of procedural rules is largely incomprehensible to non-experts and much of it is forgotten most of the time. One debate a few years ago was suddenly brought to an halt by a drunken peer losing patience with the flow of rhetoric and saying, quite clearly: 'I move that the question now be put.' No one knew what to do. It had not happened before in living memory. Eventually the Chief Whip took the *Companion* to the Deputy Speaker and they worked out how to ignore it.

Reforming the rules

For some, the House rules need no reform. Almost all observers agree that the quality of peers' work is usually high and the outcomes useful. They give more time to scrutiny than MPs and make a huge number of improvements to bills: 2557 amendments in 2001–02 and 2996 in 2002–03. Many lords believe that their debate is superior to that of the Commons and although this may be true, the complacency it engenders can act as an inertial force in discussion of change. It makes questioning Lords' procedures almost outside 'the framework of possible thought', in Chomsky's memorable phrase,[23] as though any change would automatically bring about a loss of quality. In addition, this, together with peers' occasional theatrical defeats of the government, combine to create an impression of independence that may be more illusory than real at certain times. Peers' pride in their independence encourages acceptance of the *status quo* by the same complacent mechanism and, again, resistance to change. This acquiescence may not prevail, however, because increasing numbers of new peers are beginning to question the unquestionable: the rituals themselves.

Demands for reform and for changes to procedure grow intense when the creation of new peers causes stress, and when the opposition is being effective. When the Labour party took office in 1964, it faced huge Conservative opposition in the Lords, and created numbers of peers to achieve better balance. Both these circumstances intensified demands for reform. In a report in 1971, a Group on the Working of the House explained:

the rate of creation of Peers in recent years has been greater than hitherto, and, therefore, the new recruits have taken longer than usual to accustom themselves to the ways of the House ... If the rules are to be respected, they must be understandable and command the assent of Peers; mumbo jumbo provokes dissatisfaction.[24]

Since the 1997 election, the House has been under strain once again. During 1999 in particular, there was a massive influx of peers and the House was so well-attended that it often attracted 450 peers on benches only designed to take 250. With nowhere to sit, not enough speaking time and feisty opposition, courtesies began to break down. The offenders were not always the latest arrivals. When joined by large numbers of new and more sceptical peers, old hands who had always found some of the procedures irritating became more courageous about breaking them.

In 1999 a working group concluded that the restraint of members was beginning to break down, but rather than recommending significant change, it suggested only slight adjustments, and concentrated instead on improvement of the training of peers to encourage observance of procedures. It warned their lordships that: 'courtesy should not be seen as an optional extra. Without a degree of courtesy and self-restraint, self-regulation will become unworkable, and the freedoms which enable the House to do its job will be forfeit.'[25] These reminders about the courtesies of the House received wide support, including from Earl Ferrers who made his contribution with his customary eloquence:

> In the good old days – as a schoolboy would say – if two Peers got up to speak, one would graciously give way to the other. That does not happen now. People stand like two bulls pawing at the ground, each trying to outstare the other in the hope of winning the right to speak ... When noble Lords give way, some do so without too much grace and sit down slowly. A speaker can be half-way through his question and the noble Lord who has been put out is still descending. It is rather like letting air out of a balloon with your hand over the nozzle so that it escapes slowly. It would add greatly to the courtesies of the House if noble Lords sat down quickly.[26]

Until recently proposals for change were regularly defeated by the Procedure Committee. Small changes got through but it was not until a new Leader of the House (Lord Williams of Mostyn) and new Chairman of Committees (Lord Tordoff) were installed that procedural reform gathered momentum and significant measures were taken.

In July 2001 the modernisers won a victory when a code of financial conduct was introduced. The custom of the House had been that peers had always declared during speeches a pecuniary interest in subjects on which they spoke. The register of interests was voluntary. With allegations of sleaze in the House of Commons, the increase in parliamentary lobbying, and some confusion about what declarations were appropriate, a more formal system was proposed.[28] Some peers saw the compulsory register as an intrusion into their privacy. They were, after all, unpaid, and it was said it might deter prospective peers. In the event, it got through quite easily partly because, once raised, rejecting it would have looked as if peers had something to hide. As Baroness Hilton of Eggardon, a former police officer, observed: 'I think that it is symbolically important in the same way that I think most of the criminal law is symbolically important rather than actually having much effect on human behaviour.'[29] Most accepted it, although Lord Cranborne was so horrified that he gave it as his reason for taking a leave of absence.

Peers' own evaluations of the usefulness of the rules are most revealing about what they, and their ritual contexts, mean to different participants. The dialectic between proponents of preservation and change throws a sharp light on the different messages the same rituals can convey.

Lord Williams of Mostyn proposed even more significant reforms, including pre-legislative scrutiny for certain bills, less anti-social hours and, to the disgust of the Treasury, an advisory role on money bills.[30] It was observed that while some of these would be useful, especially enabling the public greater participation in law making, they might also make life slightly easier for the government. Lord Williams knew that putting these proposals to the Procedure Committee would meet with diehard resistance from traditionalists. He strategised. He invited the Cross-bench Convenor and other parties to select representatives to join a working group to put together proposals. Ten months later, after a questionnaire to all peers and sixteen meetings, a unanimous report was published. It was debated and, with the full backing of the usual channels, referred to the Procedure Committee. The few traditionalists still hell-bent on putting a spanner in the works did not stand a chance. I was present at the meeting and their hostility caused a tension that made me blush. While other opposition members of the committee proposed useful revisions with customary Lords' gentleness, the would-be saboteurs became apoplectic. Other peers produced a low murmur as if reassuring themselves that all would be well. The dissidents railed against the government, accusing them of curtailing the rights of the opposition and of back-benchers in particular, complaining that the Chairman was not letting them speak and continually asking where they had got to in the agenda, jumpy that they might miss a chance to protest. Lord Williams of Mostyn wisely kept quiet, leaving the Conservative Leader to argue the case for change, although a Labour minister's patience snapped and, tigress-like, she demolished the argument of one protestor. Eventually the Chairman gave up and agreed to have yet another meeting:

> "I have a function that night. When will you finish?" asked the leading dissident.
>
> "I have no idea," replied a leading member.
>
> "Well, I have to know."
>
> "And I can't possibly tell you."

On this tetchy note they dispersed, looking shell-shocked. Despite these agitations, the report was finally agreed, and its recommendations approved by the House.

Aggressive though they were in style, the objectors had a point: the measures could give the opposition less time for debate. On the other hand, on balance they almost certainly improve the legislative process. But their passage was not entirely to do with their merit. Lord Williams of Mostyn outmanoeuvred the traditionalists by carefully and with steely patience rallying the support of the usual channels and back-benchers until the momentum was unstoppable.

Since then the Prime Minister has announced plans to abolish the post of Lord Chancellor, which has forced the House to review his role as the Lord Speaker. In a debate in January 2004 on a report by a committee that has proposed a new 'light-touch speaker', only one peer argued for a more interventionist speaker, and all wished to preserve self-regulation but recognised that courtesies are under strain. As Baroness Williams of Crosby put it, 'when responsibility for good behaviour is passed on to someone else, individuals no longer feel bound in the same way by their obligations to maintain good behaviour.' It is possible that 'the danger of creating a Speaker is that we will be sowing the seeds for the destruction of self-regulation'.[31]

The political significance of ritual

The complexity of Lords' rituals – both in their meanings and their consequences – mirrors the many-layered nature of the institution. In addition to the complexity of its social hierarchies and political factions, it is in the throes of huge cultural and political change. The rituals of debate, however, are above these divisive and changeable aspects of the social and political life of the Lords, and define how peers relate to each other.

The rules of debate convey the principle of equality between peers, and the sacred texts – principally the *Standing Orders* – enshrine this principle. As in other rituals, they 'can be seen as a form of rhetoric, the propagation of a message through a complex symbolic performance'.[32] The rhetorical message of equality has significant political consequences. The

Lords' usual channels obey the government in the sense that the executive alone decides on the legislative priorities, and the opposition in the upper House exercises restraint more often than not. The government is, however, regularly defeated in the Lords, and while these defeats are often reversed in the Commons, they give back-bench peers the impression that they have more control than they do. This, and the message of equality, distracts them from the limits to their influence – continual awareness of which might induce apathy and cynicism – and ensures their active but acquiescent participation.

The rituals thus subtly encourage both participation and self-restraint among peers and the principal beneficiary of this is the government, which needs time to get its legislation through. This consequence of ritual is not found in all legislative assemblies. The contrast with Weatherford's study of the US Congress is revealing. He portrayed its ritual occasions as a theatre used merely to aggrandise and increase the power of its individual members:

> The normal work day of a member of Congress is spent making series of cameo appearances in the various ritual arenas ... The politician enters one scene, is coached by a waiting assistant for a few moments, and then performs the role. His particular performance may have no relation to that of the actors who appeared just before or after him, but the pieces will be edited together afterwards by the staff. The important point is simply that he should get his appearance on record. He voted, he came for the quorum call, he asked the question of the witness, he introduced the bill, he co-sponsored the amendment, he spoke the sentence. The staff can issue all the press releases and printed speeches to show that this made him a prime mover.[33]

Members of Congress make use of rituals to improve their position and increase the impression of their power; the rituals, according to Weatherford, mean almost nothing in themselves. Peers, in contrast, when speaking in the Chamber, address their fellow peers rather than the outside world, and respond directly to each other. Back-benchers have no staff, and they very rarely issue press releases as individuals. For them, each enactment of the ritual is immanent with meaning.

This seems to be also the case in the French legislature. The anthropologist Abélès writes that debates in the National Assembly are not mere theatrical performance; they are a ritualised semiotic struggle over the meaning of texts (laws) in which the warring groups of members embody elements of civil society that are really fighting moral wars over, for example, homosexuality or state intervention.[34] As with the Lords, debates over legislation represent moral battles about how society should be ordered and governed, and what is deemed normal, natural and morally desirable. Each ritual is itself an item of cosmological warfare, and the Lords Chamber is a battleground between traditionalists and modernisers (roughly, but not exactly, represented by the Conservatives and Cross-benchers versus the Labour and Liberal Democrats). Thus, the political significance of ritualised debate is not only found in rules that express equality but, more significantly, in the expression and resolution of moral conflict between conflicting elements within society. The resolution of conflict may be relevant to most, if not all, parliaments; and both these aspects encourage peers to participate and speak as individuals but to be restrained and vote with their own side as members of moral communities.

Debates about reform of the rituals themselves become highly charged not only because peers' own social order is under discussion but because so also is their relationship with the public. When opposition peers argued against the introduction of a register of interests, they were trying to protect the principles of trust and honour that should underlie the relationship between peers as an ideal for the rest of society to aspire to. When back-benchers complained about the introduction of pre-legislative scrutiny and the carry-over of bills, much more than the procedural rules governing the passage of public bills was at stake. Some argued that these measures threatened to increase the power of the usual channels, thereby making it more difficult for peers to represent the interests of the public. Peers' complaints about transgressions, and their reiteration of the need for obedience to rules, are not only a bid to improve efficiency; they are an attempt to protect the institution's ethos, to regulate how peers relate to each other, to socialise newcomers into the House of Lords and to present a certain ideal of behaviour. It is the rituals and symbols that make people into proper peers.

Rituals in the House of Lords are not a cultural sideshow; they are the real stuff that politics is made of. Not only do they define how peers relate to each other but they permit the resolution of conflict between them. Parliamentary ritual does this so successfully that, as Kertzer writes about ritual more generally: 'it creates an emotional state that makes the message uncontestable because it is framed in such a way as to be seen as inherent in the way things are.'[35]

Notes

1   D. Kertzer, 1988, *Ritual, Politics and Power*, Yale University Press, New Haven and London, p. 132.
2   The exception to this is in election years, when the State Opening usually takes place earlier in the year.
3   Those for a taste for the detail of the parliamentary seasons and procedure could consult R. Rogers and R. Walters, 2004, *How Parliament Works*, 5th edition, Pearson Education, Harlow.

4 Bills are sent back and forth between the Houses earlier in the year as well.

5 The Yeoman Usher of the Black Rod is deputy to the Gentleman Usher of the Black Rod, the official in charge of security, the building and services to peers.

6 Forty minutes is reserved for five questions on Tuesdays and Wednesdays, and they take thirty minutes for only four on Mondays and Thursdays. Examples of 'motions' are given in Table 10.1.

7 Although every bill has to go through these stages, the intervals between them can be shorter than the rules stipulate if the opposition agree to it.

8 At present this role is performed by the Lord Chancellor. Since the Prime Minister announced his intention to abolish this post, the House of Lords has been reviewing the role of Speaker. See HL Deb., 12 January 2004.

9 If a bill receives Royal Assent during the session, ceremonial recognition of the monarch's wishes is now dispensed with. Proceedings used to be interrupted, but a procedural reform was introduced in 1967 to save time at the request of the Commons (Sir John Sainty, former Clerk of the Parliaments, personal communication).

10 Most votes are at report stage; few amendments are pressed to divisions at committee stage.

11 Lord Carter, HL Deb., 27 March 2001, cols 104–5.

12 See also Chapter 2.

13 Lords Carew and Ewing of Kirkford, HL Deb, 30 March 1999, col. 287.

14 Lords Whitty and Russell, HL Deb., 10 March 1999, cols 167–8.

15 House of Lords, 1994, *The Standing Orders of the House of Lords Relating to Public Business*, HMSO, London, pp. 16–17.

16 He later became known as Lord Longford when he succeeded to a hereditary peerage.

17 House of Lords, *ibid.*, p. 12.

18 C. Riding, 2000, *The Aura of Sacred Mystery: Thrones in the New Palace of Westminster, in the House of Parliament*, Merrell, London, p. 180.

19 House of Lords, *ibid.*, p. 12.

20 House of Lords, 2000, *Companion to the Standing Orders and Guide to the Proceedings of the House of Lords*, London, The Stationary Office, p. 55.

21 Only Black Rod in the Lords or the Serjeant-at-Arms in the Commons can send people to these cells – one in the Clock Tower and one at the north end of Westminster Hall. In 2004 a visitor to the Lords was locked up when he was found carrying something he should not and Fathers4Justice were marched to a cell after they threw a condom filled with purple powder at the Prime Minister. But such occasions are rare.

22 To avoid disturbance in the Chamber, MPs and peers have all been issued with vibrating pagers.

23 N. Chomsky, 1987, 'The manufacture of consent', in J. Peck (ed.), *The Chomsky Reader*, Serpent's Tail, London.

24 House of Lords, 1971, *Tenth Report form the Select Committee on Procedure of the House, Appendix, Report from the Group on the Working of the House.*

25 House of Lords, 1999, *Freedom and Function, Report to the Leader of the House from the Group on Procedure in the Chamber*, HMSO, London, p. 2.

26 Earl Ferrers, HL Deb., 22 March 1999, col. 976.

27 See Chapter 9 for details.

28 By Lord Neill's Committee on Standards in Public Life.

29 House of Lords, *Seventh Report of the Committee on Standards in Public Life, Standards of Conduct in the House of Lords, Volume 2: Evidence*, HMSO, London, p. 46.

30 The proposals were: that all bills should be subject to pre-legislative scrutiny; that bills could be carried over from one session to the next by agreement; that two new

committees should be set up, including one to comment on the budget and finance bill; that there should be more questions at Question Time; that more committee stages of Bills to be taken in rooms other than the Chamber; and that the House should aim to finish business at around 10 p.m. except for Thursdays which should run from 11 a.m. to 7 p.m.

31 Baroness Williams of Crosby, HL Deb., 12 January 2004, col. 390; Earl Ferrers, HL Deb., 12 January 2004, col. 417. The decision about establishing a 'light-touch speaker', who would take on some of the disciplinary duties of the Leader of the House, has been deferred until the 2004–05 session, because the House voted to refer the bill that would abolish the post of Lord Chancellor to a committee for further scrutiny.

32 Kertzer, *ibid.*, p. 101.

33 J. McIver Weatherford, 1985, *Tribes on the Hill: The US Congress Rituals and Realities*, Bergin and Garvey, Westport and London, pp. 206, 208.

34 M. Abélès, 2005, 'Politics and ritual in the French National Assembly', in E. Crewe and M. G. Müller (eds), *Rituals in Parliaments: Political, Anthropological and Historical Perspectives on Europe and the United States*, Peter Lang, Frankfurt am Main.

35 Kertzer, *ibid.*, p. 101.

11 Men in tights

The House of Lords provides almost an excess of things that excite anthropologists: myths, hierarchies, symbols, rituals and rules, all manifesting themselves within a building whose contents alone could divert a social scientist for years. The public spaces, the Central Lobby and the passageways and staircases along which *hoi poloi* must travel can be a little impersonal, very much like the back stairs in a stately home, but most of the areas where peers and clerks work, despite the grandeur, are designed on a human scale, engendering a sense of gracious informality. The Chamber itself has the uncanny quality of appearing forbidding and majestic to visitors, but almost intimate to its regular users. Its architect – familiar with the vast drawing rooms of nineteenth-century grandees – designed a hall that at once overawes and reassures depending on where you are in it. Strangers – that is, visitors not entitled to sit nearer the action – are in a gallery close to the roof, whence the Chamber appears like the Grand Canyon. One feels small. A vast void separates the gallery from the opposite wall and the floor could almost be in another country. Perhaps the physical distance between strangers and peers marks their difference in status. Contrastingly, when you are on the ground – the canyon bottom so to speak – horizontal distances retract and even the furthest corners of the floor seem within conversational distance. The peers, their guests and the clerks who inhabit this profoundly human space move among the furniture of a well-used salon. It is not exactly intimate as it is above all a battle-ground, but for a place so grand it is curiously informal and becomes more so with familiarity. The gilded ceiling is so far away it seems irrelevant, and those sitting in the galleries are out of mind. On the floor there is a closeness.

The architecture is the backdrop for much national pageantry. The Palace of Westminster itself, as conceived by architects Charles Barry and Augustus Pugin, 'was not so much a legislature as a theatre of state, a building of uniquely dramatic intensity and potential, the setting for royal ceremonies …', most especially the State Opening, a celebration of royal majesty and ordered hierarchy.[1] The Lords' Chamber is its ceremonial centre: the arena for transcendent moments of political ceremony, just as the '*puri*' was for nineteenth-century Balinese rituals:

> As the king or lord was turned into an icon by state ceremony … so his palace, his dalem or puri, or jero was transformed into a temple, a setting for the icon … the puri was a stretch of sanctified space, a fit place in which to confront the mysteries of hierarchy. It was in the lord's residence (and around it – for all Balinese temples are but the foci of the sprawling pageants which swirl in and out of them), in 'the place where he sits', that the doctrine of the exemplary center was made socially real.[2]

Of the rituals that interrupt parliamentary proceedings in the Lords, the Introduction Ceremony and State Opening are the most flamboyant, but there are many others. Some are held daily, such as the Lord Chancellor's procession into the Chamber at the start of business. Others are annual, such as Royal Assent (transforming bills into Acts), Prorogation (bringing the parliamentary session to an end), the Lord Chancellor's breakfast reception for the judges at the opening of the judicial year, and the Loving Cup ceremony, an intimate little occasion to present the Lord Mayor of London to the Lord Chancellor for the Sovereign's Approbation. A few occur less often, such the most important British political ritual of all, the general election. Those ceremonies and symbols that have significant consequences for the social position of peers are the principal focus of this chapter.

The Introduction Ceremony

Peers rash enough to sit in the Chamber before being introduced and taking the oath can still be fined £500.[3] Peers' reaction to proposals for changing the Introduction Ceremony – vehement on both sides – demonstrates its importance to them. Of all the ceremonies, it is the most kicked political football. It dates from 1621, when the monarch ceased to confer peerages personally, probably to distance himself from the ennoblement of favourites or in return for cash.[4] The same procedure has been followed ever since (with some modifications in 1998), each time a new peerage is created. The ceremony takes place at the start of an ordinary sitting.[5] Before 1998, the Lord Chancellor sat on the Woolsack wearing court dress, gown, wig and tricorn hat. The Gentleman Usher of the Black Rod (also wearing court dress), and Garter King of Arms (in his black, red and gold tabard) led the junior supporter, the new peer and the senior supporter into the Chamber, all in black tricorn hats and red robes with ermine trim. At the bar each bowed in turn to the Cloth of Estate. They made their way towards the Throne, bowing (again) as they reached the Table and for the third time as they came level with the Judges' Woolsack. At the Lord Chancellor's Woolsack, the new peer kneeled on his or her right knee and presented his writ of summons and patent to the Lord Chancellor, who handed them to the Reading Clerk. The senior supporter led the procession, now including the Clerk, to the Table. Unless female, the new peer put his hat on it (women peers kept it on throughout). The Clerk read out both the patent and writ. Then the new peer took the Oath of Allegiance ('I [giving name and title] do swear by Almighty God that I will be faithful and bear true Allegiance to Her Majesty Queen Elizabeth, Her Heirs and Successors, according to law. So help me God'), or, if he or she preferred to keep God out of it, the Solemn Affirmation; after which he or she signed the Roll of the Lords. (Welsh peers have repeated the oath in Welsh; Scots in Gaelic; Jews have sworn on the Old Testament, and Baroness Uddin and Lord Ahmed took the oath on the Koran instead of the Bible.)

The peer then retrieved her or his hat and processed back down the Chamber to the bar. Garter "placed" the new peer and his supporters on the bench 'appropriate to their degree in the peerage' (although in practice, all new peers have been barons in recent years). There they sat down, put on their hats, rose, took off their hats again and bowed to the Lord Chancellor, and then sat down again. They repeated this three times.[6] The Lord Chancellor lifted his hat in reply and as the procession left the Chamber the new peer shook his hand. Watching peers then, by custom, greeted the new peer by murmuring 'Hear, hear'.

The early 1960s and the 1970s were both periods when the numbers of introductions increased greatly, causing peers to complain that the ceremony wasted time and was out of date. These arguments emerged again, for the same reason, in 1997. It is said that this was partly the fault of officials who had, a few years earlier, started encouraging a huge tennis swing movement with the hat, instead of the previous, discreet style of doffing.

Lord Richard, then Leader of the House, argued to the Procedure Committee that because the ceremony had scarcely changed in nearly four hundred years it seemed 'out of tune with perceptions of how Parliament should operate at the end of the twentieth century. Moreover the dignity of the occasion is bound to suffer when repeated as nauseam'.[7] The Procedure Committee set up a Select Committee whose members held such strong views they almost came to blows before and while they took evidence from other peers. Among those giving evidence, the late Duke of Norfolk (who as Earl Marshal was in charge of the Heralds) suggested that the Introduction Ceremony 'wants cutting like hell'.[8] The chief

Herald, Garter King of Arms, disagreed with his boss about that, and about the three bows:

> The Earl Marshal has told us that the three bows are to do with the Trinity, I think that is a nonsense, nobody knows. Somebody else has suggested that it has something to do with England, France and Ireland. Nobody knows. I think that it is simply a dignified number. One was not sufficiently important or dignified, so let us go for three.[9]

Lady Saltoun of Abernethy suggested that the hat-doffing three times may have had Christian roots and the nine bows during the ceremony resonated with ancient mysticism.[10] The Earl of Northesk suggested that the number three represented the constitutional trinity: the Crown, Parliament, and the people.

It was those aspects of the ceremony of which the meaning was uncertain or, if known, was unpopular, that many wished to reform. They found hat-doffing and repeated bowing comic and incomprehensible. Kneeling before the Lord Chancellor they found out-of-date and humiliating; and they felt that 'placing' was inconsistent with their ethos of being 'peers' or equals.[11]

But its defenders were fierce: many dwelt on the importance of the ceremony to individual peers; Lord Naseby pointed out that for some it is the most memorable event of their lives.[12] For Lord Denham, it was 'validated by 376 years. Shorten it or tamper with it in any way and it will only go back to 1997 ... the House works by tradition. Take away this most spectacular one, the first to be encountered by every new Peer, and which of the remainder will be safe?'[13] He was among many in arguing that shortening the ceremony might lead to the unravelling of a ceremonial totality that is not understood. Some opined that even a small reform could lead to total abolition once a pattern of change had been established. Lord Chalfont had felt history coursing through him during his introduction and argued hard to have it preserved in its entirety, while Lord Campbell of Alloway hotly defended the 'spirit of affinity with the Sovereign', that the affirmation of allegiance to her during the ceremony engenders.[14] Lady Saltoun of Abernethy argued that it might be no bad thing if new peers were made to feel ridiculous during their introductions: 'it may even be quite good for those – very few, but there are a few – who come to this Chamber puffed up with a sense of their own importance.'[15]

Garter King of Arms was almost thrown out of the ceremony but was rescued by the Duke of Norfolk (who insisted that as the Crown's representative he had to be there) in alliance with the Clerk of the Parliaments, who saw no reason to get rid of a dash of colour. A tactical move for delay was defeated in the House: a small majority had lost faith in the overall effect of the ceremony, so, with the Queen's permission, reforms came into effect in April 1998: they abolished hats, replaced the 'placing ceremony' with a short procession through the Chamber, deleted the kneeling and the reading of the writ of summons and added a new convention (that the peer and supporters should return to the Chamber without robes and sit with the group that the new peer intends to sit with in future).[16] Despite the vehemence of protests, I am unaware of complaints that the ceremony has lost its way. In fact, the abolition of doffing probably ensured its survival.

It is significant that the abolition of the entire Introduction Ceremony was not proposed. It is agreed that newcomers need initiation into their role as parliamentarians, but what raises eyebrows outside the Lords (more than in it) is the transformation into a peer. This is marked by the adoption of the title – in effect a new name – publicly declared during this ceremony.[17] Titles are seen by most peers to have a dual significance – they have a function in parliamentary ritual, and they raise their status in relation to the rest of society[18] – although they plainly do more than just these two things as well. The ritual function is described in terms of the impersonality of address, whereby a peer speaking in the Chamber refers to 'the Noble Lord' and never 'you', thus reducing the risk of angry confrontation; but it is questionable whether permanent titles are necessary for this. It is achieved in the Commons by MPs referring to each other as 'the member for so and so'. The change of status, on the other hand, is much more complex. When I asked peers why the status was important, most explained that titles are either an honour they deserve or a reward for their unpaid work. Many put it bluntly that without prestige and importance it would be difficult to get so much of people's time for nothing.

Assuming a new identity along with shouldering exalted responsibility is be no means uncommon. 'Throne names' have quite often been taken by European monarchs, and elsewhere: popes invariably adopt new names on taking office, and Tallensi earth-priests, among many dignitaries outside Europe, receive a new name at their installation, symbolising a new identity and setting them above the rest of society. There may be an element of abandoning a previous identity – which may have even manifested inferior characteristics – and replacing it with a new, superior one, differing in essence from other people, in order to meet with perfect integrity and sagacity the greater responsibilities that go with the office.

In addition, as the French anthropologist Bourdieu observes, names can carry symbolic capital: 'titles of nobility, like educational qualifications, represent real titles of symbolic property which give one a right to profits of recognition.'[19] Peers, on the whole, would not disagree, though they might argue as to whether or not such privilege is morally desirable. Only a few treat it as a joke and a minority would do without titles quite easily, but most of those I interviewed would prefer to keep them. An honours peer expressed the view of many in holding that she would not mind being called a senator, but she would not like the honour to be taken away. It means a lot: the appeal of being seen to be valued by the nation, above the rest and equal to all other peers, is great.

When changes were suggested to the introduction ceremony, none took the opportunity to complain that it entailed the adoption of a noble name and status. The areas of agreement between traditionalist and modernising peers – often greater than those that divide them – are sometimes lost in the polarised debate between them. The former tend to misrepresent their opponents as wanting to salami-slice tradition until there is none left. In practice this would be true of only a quite small minority of peers. Most are agreed that titles, rituals and ceremonies on the whole enhance the reputation and ease the business of the House and because this is taken for granted, it is often left unsaid.[20]

Both sides value the symbolic capital conferred on them by their status as peers. All have an investment in how the House is perceived by outsiders, and do not wish to see its dignity diminish because their symbolic capital would fall in value as a consequence. The disagreement between traditionalists and modernisers is about how the dignity of the House is best maintained. To traditionalists, it is above all the past that confers dignity, so that the more clothes, symbols or rituals can be seen as a legacy from, or continuum with, the past, the greater their lustre and value; and, up to a point, the more of them there are, the greater the dignity of the House. This would represent optimisation of the value of their symbolic capital. Most modernisers show no less ardour in protecting their investment, but they see it as endangered by too many relics from the past. There are many shades of opinion among the modernisers, but the most common view is that over time some of the antique relics become ridiculous, and there can be too many. They found the doffing of hats, for example, comical. They believe in constant judicious pruning of ceremony to keep the House on the path of optimum dignity between tendencies toward comic opera on the one hand and, on the other, the Brussels-style, atmosphere-free, unceremonious rituals that accrue little status to their participants.

State Opening

This polarisation in attitudes to the past also extends to the opening of Parliament. Each session begins with this state ceremony: peers and visitors love it, millions abroad (according to peers) are glued to their TV sets, and even one of the jeans and T-shirt generation of peers called it 'the best show in town'.[21] The Queen processes first in a coach and cavalcade from Buckingham Palace to Westminster, and then on foot to her Robing Room in the Palace of Westminster and thence to her throne in the Lords' Chamber to read a speech to peers and MPs.

A carriage rehearsal is held before dawn the week before, an event that is in some ways better than the real thing. In the silence, watching the Guard of Honour marching from the distance like toy soldiers through the winter darkness, followed by the eerie clip clop of the Household Cavalry, was not quite of this world. The cavalcade of coaches was also observed by construction workers wearing their hard yellow hats; beside them on the slick black road stood the smooth mafia of Buckingham Palace officials in bowlers. Some days later the Lord Great Chamberlain carried out his official search, inspecting the Queen's 'line of route' in the Palace of Westminster. The guards' swords and spurs clanked and jingled heroically as they marched in to take their places lining the Sovereign's Staircase, but their faces were nervous. Their NCO instructed them, 'Find something to look at on the opposite wall, don't catch anyone's eye'. The run-through by the Gentlemen at Arms and Yeomen of the Guard was directed by a tyrant from the palace: 'We have to start from first principles,' he shouted, showing them how to walk. When a herald was asked to speak up he snarled: 'I've never been asked to bark at State Opening before.' The procedure culminated in the rehearsal of the Sovereign's procession from the Robing Room to the Chamber. The late Duke of Norfolk, like a kindly theatre director, gave gentle instructions. Finally, on the Lord Great Chamberlain's signal, two doorkeepers pulled wide the magnificent double doors of the Robing Room ... and nothing happened. The Duke said softly: 'All is fine but we haven't got a Queen.'

The big day itself begins with a reminder of a seventeenth century triumph of the forces of stable government over fanatical religious terrorism: Guy Fawkes' Catholic plot to blow up James I in Parliament. All year, a Public Works Department engineer keeps an immense key in safety. There is no door in the palace that it fits. As they have done annu-ally since the gunpowder plot, the Yeomen of the Guard, the royal body-guards, gather in the morning ceremonially to search the cellars for plotters, an officer leading, carrying this magnificent key, and the others bearing lanterns. He leads them through the rabbit-warren twists and turns of the basement, stooping slightly at the low ceilings but marching quite fast. (One year they got lost and wandered past the shooting range, the clock repairer's workshop and other features of the cellars until someone rescued them.) When I was there, after inspecting the cellars they found their way unerringly to the terrace, where we were given a glass of port by the Lords' barman. This overture to the main ceremony is unseen by outsiders, but still has a resonance that explains its survival over four centuries.

Meanwhile the corridors teem with lords in their pantomime robes – inherited, bought or hired for £100 – while ladies parade in ballgowns and tiaras and staff and visitors go to parties in various panelled rooms. The State Opening is composed largely of waiting for something to happen. At its centre is the monarch, upon whom all wait and whose immense exaltation is greatly heightened by the time spent waiting for her. It consists of a number of different events, some concurrent, which renders it a different ceremony depending upon where you are. In 1999 I watched the procession to Westminster from the Clerk of the Parliaments' office window. After the Queen has arrived at the palace, custom dictates that while those who have seats in the public rooms wait for her to emerge from the Robing Room, the less privileged descend narrow stone staircases to one of the many courtyards, and join a behind-the-scenes ritual: feeding Her Majesty's horses. Along with staff clutching the hands of children, my daughter and stepson gave the towering sleek black horses carrots and I took photographs. We then returned to the office, where it is also customary to wait until after the Queen's speech before opening the champagne. Another year I sat in the long, gilded Royal Gallery, where the frescoes of Waterloo (along one wall) and Trafalgar (opposite) were obscured by banks of seats for dignitaries and peers' guests to sit upon while they wait for the sovereign to emerge from her Robing Room. After, and punctuated by, much waiting, we saw various royal processions: the Yeomen of the Guard marching in to line the route; followed by the Gentlemen at Arms; then the Crown, the Cap of Maintenance and the Sword of State, the first two carried on cushions by peers; and then finally the Sovereign's Procession. In 1998 (the year the Queen was interrupted when she promised her government would remove hereditary peers) I sat in the Chamber itself, and watched from close quarters the climax of the whole event when all the disparate groups – peers, MPs, the Queen, visitors – come together in the Lords and are treated to a speech by the monarch acting as mouthpiece for the elected government. Each experience was quite different from the others.

The aspects of the ceremony that are so well known as to be public property include the procession from Buckingham Palace to Westminster; MPs slamming the door of the Commons in Black Rod's face, his knocking three times to demand their attendance on the Queen in the Lords; and the Queen's speech from the throne. The first of these, the procession – an elaborate affair comprising a small show of military power and a lot of the colourful and extraordinary, with the Queen in one hugely ornate coach and her crown in another – is clearly a reminder of the potency and majesty of the monarchy past and present.

Of the second aspect, it is widely understood that when the Queen sends Black Rod to fetch MPs, his dismal reception in the Commons is intended to indicate MPs' independence from the Crown. Never again will a monarch so over-reach themselves as Charles I did in 1642, precipitating civil war by riding to Parliament to arrest five MPs. Dennis Skinner, a republican, customarily makes a small personal demonstration, such as replying to Black Rod's summons by shouting 'Let's close the doors again', and remaining seated in the Chamber when the others depart for the Lords. Tradition dictates that on their walk from the Commons to the Lords, MPs amble, talking noisily and joking, thereby asserting their independence and that though the monarch may summon them with the pomp of apparent authority, they obey only voluntarily and in their own time and manner.

Once in the Chamber, in the third well-known part of the ceremony, MPs are uncomfortably jostled together in the small space between the entrance and the bar, at the opposite end of the Chamber from the Queen on her magnificent throne, to listen to her speech. The Prime Minister and opposition leader stand in front. The Queen is surrounded by judges and peers, and kept at the greatest possible distance within the Chamber from those with political power, the MPs. MPs are not even given seats. This is not usually remarked upon by parliamentarians, but worries Lord Gordon of Strathblane:

> Even the Prime Minister and others are summoned as though second-class citizens to the Bar of the House to hear the Queen's Speech. That is wrong. I do not think that anyone has taken drastic offence so far, but it is only a matter of time before someone does. Let us change such practices ... the reality is that the House of Commons virtually ignores the House of Lords.[22]

Parliamentarians in the Queen's procession through the Royal Gallery include the Lord Privy Seal (often the Leader of the Lords although currently the Leader of the Commons), the President of the Council, the Lord Chancellor, the Lord Great Chamberlain, the Earl Marshal, the Captain of the Yeomen of the Guard, the Captain of the Honourable Corps of Gentlemen at Arms, and others in the Royal Household. It is significant that usually only three of them are MPs: either the President of the Council or the Lord Privy Seal, the Comptroller of Her Majesty's Household and the Treasurer of Her Majesty's Household. However, the Vice-Chamberlain of the Royal Household, who is given a 'white stave'[23] and a glass of sherry by the Queen and held hostage in Buckingham Palace until she returns, is always an MP.

There is a disjunction between the Commons' political primacy and its ceremonial inferiority. For most peers, and perhaps even for the monarch, the procession and the seating during the speech are most satisfactory. The peers' benches continue to be packed each year and so many spouses or partners are keen to attend that their names have to be entered into a ballot. Peers' prominence in Parliament's most public spectacle has gradually evolved from being an expression of the realities of power to being part of a package of compensation for the political power that the upper House has lost. Some MPs seem to recognise this, and regard State Opening with the patronising air of adults humouring children. Others are beginning to mutter that it needs modernising.

Clearly, from their different perspectives, the ceremony holds markedly different meanings for MPs and for peers. As Kertzer explains, that the same symbol may be understood by different people in different ways is important for building solidarity in the absence of consensus. In fact, the uncertainty of meaning in symbols can be the source of their strength.[24] When asked, peers give a variety of answers. Nearly all agree that it is the main illustration of the Queen in Parliament, symbolising the unity of the nation by bringing the Crown, Lords and Commons together. Beyond that, the views of traditionalists and modernisers diverge.

Only a very few peers can be heard rubbishing the entire ceremony, none as emphatically as this member of staff – "Most ceremonies are nineteenth century and it's all about bolstering the monarchy and keeping in with the gothic crap" – or even as dismissively as Richard Crossman in 1967, when he compared it with 'the Prisoner of Zenda but not nearly as smart or well done as it would be in Hollywood. It's more what a real Ruritania would look like – far more comic, more untidy, more homely, less grand.'[25] Though most modernisers enjoy it, some would like details changed – the uniforms, the walking backwards, or the length of the procession – to maintain it as a magnificent spectacle rather than being so overblown as to be embarrassing.

For many traditionalists, on the other hand, it is a day when past and present fuse in a manner that seems almost to have elements of the mystical. Visually, it is extremely beguiling. For those peers who revere the historical, it is historicity that imbues the symbols with power and beauty. The day when the symbols are paraded in full panoply of potency and the ancient associations made manifest in rituals that are seen as centuries-old, enacted in dazzling antique dress, can be, for them, a profound expression, not just of the national spirit, but of the place of the nation and the body politic in the unchanging moral universe. One wrote:

> All the protocols and procedures that reinforce the idea of the superiority of Parliament are important. During the State Opening there are many curious symbols carried about by odd bods in fancy outfits that represent the

enormous achievement of a settled government. To an outsider they may seem ludicrous, arcane and irrelevant: however these should be paraded from time to time just as reminders that they represent 600 years of stable government.[26]

The visible presence of history is seen as powerful in itself: as Bourdieu points out, to possess things from the past is to master time, and this mastery is a form of social power.[27] Those who wish to change the historical ceremonies, traditionalists argue, do not understand their symbolic importance.

An aspect of this view of history is that precise historical continuity is not required. Even were it true that government has remained stable (Cromwell's abolition of the monarchy and the House of Lords are not taken into account), the context and meaning of the royal ceremonies have not. Cannadine observes that royal rituals were magnificent in the sixteenth and seventeenth centuries, straightforwardly reflecting the power of the monarch, but that they were seen as ridiculous in the early nineteenth century, when State Opening was scarcely an event. Between 1861 and 1886 Queen Victoria opened Parliament only six times. It was then that the tremendous showman Edward VII brought back full ceremonial dress and the procession in the state coach, and personally read the speech from the throne: 'this was more than the revival of a state theatre that had been moribund since 1860: for Edward was Emperor of India and ruler of the British dominions beyond the seas, an imperial monarch in full finery in his imperial Parliament.'[28] Now, what was once an affirmation of imperial greatness may have become merely a collective longing, or at least nostalgia, for past glories, achieving its heyday in the 1950s with the advent of TV and the colossal popularity of the young Queen.[29]

Perhaps to keep criticism to a minimum, incremental reform of State Opening is continual. While the Introduction Ceremony (a parliamentary ceremony) required two committees and two full-scale House of Lords' debates before change was possible, royal ceremonies require no formal discussion. The Earl Marshal, Lord Great Chamberlain and the Queen trim and modify at will: recently they have reduced the numbers in the processions (abolishing 'Silver-Stick-in-Waiting' for example), let the Lord Chancellor off walking backwards,[30] and allowed Black Rod to begin his walk at Central Lobby rather than from the bar. Some participants have sneaked changes through on personal initiative. The then Captain of the Honourable Corps of Gentlemen at Arms (Lord Carter) and the Captain of the Yeomen of the Guard (Lord McIntosh of Haringey), thoroughgoing civilians both but dressed in the spectacular military uniforms of some other century, found it difficult to hold their helmets in one hand and their swords in the other. Seeing no one else wearing helmets they quietly abandoned them, one remarking to the other 'Ah, so that is how 500 years of procedure is dispensed with'. Change to royal ceremonies is easy at the top, but may require a bit more persistence if initiated from below. Women heirs were not permitted to sit with male heirs during State Opening until the Countess of Mar, losing patience with being denied repeatedly, crossed out 'son' and wrote 'daughter' on her ticket. Since it said 'full evening dress uniform or morning suit', she sought advice as to what her daughter should wear. Again she was told it could not happen because it had never happened before. Her daughter attended wearing a black dress and pillbox hat and *fait accompli* once again carried the day.

As with the Introduction Ceremony, attitudes towards reform of the State Opening shed light on the meaning of the ceremony to participants. While many modernisers have ideas about how to make it more dignified, very few desire its abolition. Only two of those interviewed suggested that it should be replaced with a less colourful event. It is a royal and state occasion, beyond the control of peers or MPs. State ceremonial is the last preserve of the monarch, the foundation of her social, but no longer political, status. Most peers seem content with that state of affairs.

The Lord Chancellor's breeches and other symbols

In October 1998 the Lord Chancellor proposed that his breeches, stockings and buckled pumps should be replaced by trousers and shoes, and that when participating in debate he should leave the Woolsack and speak from the government front-bench. Until then, the Lord Chancellor had merely stepped to one side when speaking (and still does occasionally to answer questions) to indicate that he is answering as a minister rather than as Speaker. This made good sense to most peers.[31] But already flustered by changes to the Introduction Ceremony, some Conservatives and Cross-benchers saw this as more 'salami-slicing' of tradition. In a meeting of the Procedure Committee (the first and most fraught meeting I was permitted to observe) the argument that trousers would bring his appearance up to date and thereby avoid ridicule was strongly resisted. Traditionalists protested that ceremonial dress confers dignity to an office of the very highest importance. The committee was deadlocked: on the one hand, if it were taken to the House, parliamentary sketchwriters would have a field-day; on the other, if it were passed in committee (probably narrowly), a peer could raise it in the House in any case. The Chairman of Committees referred the matter to the House.

In the House, Earl Ferrers championed the *status quo*:

The office of the Lord Chancellor is one of the highest in the land. The ceremonial which goes with that office, and the uniform which attaches to that office, are very important. They are a reminder to all of us – your Lordships, members of another place and the general public – of the stature, dignity and, indeed, the awe with which the office of Lord Chancellor is held.[32]

Lord Graham of Edmonton, on the Labour side, pointed out that those advocating change are just as determined to maintain the dignity, richness and colour of the House.[33] Once again, while traditionalists feared history was being abandoned, modernisers, uninterested in the past as a route to respect, warned of the House losing credibility by looking anachronistic. One warned of the dangers of the House acquiring an "Iolanthe theme-park image". Another spoke of the absurdity of taking historical accident so seriously; and a Liberal Democrat pointed out that the breeches and tights go back only as far as the eighteenth century in any case.[34] (Several had a dig at the extravagance of the Lord Chancellor in renovating his apartment in contrast to his careful attitude to breeches.[35])

With Labour and Liberal Democrat support and a sprinkling of Tories and Cross-benchers, the motion was passed. When the result was announced in the Chamber a peer exclaimed with perfect timing, 'Get 'em off then'. The Lord Chancellor carried on wearing breeches for a while to maintain the suspense, and then no one seemed to notice when he one day put on trousers. He apparently took it in good humour when Earl Ferrers subsequently put on the bottom of an invitation to his seventieth birthday party, 'buckles and breeches'.

Of course both sides recognise that breeches have no value in themselves, they are symbolic. And both sides take for granted that symbols transform people. When a traditionalist was given the role of carrying the Cap of Maintenance at State Opening one year, he did a rehearsal in plain clothes and it meant nothing; when they had the real uniforms and he held the symbolic cap on a red cushion, he was transformed, he said, into the latest incumbent of an office of state. But modernisers too will tell you that the person of Derry Irvine was transformed by symbols, into Lord Chancellor when he wore a wig and robe and sat on the Woolsack, and to a government minister when he removed the wig and stood at the despatch box. The Earl of Clancarty, who was more radical in this than other peers, argued that relaxing the dress code would bridge the gulf between between peers and visitors, open up Parliament, and break down the House as an exclusive club.[36] Nevertheless, all peers value the dignity of the House; it is only their perception of what is dignified, and how to maintain it, that is contested.

Cosmological contests

The argument about tights may seem at first glance to be about whether signification through costume is necessary, but that is only a tangential issue. The passion peers demonstrate when arguing over custom and ceremony arises more from a desire to protect their investment of symbolic capital. While few peers challenge the gift of status that ennoblement offers them, they argue endlessly about how it is most effectively symbolised. They all wish for their status to be presented to the best advantage, but each according to their own lights. Hence the conflict.

The theme underlying peers' discussions of rituals and symbols is a profound disagreement about the relevance of history, and of historical hierarchies, to the present. Traditionalists defend ceremonies for the role they play in Parliament, the constitution and the nation; they are, in the words of one, "the traditional cement which holds together the structure of the House. They confer dignity on the offices of Parliament, and the institution itself, and give pleasure to participants and visitors alike." Many Conservatives and Cross-benchers believe that respect for tradition – with which the monarchy is intertwined – provides the sense of history that underpins the stability of the constitution. A stable constitution guarantees a stable country, and "a self-confident nation reveres past traditions", as Lord Strathclyde put it. Another told me: "a second chamber aware of its historical context and understanding that it is floating on the river of history is more likely to preserve the freedoms of the people against the executive than one that has been politicised and shorn of its past." In this view, continuity is of immense value: traditions that have stood the test of time are best, those that survive do so because they work, and the more ancient a symbol or ritual, the more useful it is likely to be. Traditions are important also to Britain's place in the world. A Conservative peer sent me this in an email:

> Their importance lies in the fact that the symbols of sovereignty, constitution, parliamentary government and union must be publicly seen as backing for the elected government of the nation in the eyes of the voters and the representatives of other nations at the Court of St James. These symbols of sovereignty also represent British tradition, beliefs and way of life and are a visible reminder of what the UK stands for globally.

In defending symbols and rituals, traditionalist peers see themselves as guardians of the House, Parliament, the constitution and even of British culture. There is an admirable humility in their respect for the past; but sometimes there may also be a touch of arrogance in their collective longing for Britain's former glory and nostalgia for hierarchies that conferred the highest status on the aristocracy.[37]

In contrast, for most modernisers history of itself confers nothing in particular, but they would like the nation to distance itself from our morally tarnished imperial past. They would prefer a 'modern' multicultural Britain, where there should be equality of opportunity, and few associations with the nation's unjust, racist and class-ridden history. They tend, for instance, to see too much engagement with the past as an encumbrance in seeking global influence in the twenty-first century world. One said:

> "There is lots of ritual. Some of it could be reduced. Britain should avoid being turned into an 'old curiosity shop', otherwise it could harm her image and, therefore, trade. If we were still an imperial power it would be fine, but we are not. It just looks curious and quaint and we can not afford that ... We can only afford the luxury of ritual when we are top dog."

Some traditions grate on the nerves of modernisers more than others. Peers' robes are seen by quite a few to have an adverse effect in setting peers apart from the public and from MPs, while several object to the bicorn hats worn by the Royal Commissioners (Privy Counsellors standing in for the Queen during ceremonies). Others are exasperated by the old-fashioned eccentricity of the place:

> I may alienate some in the House by saying that, if an idea were put forward to bring this House into the same time zone as the rest of the country so that we no longer greeted each other in the afternoon with 'Good morning', I would not regard that as the end of civilisation as we know it.[38]

Some, particularly newcomers, are even embarrassed by Lords' ceremonies; they find them comic, tedious and stultifying, and complain that they increase the self-importance of peers, waste time, dampen radicalism and preserve the establishment. They believe that they reinforce and justify the view of many outside the House that it is out-of-touch and out-of-date.

Details of costume and custom may at first appear trivial almost to the point of frivolity, and not even a proper subject for grown-up debate, but to dismiss them on these grounds would be to miss the point that they are subjects that engender passion. Peers may talk dispassionately or humorously about them outside the Chamber, but when battle is joined in debate, the nature and quality of the exchanges (on the whole, repetitive and polemical) reveal that peers' political passions are heavily invested in them. As already mentioned, there are two reasons for this passion: first, they are bound up with the symbolic capital of ennoblement; and, secondly, they offer an outlet for the more profound conflict between battling moral communities.

The same differences about the importance of history arise during debates on other issues that engender passion in the Chamber and which also reverberate in wider society. For much of the twentieth century the most polarised debates were about the economic system – state control versus the unfettered market. Now parliamentarians seem to bring the same passion to certain cultural and social traditions. In this they have become reliably predictable. Besides ritual, issues that peers have reacted with heat about include:

- *hunting*: Labour has been trying to ban hunting with dogs in England and Wales, while traditionalists have tried to defend it, and others support a 'middle way' that allows hunting with licenses;
- *homosexuality*: Conservatives and some Cross-benchers attempted to champion the 'traditional' family and delayed Labour and Liberal attempts to liberalise legislation on homosexuality;
- *the reform of the Lords*: Conservatives and some Cross-benchers have tried to prevent the exclusion of hereditary peers, the abolition of the Lord Chancellor, and the establishment of a supreme court.

These issues all concern relationships within society: liberalising laws on homosexuality goes to the heart of relationships within the family and between the church and state, and has come to symbolise the moral decay of British society for many traditionalists (see Chapter 7); while reform of the Lords relates to parliament and the judiciary, but also represents a form of class conflict (see Chapters 4 and 12). Hunting arises partly from a clash between rural and urban cultures. Arguments about animal cruelty are invoked, but for some on the left the issue has become one of ending unedifying aristocratic privilege. When asked why the government was spending so much time on this relatively narrow issue, relative at least to the crisis in the countryside or to rural poverty, one Labour back-bencher replied: 'I return to my starting point on the question of morality. We have to ask questions about the kind of society in which we live and, more importantly, the kind of society which we are hoping to create.' Another claimed that it was a 'sport unworthy of Britain in the 21st century ... It is just not British'.[39] Despite the oft-repeated, and sometimes highly emotive, accusations of cruelty to foxes, hunting with dogs has become more about people than animals. The Labour peer Lord Stoddart of Swindon puts it bluntly: 'I believe that this Bill is more about class hatred than about the welfare of animals. If it were not, its provisions would be cast far more widely to cover many other kinds of field sports and activities involving the killing of animals for sport.'[40] As gay rights are to the traditionalists, so hunting with dogs is to many modernisers.

On these cultural and social issues – hunting, homosexuality and lords – in general tradition commands Conservative loyalty and that of a majority of Cross-benchers; and Labour and Liberal Democrats champ the bit of modernisation; though there are exceptions to these tendencies. It is back-benchers who galvanise debate on homosexuality and hunting, with the quiet support, or neutrality, of their party leaders. They reflect substantial polarisation among the public.

Although the moral character of the nation is an ever-present issue for peers, it is seldom or never talked about directly; it has more the character of the 'elephant in the room'. Debates about ceremonies, symbols, hunting and homosexuality provide an opportunity to do so. The most contentious matters of all are thus debated by symbolic means; and because such debates are relatively infrequent and the issues they symbolise so vast, accumulated passions are often given vent. Ceremonies, rituals and ritual dress are symbols of the character of the nation, and act as the focus of the moral argument about what sort of country Britain should be. The subject matter (symbols) is itself a symbol. This doubly symbolic way of addressing the biggest issues allows the most emotionally charged debate to take place principally at the most abstract level. The same symbolic status has been conferred on civil liberties, gay rights and the reform of Parliament. All provide rare opportunities to engage with the 'elephant in the room'.

The polarisation between the political parties – together with a suspicion of each other's motives and morality – propel both sides towards fanaticism on these issues. Both tend to be blinkered by a sense of the moral superiority of their own position and have difficulties in seeing merit in the opposing view. In the fight between continuity and change, particularly in parliamentary rituals and ceremonies, each side has become so entrenched and frustrated that virtually any innovation is bad to traditionalists and good to modernisers. It is possible that this stalemate may only be resolved by such profound changes in the intellectual climate that other issues replace them as the focus of peers' political passions.

Notes

1 D. Cannadine, 2000, 'The Palace of Westminster as palace of varieties', in C. Riding and J. Riding (eds), *The Houses of Parliament*, Merrell, London, pp. 16–17.

2 C. Geertz, 1980, *Negara: The Theatre State in Nineteenth-Century Bali*, Princeton University Press, Princeton, p. 109.

3 Under the Parliamentary Oaths Act of 1866.

4 A. Wagner, and J. Sainty, 1967, *The Origin of the Introduction of Peers in the House of Lords*, Society of Antiquaries of London, Oxford.

5 Law lords have the same ceremony, which they can undertake at a judicial sitting during Prorogation or recess as well. Lords spiritual have a similar but shorter one, wearing white rochet with black bands, black chimere and scarf and mortar boards.

6 Select Committee on Procedure of the House, The Ceremony of Introduction, Memorandum by the Clerk of the Parliaments. PC/1997–98/2, 5 October 1997.

7 Memorandum by Leader of the House, the Ceremony of Introduction, PC/1997–98/1, 20 October 1997.

8 House of Lords, 1998, *The Introduction of New Members to the House of Lords, Volume II – Evidence, Select Committee on the Ceremony of Introduction*, HMSO, London, pp. 6–7.

9 House of Lords, *ibid.*, p. 15.

10 She also argued that the ceremony was important for introducing newcomers. When Lord Richard asked why it did not apply to hereditaries, he was told that they were already known.

11 Select Committee on Procedure of the House, the Ceremony of Introduction, *ibid*.

12 House of Lords, *ibid.*, p. 36.

13 Lord Denham, HL Deb., 27 October 1997, col. 921.

14 Lord Chalfont, HL Deb., 30 April 1998, col. 411; and Lord Campbell of Alloway, HL Deb., 30 April 1998, col. 412.

15 Lady Saltoun of Abernethy, HL Deb., 27 October 1997, col. 923.

16 For a detailed description of the present ceremony, see House of Lords, 2000, *Companion to the Standing Orders and Guide to the Proceedings of the House of Lords*, The Stationary Office, London, p. 229.

17 Hereditary peers adopt a new name the moment they succeed to their title, that is when the last holder dies, while those receiving new peerages do so (after the title has been agreed with Garter King of Arms) when their letters patent is stamped with the Great Seal.

18 The fact that the higher ranked titles have more ermine stripes on their robes was not mentioned by any peer and has become unimportant because distinctions of rank between peers scarcely matter any more. New hereditary peerages are most unlikely ever to be created again, except perhaps among the royals.

19 P. Bourdieu, 1990, *In Other Words: Essays towards Reflexive Sociology*, Polity Press, Cambridge, p. 135.

20 P. Bourdieu points out that '*what is essential goes without saying because it comes without saying*; the tradition is silent not least about itself as a tradition', (1977, *Outline of a Theory of Practice*, Cambridge University Press, Cambridge, p. 167, original emphasis).

21 Lord Addington, HL Deb., 16 December 1998, col. 996.

22 Lord Gordon of Strathblane, HL Deb., 22 January 2003, col. 766. A similar point was made by Lord Weatherill about the tradition that requires the newly elected Speaker of the House of Commons to go to the House of Lords to seek the approbation of the Queen. He warned that it gives the impression that the Lords is more important than the Commons and suggests that approbation should be sought by sending a message directly to the Queen instead. HL Deb., 12th January 2004, col. 410.

23 This is a ceremonial wand of office which is symbolically snapped in two by the Queen when the Vice-Chamberlain leaves office.

24 D. Kertzer, 1988, *Ritual, Politics and Power*, Yale University Press, New Haven and London, p. 11.

25 As quoted by C. Silvester, 1997, *The Pimlico Companion to Parliament: A Literary Anthology*, Pimlico, London, p. 120.

26 Response to questionnaire, 1999.

27 P. Bourdieu, 1979, *Distinction*, Routledge and Kegan Paul, London, p. 71–2.

28 Cannadine, *ibid.*, p. 23.

29 D. Cannadine, 1983, 'The context, performance and meaning of ritual: the British monarchy and the "invention of tradition", c. 1820–1977', in E. Hobsbawn and T. Ranger (eds), *The Invention of Tradition*, Cambridge University Press, Cambridge, pp. 101–64.

30 In 2003 the new Lord Chancellor, Lord Falconer of Thoroton, resurrected the respectful custom of walking backwards after he has taken the speech from the Queen, while the Earl Marshal and Lord Great Chamberlain refrained from doing so during the Sovereign's procession.

31 Some peers claim he has to take a step because the Woolsack is not part of the Chamber, while clerks describe this as nonsense.

32 Earl Ferrers, HL Deb., 16 November 1998, col. 985.

33 Lord Graham of Edmonton, HL Deb., 16 November, col. 1005.

34 Lord Lester of Herne Hill, 16 November 1998, col. 988.

35 For more about Lord Irvine of Lairg's expenditure on wallpaper, see J. Jones, 1999, *Labour of Love*, Politico's, London.

36 Earl of Clancarty, 1998, 'A dressing down for the Lords of convention', *Evening Standard*, 27 October 1998.

37 See Cannadine, 1983, 2000 *ibid.*

38 Lord Gordon of Strathblane, HL Deb, 2 January 2003, col 765.

39 Lord Watson of Invergowrie, HL Deb., 12 March 2001, col. 602; Lord Harrison, HL Deb., 12 March 2001, col. 612.

40 Lord Stoddart of Swindon, HL Deb., 12 March 2001, col. 622.

12 Opening up Parliament

Should the House of Lords be abolished, elected, appointed, kept as it is or some combination of these? Commissions have reported, parliaments overseas been examined,[1] proposals made and Parliament has debated. What more can be said on the subject? An anthropological perspective offers no obvious answers, but perhaps a slightly different way of looking at it.

Until this study, there had been no detailed analysis of how Lords' cultures play a part in their politics and how their rules, rituals and symbols relate to power structures and relationships within the House. Before suggesting the implications of these, I will sketch the main proposals that are on the table.

Proposals for reform

There is no shortage of ideas, but the two main positions are irreconcilable. Baroness Hollis sums succinctly:

> [C]onstitutional reformers want to have a distinct and independent mandate that comes from election which then acts as a brake on the Commons. Whereas of course, political parties just want to get their business through and they want the Lords to be virtuous in the sense of cleaning up the draughtsmanship.[2]

As soon as it became clear that Labour were likely to form the next government and intended to reform the House, the political parties and the Cross-benchers started producing reports on it.[3] When, in 1999, the government expelled most hereditary peers, complaints that this was a piecemeal approach were held at bay by their setting up the Royal Commission on the Reform of the House of Lords, chaired by Lord Wakeham. Its main recommendations were that the House should be composed of two types of peers: appointed members and a minority of indirectly elected members, all serving for fifteen years.[4] For the government, the fact that the proposed new House would not have the legitimacy to block their legislation was welcome. Many parliamentarians were unhappy. Outside Parliament (at least, among those who took an interest at all) there was derision. Although the Commission had argued that to be democratic the second chamber should not challenge the primacy of the first (elected) chamber, most felt that a modern chamber of Parliament should contain directly elected representatives.[5]

In late 2001 the Lord Chancellor's Department produced a white paper based on the Royal Commission's recommendations. Although 89 per cent of those consulted by his department had favoured a House that was 50 per cent or more elected,[6] it proposed 480 nominated members (mostly chosen by the parties) and 120 directly elected members, also chosen by the parties. The idea of parties controlling both appointments and elections was lampooned in the press (the *Daily Express* dismissing its 'medieval systems of patronage'),[7] and it failed to achieve support.

It became apparent that most MPs of all parties wanted a largely elected chamber. It was the official policy of both the Conservative and Liberal Democrat parties and had the support of many Labour peers. A report produced by the Commons Public Administration Committee proposed a 60 per cent elected House and that the final say on even political nominees should rest with an Independent Appointments Commission. This did not go down well with the government.[8] By May 2002, after months of deadlock in cabinet, it had become clear that the Lord Chancellor had failed to resolve Lords reform. The hot potato was handed to the Leader of the House of Commons, Robin Cook. He set up a Joint Committee[9] to produce a range of options and promised a free vote in both Houses. On 4 February 2003 the two Houses were invited, one after the other, to vote on seven options: all appointed, all elected, and five hybrids. The contrast between the Houses was telling: peers, recognising that everything to be said about reform had been said more than once already and wanting to avoid another 'groundhog day',[10] scarcely debated the issue but walked straight into the lobbies seven times. The result in the Lords was a clear win for an appointed chamber. Peers had voted for people like themselves. MPs launched into yet another ferocious debate before the vote, with some arguing that only elections could guarantee a democratic political system, while others insisted that more elections would throw up second-rate candidates, bore the electors and challenge the Commons. Ten days earlier, Prime Minister Tony Blair had announced his preference for an appointed Chamber. Despite it being nominally a free vote, Labour whips put their MPs under considerable pressure to support this option but were ignored. An elected upper House was the choice of many more MPs than an appointed one. Like peers, MPs voted for people like themselves; but, taken singly, each option was rejected.[11] The most popular, a 80 per cent elected House, was the one proposed by the Conservative party: it was defeated by only three votes.

This patently unsatisfactory result meant that the issue of Lords reform would still not go away. The continuing presence of ninety-two elected hereditary peers in the House exacerbated it. The following month, Lord Ullswater was elected to replace one who had died. It is partly this system of by-elections to replace hereditaries when they die, described by Earl Ferrers as a self-perpetuating oligarchy, that has left the government in a tight spot.[12] It ensures that hereditaries remain until a government manages to repeal the Weatherill Amendment or at least the clause about by-elections. In February 2003 Lord Weatherill introduced a bill to repeal this clause which would have allowed hereditaries to disappear gradually over the next fifty years without being replaced, but the Conservatives (whose policy is to have a mostly elected House) declined to support it. They wanted to prevent the creation by stealth of an all-appointed House.

In June 2003 the Prime Minister without any warning announced the abolition of the post of Lord Chancellor and its replacement by a Secretary for Constitutional Affairs (Lord Falconer of Thoroton). It was announced to the press, rather than Parliament, and provoked the Earl of Onslow to accuse Tony Blair of 'an abuse of power, of privilege and of office'.[13] This inept reform was found to be unconstitutional. Lord Falconer of Thoroton became the new Lord Chancellor and when legislation was introduced the following March to abolish him, as well as set up a separate supreme court and independent Judicial Appointments Commission, it was referred to a committee for further scrutiny by an alliance of Cross-benchers and Conservatives. By supporting this tactic, Lord Strathclyde frightened the government into abandoning a further bill that would have removed the remaining ninety-two hereditary peers. Such a bill would have entailed breaking the Lord Chancellor's promise to Parliament, made on 30 March 1999, that the remaining hereditary peers 'would only go when stage two has taken place. So it is a guarantee that it will take place'.[14]

Although long-term reform remains unresolved, new peers are still being appointed. In May 2000 the Prime Minister set up a House of Lords Appointments Commission. It received over 3000 nominations from people wanting to be peers.[15] To the disgust of many whose expectations had been raised by Downing Street Press Office spin about 'people's peers',[16] the Commission's choice turned out to be much the same kind of people normally chosen – establishment high achievers.

While politicians flounder, constitutional reformers make more imaginative proposals. The Fawcett Society campaigns for more women in Parliament, the Hansard Society for greater public accountability, the Constitution Unit for a separate supreme court, and Demos for a people's lottery. And then there is the singer-songwriter Billy Bragg, who has battled for a democratic upper Chamber for years. Although he initially raised noble eyebrows he now tends to attract favourable attention. One minister said to me: "Charter 88 want politics without politicians, the *Guardian* is spiteful and unrealistic but Billy Bragg has some interesting ideas." When MPs voted on reform in February 2003 I noticed several nodding greetings to him in the gallery. His ideas are thought-out, clearly expressed and stubbornly adhered to; he suggests that 600 members should be indirectly elected according to votes cast at general elections.[17] This proportional representation model, with closed lists drawn up by parties, ensures that two critical issues are addressed: the primacy of the Commons is protected while the will of the people is expressed. But it has three flaws: his hope that regional lists would be compiled democratically by party members, rather than centrally controlled, seems forlorn; a wholly elected upper House would probably lead to a reduction of its powers; and non-party peers would be lost.

Many members of political parties would view the end of the Cross-benchers as no great loss: but they underestimate the value of Cross-benchers' work, especially their less obvious roles of informing debate and contributing to committees and inquiries. Some fail to appreciate that the Cross-benchers give substance to the Lords' ethos of independent thinking. This does not mean independence from *any* interest groups or ideological viewpoints, but it does entail refusing to follow the whole agenda of any political party represented in Parliament. The contributions of Cross-benchers might receive more recognition if they took greater account of public opinion. If Cross-benchers improved their links with the public (as many of them already have), and with the press, they could possibly help rekindle interest in Parliament amongst those disillusioned with party politics. For this they deserve far more generous financial backing. So a combination of the Bragg elections and appointed cross-benchers might attract substantial popular support.

Most proposals for Lords reform concentrate on composition but other areas of concern include public perception of, and access to, the Lords, and public participation in the work of the upper House. The value of titles has been questioned. According to the *Guardian*, 120 peers have signed a 'Commoners' Register' on the grounds that 'titles are symbolic of a social system which can be very offputting for people coming from the wrong side of the tracks'.[18] Although honours peerages continue to be given to those whose offices entitled them semi-automatically to a peerage on retirement[19] – for former Speaker Betty Boothroyd, former Chief of the Defence Staff General Charles Guthrie, former Cabinet Secretary Richard Wilson, and former Bank of England Governor Edward George – the system appears to be evolving into an establishment of working peers. If this is the case, titles constitute a form of remuneration as peers receive no salary. It is arguable that this form of reward compromises their ability to be accessible because it sets peers above other people. The pyramid of social status, of which peerage titles are a part, may be fading in potency, but it has become an anomaly that can engender either complacency or embarrassment in peers, and misplaced deference or, increasingly, ridicule in sections of the public. The arguments for detaching peerage from Parliament may be gaining ground.

Social distance between peers and the public is compounded by the difficulties of outsiders physically getting into the Houses of Parliament.[20] While members of the public can always demand to see their MPs, and can even sometimes get a meeting in Central Lobby for a few minutes, you have to be invited or make a formal request to meet a peer. People tend not to realise they have the right to watch Lords' proceedings from the Strangers' Gallery. Most peers are wary of and formal with strangers, especially if they might be journalists – they have been ridiculed far too often. As a Conservative peer explains:

> "to some extent peers want to get on with their work in glorious isolation ... They do not want attention from hacks. They are usually not popular because they only pay attention when a peer is saying something silly. If the institution is exposed too much, open to too much scrutiny, then they will destroy the mystique, destroy the virtue. Publicity is a two-edged sword."

But for the upper House to be respected, this will have to change. Many have recognised this already. The parties, the committees and the House itself,[21] along with an increasing number of individual peers, endeavour to cultivate the press.

One reason peers have been forced to be more outward-looking is the increasing public disenchantment with politics. It has been said of European and American politicians that 'there is no doubt that distrust and alienation have risen to a higher level than ever before. It was always fairly prevalent; it is now in many regards almost universal.'[22] Dalton suggests that since electorates have become more critical of political elites, parliaments have either to re-establish their political authority or accept that they are entering into new period of democratic reform that allows more citizen participation and different forms of accountability.[23]

If two chambers of Parliament are constituted differently, as in Britain, they should be accountable to the public in different ways. MPs account to the ballot box. Representative democracy may be the least worst form of government, but one of its many problems is the potential for tyranny of the majority (the 'elective dictatorship', Lord Hailsham called it); most acute in the British 'first-past-the-post' system of voting.[24] It has been argued that elections – whereby the political preferences of 'the people' are collectively expressed through representatives – allow no direct participation and are even designed so that distance between people and government can be maintained.[25]

New ways are needed to ensure public participation in all Western democracies. House of Lords reform offers a rare opportunity to develop other forms of democracy and accountability, perhaps through direct participation and transparency rather than elections alone. Outside lobbies are already pursuing peers more vigorously and in more sophisticated ways – targeting peers according to their interests for example. Because the Lords considers legislation in greater detail, parties there are perceived as less cohesive, and as the government can be more easily defeated in the upper House (especially when they have a large majority in the Commons), lobbying there is on the increase.[26] But much could be done to make the House of Lords more accessible and open to a wider range of interests. Rather than allowing the continued dominance of the 'triumvirate of business-labor-government' found in most industrial democracies, diverse interest groups, and especially those that are usually hidden or forgotten, deserve attention.[27] As Lord Dahrendorf suggests, 'representative government is no longer as compelling a proposition as it once was. Instead, a search for new institutional forms to express conflicts of interest has begun.'[28] Traditional forms of participation in democracy – voting, party work, party campaigning – are declining and new forms are on the increase, including a growth in citizen action groups, direct-democracy methods (such as referendums), citizens' use of the courts, and protest politics.[29]

Ideas for improving the relationship between Parliament and citizen, and finding new ways for groups and individuals to express their views, are not in short supply and some are already being implemented. Recent British constitutional reforms include devolution of powers to the Scottish, Welsh and Northern Ireland assemblies; the introduction of proportional representation for those bodies and for elections to the European Parliament; increasing the rights of the individual through the Freedom of Information and Human Rights Acts; and 'modernisation' of Commons procedure, including pre-legislative scrutiny. The Hansard Society, the Norton Commission to Strengthen Parliament and academics have made other wide-ranging suggestions for our national Parliament as follows.

- *Better communication*: press reports on parliamentary debate have shrunk over the last fifty years but the broadcast media and new information and communication technologies offer opportunities for informing the public. The internet and satellite technology could be better harnessed to expand public education about Parliament.[30]

- *More transparent decision-making*: the secretive processes by which the usual channels of each House negotiate their agenda of legislation behind closed doors could be unveiled. The Hansard Society has begun to expose who they are and what they do, and several organisations have suggested that they should be replaced by a Public Business Committee, like that of the Scottish Parliament, so that back-benchers could be better informed about negotiations.[31]

- *Strengthening and expanding committees*: the demand to strengthen committees, so that Parliament can hold the government to account more effectively, has been growing as the influence of committees in the Commons has been eroded. The government has weakened the committee stage of some bills in the Lords by taking them off the floor of the House into committee rooms, where votes are not allowed. It has been argued that pre-legislative committees are the 'ideal vehicle for the expansion of public participation in policy making'.[32] They could be made less formal and more accessible by holding meetings around the country rather than just in Westminster; they deserve to be better resourced and could be given the right to summon witnesses. It has been suggested that they might have a role in post-legislative inquiry as well as pre-legislative scrutiny.[33]

- *Civic participation*: opening up Westminster to greater civic participation could be achieved by adopting some of the principles and practices of the Scottish Parliament. Founded on the principles of 'Access and Participation, Equal Opportunities, Accountability and Power Sharing in the work of the Parliament', it has a Petitions Committee and a Civic Forum, and its Procedure Committee has already reviewed its engagement with civil society, making 135 recommendations about how to improve practice ranging from improving scrutiny to encouraging school visits.[34]

- *Recognition of the legitimacy of citizen action*: some governments are becoming more responsive to citizen's demands. In Germany local citizen action groups have won changes in administrative law to allow for citizen participation in local administrative processes; citizen groups in the US make greater use of referendums to involve the public directly in policy-making; citizens elsewhere are making better use of courts to guarantee rights of democratic access and influence.[35]

Adopting a more open approach in Westminster would require a cultural *volte face*. During a meeting of parliamentarians and academics on this subject, a peer's suggestion that: 'it is time to stop the mumbo jumbo business of the usual channels, it is not necessary to have all the secrecy anymore. The time has come for openness, transparency and a more grown-up attitude', was not well received. Usual channels from the Lords pointed out that if they disclosed deals too early they would be badgered about which bills or amendments to prioritise, the press would harangue them and their negotiating positions would be jeopardised. But business committees already work well in the Welsh Assembly and Scottish Parliament. The usual channels in those parliaments continue to strike deals before the committees convene to discuss the agenda in public; the secret deals remain confidential, while the public discussion of the timetable keeps outsiders better informed. Although business becomes inflexibly set, thereby making it difficult for back-benchers to intervene beforehand, once debate starts changes can be made to the agenda. It is not practical objections that stop the idea in its tracks: it is the government and the usual channels who are reluctant to introduce greater transparency because it would diminish their room for manoeuvre and control.

The need for reform is agreed, workable ideas are plentiful, but the will to implement them is lacking. Why do the back-bench peers and MPs put up with this state of affairs? To answer that, the cultures of Parliament have to be understood.

Manners, rituals and power in the House of Lords

There is a common assumption that ritual is unimportant in politics because of its association with religion; and since religion and politics are usually kept separate in Western democracies, it is supposed that rituals found in politics must be insignificant. Anthropologists have not taken much notice of Hocart since, in the 1930s, he raised the importance of rituals in politics:

> ritual is not in good odour with our intellectuals. It is associated in their minds with a clerical movement for which most of them nurse an antipathy. They are therefore unwilling to believe that institutions which they approve of, and which seems to them so eminently practical and sensible as modern administration, should have developed out of hokus-pokus which they deem ritual to be. In their eyes only economic interests can create anything as solid as the state.[36]

Whether or not it was ritual organisation that evolved into systems of government, his work illustrates that rituals are a key part of the political process.

Similarly political anthropologists thought it proper to divorce politics from culture and reduce political ritual to its function, structure or process.[37] Some of those who recognise the importance of ritual portray it as a tool for deliberately reinforcing the *status quo*. Weatherford endorses this idea, suggesting not only that rituals in Congress perpetuate a theatrical system and have themselves become self-perpetuating, but further that instead of facilitating political decision-making, the rituals of Congress have become empty of substance. Congress, he suggests, has been reduced to nothing more than a ritualistic show:

> Congress preserves the format of legislative procedure – the appearance of debate and decision without any of the substance ... The greatest deliberative body in the world has become the greatest ceremonial body in the world, and the talents of its members are devoted less to deciding matters of national policy than to arranging and considering minute points of ceremony ... In most civilizations in which the leaders of the nation were more involved in pageantry and ritual than the affairs of the nation, power temporarily passed into the hands of those 'servants' around them.[38]

Weatherford's interpretation of Congress hinges in part on his view that 'ritual prevents interaction'.[39] Evidence points to different conclusions for other legislatures. In fact, almost the opposite is true of the House of Lords. Lords' ritualised debates are serious struggles between opposing moral communities; many of the conflicts engaged in through ritualised debate are not only significant in themselves, but have important outcomes. Peers are doing real politics through ritual: it is the anvil of politics, on the smooth surface of which legislation is forged (see Chapter 10, p.183). The wrangling over clauses in bills is a real moral conflict between political parties representing divisions in wider society.

Something similar takes place in France. Abélès writes that in the French National Assembly words, acts and objects are manipulated in ritual to bring into play the symbolism of relations between political power and civil society.[40] In 1999 when some French Assembly Members proposed a law to give legal status to homosexual couples, conservatives clashed with liberals. They battled over the text – especially whether the new status should be an 'agreement' or a 'contract' – shouted, insulted each other, even burst into tears. This ritual struggle was an 'effective and violent confrontation of people who incarnate intellectually and physically different elements of civil society'.[41] It is more than just theatre, or 'showmanship' as Weatherford describes it,[42] because, in the British and French parliaments, such ritualised debates constitute real arguments that engage passions in the nation. Accommodation or compromise are reached through rituals in Parliament, on behalf of the nation, and by the same means made acceptable to the nation.

Political rituals are thus important events in themselves. There are two significant forms of ritual in the British Parliament: ritualised debates, and the ceremonies that interrupt business. Both are inherently political. Do the ceremonies that do not deal with law-making or policy debates really matter? Geertz, in his book on nineteenth-century Bali, argues that they do, that culture and politics are inseparable, and that ceremony and symbolic action constituted the politics of Bali:

> That Balinese politics, like everyone else's, including ours, was symbolic action does not imply, therefore, that it was all in the mind ... The dramas of the theatre state, mimetic of themselves, were, in the end, neither illusions nor lies, neither sleight of hand nor make-believe. They were what there was.[43]

State ceremonies turn the Balinese King into an icon. The same might be said of our monarch. It is through state ceremonial that the Queen performs her political role.

Shils and Young explained the significance of the Coronation in terms of creating social solidarity; they claimed (following Durkheim's approach to ritual) that it had an impact on the nation in that it 'reaffirms the moral values which constitute it as a society and renews its devotion to those values by an act of communion'.[44] This, they suggest, contributes to a well-governed society. Lukes, however, argues convincingly that such a view simplifies 'what holds society together'. He challenges the assumption that moral values are shared nationally when there is often little consensus on what is good or desirable. He proposes that ritual plays 'a cognitive role, rendering intelligible society and social relationships, serving to organise people's knowledge of the past and present and their capacity to imagine the future.' Rituals, in addition to having these structural functions, ensure acquiescence by 'mobilising consent':

> A role which is, moreover, made the more effective by the occasional, overt and successful performance of their instrumental functions. The occasional success of back-benchers in checking or even reversing government policies greatly enhances the symbolic effectiveness of Parliament as a mobiliser of consent.[45]

This seems more solid than the idea that rituals necessarily engender solidarity in the nation – particularly as these in the Lords escape the notice of most of the British public. So how do such rituals mobilise consent? The occasional success of the back-benchers in the endless ritual struggles, and the rules stressing the equality between peers, give an impression that they have more power and control than they actually do. Whether peers are present at the ceremonies or not, they confirm peers' ownership of their symbolic property (titles and ceremonial prominence) that some convert into objective power in the nation's boardrooms, charities and media and give pre-eminence even to those who do not.[46] Add to that the ethos of independence and the emotional loyalty felt by many to their moral communities (political parties), and the result is a layer-cake of sweeteners to make the pill of limited political power more acceptable. The state ceremonies and the rituals of debate, taken together, provide back-bench peers with quite a powerful disincentive to challenge the *status quo*.

The experience of disjunction between status and power, whereby social rank compensates for lack of political clout, is shared by back-bench MPs. Matthew Parris reports that as a new MP 'only slowly does it sink in that though the world will doff its cap to you ... and though the local newspaper will print your thoughts on any subject ... nobody is actually taking any notice'.[47] This is not to suggest that the status of parliamentarians is created with this intention, but merely that an effect is to encourage acquiescence.[48]

MPs too engage in moral battles that represent cleavages within wider society. They differ from peers in their relationship with the executive; MPs have more formal power to defeat government motions or bills, but peers sometimes have greater influence in practice partly because they can just stay away from the Chamber when they disagree with their party. Except for front-benchers, peers may also have less incentive to resort to well-worn orthodoxies. A letter to *The Times* in 1953 pointed out that,

> It often puzzles historians, as well as other people, how governments, staffed by intelligent men, can be so slow to accept unwelcome facts. The reason is, surely, that in a government office, as in a church, those who accept current orthodoxies most easily rise to the top most frequently, while those with cross-bench minds get out most frequently.[49]

So do peers with 'cross-bench minds' have any power or influence in the Lords? As a result of the contributions of individuals, in committees as well as in the Chamber, the detail of legislation is vastly improved and government is forced to answer some testing questions. The sum of these contributions is seen as having great value, particularly by those who understand Westminster. The rituals, emphasising equality and independence as they do, give the back-benchers the feeling that they are transcending their individual powerlessness to become important components of an influential whole, which in some important senses they are.

However, when the same individuals are viewed as back-bench members of political parties, a different picture of power emerges. The influence of individuals varies dramatically according to where they sit. The power of the parties in the Lords has depended on which party was in government and how large their Commons majority was. Before 1999, the Conservative preponderance in the Lords meant that the upper

Chamber was most effective when the Conservatives were in government because when defeated by their own back-bench peers, they found it politically more difficult to reverse unwelcome amendments, especially when their Commons majority was small. By contrast the present Labour government has been defeated about three times as often.[50] But because of its substantial majority in the Commons the government easily overturns defeats when the legislation returns to the lower House.

The position of the Lords has changed, and continues to change, although such shifts are not easy to measure. Sir Michael Wheeler-Booth points out that the impact of the House of Lords Act 1999 is difficult to assess because 'there is an understandable wish in those who laboured for the cause to magnify their achievement. Ministers and civil servants may wish to dignify, as well as conceal, the process of government; while oppositions need to magnify their achievements to keep up morale.'[51] With most of the backwoodsmen expelled and near parity in numbers between the two main parties, the perception of greater legitimacy is increasing peers' confidence.[52] The opposition may be showing signs of being slightly braver, winning an amendment to the Queen's speech in 2003, for example, for the first time in over eighty years, and defeating the government eighty-three times in the last session, in addition to insisting on further scrutiny of plans to establish a supreme court. Conservatives, Liberal Democrats and Cross-benchers have protected various civil liberties that the government attempted to erode, for example, to a trial by jury, for candidates to send out election addresses, to privacy (against the government's infamous 'snooper's charter'[53]), and for detainees to have a trial. The Liberal Democrats have held the balance of power since 1999. Co-operation between Lib Dems and Tories has become a normal part of business. Where once the Tories did not need their help, it is now Lib Dems who usually decide when the opposition should win and they were active, among other things, in forcing the government to accept improvements to the Anti-Terrorism Act 2001. So far, though, peers have on the whole continued to make sure that the government is able to get its way in the end.

The even balance of the two main parties has heightened the competition between them; in the words of Lord Dahrendorf,

> I regret that reform of the Lords so far seems to have led to strengthening the role of parties, and that the next stage of reform will do so again. To talk about 'Tony's cronies' is a red herring. What really happens is that, one way or another and whether through appointment or election, party membership, party interest, party loyalty and, above all, the influence of party leadership, gain in importance and the independence of the whole Chamber is reduced. The House is becoming more tribal and, by the same token, less independent.[54]

Whips are more active, and back-benchers more prepared to co-operate. Government defeats appear to be increasing, but parties in the Lords may be becoming more important and their decision-making more centralised. This can only be at the cost of the power of back-benchers. The tendency of party managers (and others) to try to centralise power into their own hands, and expect back-benchers to comply, is an unfortunate aspect of political hierarchies, not a criticism of individuals. Peers are fond of quoting Lord Acton's letter of 1887: 'power tends to corrupt, and absolute power corrupts absolutely ... There is no worse heresy than that the office sanctifies the holder of it.'[55]

The power of individual peers varies depending on which party is in government, and on their role within that party. Places in the Chamber are ritually prescribed and the power visually expressed; Government ministers always sit on the front-bench to the right of the Throne, while the opposition sit on the left. This gives a physical immediacy to shifts in power such as changes of government or the promotion or demotion of an individual (see Figure 2.1).

But what exactly does the 'dominance' of political parties comprise? Many observers of politics take a behaviourist view, stressing power in the realm of decision-making, and especially the control of votes. In this view, a person has power over another if he or she gets the other to do something that they would not otherwise do, such as whips obliging back-benchers to vote against their conscience.[56] This happens less in the Lords than in the Commons. As far as power between the two Houses is concerned, peers do sometimes force the government to accept amendments, and even occasionally bills, that they would not otherwise approve. But power involves decisions that are not made, as well as ones that are, and most importantly it can involve control over a process of 'confining the scope of decision-making to relatively "safe" issues'.[57] The scope of decision-making – that is, the business to be debated in Parliament as a whole – is almost exclusively in the hands of the government. It is clear that back-bench peers have minimal power at this more fundamental level of control and on most issues those with serious grievances, whether covert or overt, are prevented from expressing them.

An effect of Lords' rituals may be to obtain back-bench party peers' acquiescence to the party system and the dominance of the executive, but that does not necessarily mean that all rituals require reform. Self-regulation is rightly valued by most peers because it emphasises that the whole House – a collection of individual peers – is responsible for all that goes on in the Chamber. It projects an idealised version of the House of Lords, how it could and should be: full of conscientious, equal and specialist peers who regulate their own debates. It is not these parliamentary rituals that need drastic or wholesale revision – they are judiciously adjusted and pruned from time to time – but the power structures in both the parliamentary and the wider political system as a whole. Re-evaluation of our parliamentary system – Commons and Lords – is widely recognised as overdue. Barry Sheerman MP warns: 'those who have been Members of Parliament for some time know that this place is dying on its feet. If we do not find a proper role for Parliament, we shall become merely subservient to Ministers and the Executive.'[58] There is no shortage of ideas for challenging the power structures in Parliament and strengthening the position of the Cross-benchers, some of which have been mentioned earlier in this chapter. At the time of writing it seems possible that proposals for Lords' reform may result in a part-elected House, which would increase democratic legitimacy, and part-appointed House, which could offer an opportunity to: (a) retain, or better still increase the number of independent, non-party peers, (b) combat forms of under-representation, such as those based on gender and ethnicity, and (c) develop strategies for participatory democracy to complement direct democracy.[59] Greater legitimacy could transform the power dynamic within Parliament, and the ritualisation of Lords' debates (expressing equality between peers), and parliamentary ceremonial (conveying dignity to the House and those that serve it), might have more meaning.

Political ritual must not be lightly dismissed. The ideological baggage of many on the left leads them to regard it as trivial and backward-looking. But there is a great deal at stake; after all 'far from being window dressing on the reality that is the nation, symbolism is the stuff of which nations are made.'[60] Ritual continues to capture the popular imagination. While rituals should not be preserved heedlessly, they should not be abandoned heedlessly either – we could perhaps distinguish more carefully between those that resonate successfully with imagination of participants and the public, and those symbols that create social distance between peers and the public. We can help protect or refashion our nation through its rituals and symbols.

Notes

1 See M. Russell, 2000, *Reforming the House of Lords: Lessons from Overseas*, Oxford University Press, Oxford.

2 As quoted by A. Mitchell, 1999, *Farewell My Lords*, Politico's London, p. 166.

3 To take just three examples, a small group of Cross-benchers and Conservatives defended the presence of hereditary peers (the Earl of Carnarvon, the Lord Bancroft, the Earl of Selborne, the Viscount Tenby and Douglas Slater, 1995, *Second Chamber: Some Remarks on Reforming the House of Lords*, Douglas Slater, London.) The Liberal Democrats' *Policy Review Commission Report, Constitutional Affairs*, 8 June 1998, recommends a Senate with 300 members, 250 of whom would be directly elected. The Conservative Party leader William Hague established a constitutional

commission, chaired by Lord Mackay of Clashfern, which proposed two choices for a new Senate: a mixed house with appointed and elected peers or a Senate based on direct elections (Lord Mackay of Clashfern, 1999, *The Report of the Constitutional Commission on Options for a New Second Chamber*, Douglas Slater, London.) Many others, including various government papers, are listed in: House of Lords, Library Note LLN 98/004, *Proposals for Reform of the Composition and Powers of the House of Lords*, 1968–1998.

4 Royal Commission on the Reform of the House of Lords (Chairman: Lord Wakeham), 2000, *A House for the Future*, HMSO, London.

5 House of Lords Library Note LLN 2000/002, *Press Reaction to the Royal Commission on the Reform of the House of Lords, A House for the Future*, 28 February 2000.

6 Lord Chancellor's Department, 2002, *Reform of the House of Lords, Analysis of Responses to the Government White Paper 'The House of Lords – Completing the Reform'*, HMSO, London.

7 House of Lords Library Note LLN 2001/009, *Press Reaction to the White Paper, 'The House of Lords: Completing the Reform'*, 21 December 2001.

8 House of Commons, 2002, *Report of the House of Commons Public Administration Committee, The Second Chamber: Continuing the Reform* (Fifth Report, Session 2001–02, HC 494-1, February 2002). The government's response was published in an appendix to the committee's sixth report.

9 That is, a committee with a membership drawn from all parties and both Houses.

10 Lord Strathclyde named the endless debates on reform after the film in which a man continually relives the same day, HL Deb., 22 January 2003, col. 826.

11 Two of the options were 'negatived', i.e., defeated without a division.

12 Earl Ferrers, 1999, *Select Committee on Procedure of the House*, Third Report, Session 1998-99, HL Paper 81, p. 13. For an explanation of these by-elections see Chapter 4.

13 The Earl of Onslow, HL Deb., 12 June 2003, col. 436.

14 Lord Chancellor, HL Deb., 30 March 1999, col. 207.

15 House of Lords Appointments Commission, 2001, *Response to the Government's White Paper, 'The House of Lords – Completing the Reform'*, 21 January 2001.

16 When the Chairman was asked about their choice, he replied: 'You haven't got your hairdresser in this list, but if you go back to our criteria one of them is that the human being will be comfortable operating in the House of Lords.' (Lord Stephenson as quoted by Anne Perkins, 2001, 'Selection lacks the common touch', *Guardian*, 27 April, p.13.) The Commission recommended another seven candidates for Cross-bench peers in May 2004; all were accepted by the Prime Minister.

17 Billy Bragg, 2001, *A Genuine Expression of the Will of the People: A Viable Method of Democratic Lords Reform*, www.dorset.net, Dorchester.

18 David Leigh, 2001, 'Off with their silly titles', *Guardian*, 27 April.

19 The Prime Minister has continued to appoint the occasional honours peer, who then sits as a Cross-bencher, as well as party political peers. Law Lords also continue to be appointed as usual until the government implements its plan to establish a separate supreme court, as do party political peers in small numbers.

20 J. Ashley, 2000, *I Spy Strangers: Improving Access to Parliament*, Hansard Society, London.

21 The Parliament Office has its own Information and Press Officer.

22 I. Crewe, as quoted by Russell J. Dalton, 2002, *Citizen Politics*, Chatham House, New York and London, p. 236.

23 Dalton, *ibid.*, pp. 253–5.

24 P. Dunleavy, 1999, 'Electoral representation and accountability: the legacy of empire',

in I. Holliday, A. Gamble and G. Parry (eds), *Fundamentals in British Politics*, Macmillan, London, pp. 204–30.

25 G. Parry, 1999, 'Introduction', in Holliday *et al.*, *ibid.*, p. 5.

26 N. Baldwin, 1990, 'The House of Lords', in Michael Rush (ed.), *Parliament and Pressure Politics*, Clarendon Press, Oxford, pp. 152–77.

27 Dalton, *ibid.*, p. 255.

28 As quoted by Dalton, *ibid.*, p. 257.

29 Dalton, *ibid.*, and B. E. Cain, R. J. Dalton and S. E. Scarrow, 2003, *Democracy Transformed? Expanding Political Opportunities in Advanced Industrial Democracies*, Oxford University Press, Oxford and New York.

30 More detailed ideas have been elaborated by Lord Norton's Commission in The Conservative Party, 2000, *The Report of the Commission to Strengthen Parliament*, July, pp. 54–7.

31 These include Charter 88, the Conservative party Commission on Strengthening of Parliament, the Hansard Society Commission on Parliamentary Scrutiny, and the Liberal Democrat party (as quoted by M. Rush, C. Ettinghausen, with I. Campbell and A. George, 2002, *Opening Up the Usual Channels*, Hansard Society, London.)

32 Nicholas Hopkinson, 2001, *Parliamentary Democracy: Is There a Perfect Model?*, Commonwealth Parliamentary Association, Ashgate, Aldershot, pp. 69–71.

33 Michael Ryle, House of Lords Minutes of Evidence, Taken before Select Committee on the Constitution, Parliament and the Legislative Process, Wednesday 19 May 2004, Ev 2, unrevised proof copy, pp. 15–16.

34 Procedure Committee, Third Report 2003, SP Paper 818, accessed from: http://www.scottish.parliament.uk/official_report/cttee/proced-03/prr03-03-vol01-01.htm.

35 Dalton, *ibid.*

36 A. M. Hocart, 1970, *Kings and Councillors: An Essay in the Comparative Anatomy of Human Society*, 2nd edition, the University of Chicago Press, Chicago and London, p. 35 (1st edition 1936).

37 J. Spencer, 1997, 'Post-colonialism and the political imagination', *Journal of the Royal Anthropological Institute*, vol. 3, no. 1, p. 4.

38 J. McIver Weatherford, 1985, *Tribes on the Hill: The US Congress Rituals and Realities*, Bergin and Garvey, Westport and London, pp. 177, 266, 268–9.

39 Weatherford, *ibid.*, p. 195.

40 M. Abélès, 1988, 'Modern political ritual', *Current Anthropology*, vol. 29, no 3, p. 393.

41 M. Abélès, 2005, 'Parliament, politics and ritual', in E. Crewe and M. G. Müller (eds), *Rituals in Parliaments: Political, Anthropological and Historical Perspectives on Europe and the United States*, Peter Lang, Frankfurt am Main.

42 Weatherford, *ibid.*, pp. 174–5.

43 C. Geertz, 1980, *Negara: The Theatre State in Nineteenth-Century Bali*, Princeton University Press, Princeton, p. 136.

44 E. Shils and M. Young (1953) 'The meaning of the coronation', *Sociological Review*, vol. 1, p. 67.

45 S. Lukes, 1977, *Essays on Social Theory*, Macmillan, London, pp. 68, 69, 209 n. 75.

46 P. Bourdieu's claim that 'objective power relations tend to reproduce themselves in symbolic power relations' may also work in reverse for the Lords (1990, *In Other Words*, Polity Press, London, p. 135).

47 Matthew Parris, 2003, *Chance Witness: An Outsider's Life in Politics*, Penguin, London, p. 241.

48 Bloch explains that political systems, including the disjunction between rank and power that can be found in many societies, can only be understood by tracing their historical development rather than by reducing them to a conspiratorial function (M. Bloch, 1989, *Ritual, History and Power: Selected Papers in Anthropology*, Athlone, London, p. 47).

49 A. R. Burn, 1953, Letters to the Editor, *The Times*, 28 July, p. 4, col. F.

50 This is based on figures for 1975–2003: the average number of defeats during eighteen years of Conservative administration was thirteen, while Labour averaged forty-nine over ten years in the 1970s and since 1997; see Table 4.1 for details.

51 M. Wheeler-Booth, 2003, 'The Lords', in R. Blackburn and A. Kennon (eds), *Griffith and Ryle on Parliament, Functions, Practice and Procedures*, Sweet and Maxwell, London, p. 712.

52 The government even encouraged this when Baroness Jay said both before and after the House of Lords Act that excluding the hereditaries would make it a more legitimate house (HL Deb., 14 October, col. 926 and 24 November 1999, col. 572).

53 This revision to legislation was dubbed the 'snooper's charter' because it would have allowed government agencies greater access to email and phone data to protect national security and public safety and investigate crimes.

54 Lord Dahrendorf, HL Deb., 9 January 2002, col. 591.

55 The present Lord Acton kindly gave me a photocopy of the original letter.

56 This behavourist view of power has been criticised by the philosopher Stephen Lukes for being too narrow (1974, *Power: A Radical View*, Palgrave, Basingstoke, p. 11).

57 Bachrach and Baratz, as quoted by Lukes, *ibid.*, p. 18.

58 As quoted by B.K. Winetrobe, 2000, *Shifting Control? Aspects of the Executive-Parliamentary Relationship*, Parliament and Constitution Centre, House of Commons Library, Research Paper 00/92.

59 The case for a reformed upper House, including an independent judiciary, has been convincingly made by many, but it is beyond the scope of this book to comment on these. See various publications by the Constitution Unit, University College London, including M. Russell and R. Hazell, 2000, *Commentary on the Wakeham Report on Reform of the House of Lords*, The Constitution Unit, London.

60 D. Kertzer, 1988, *Ritual, Politics and Power*, Yale University Press, New Haven and London, p. 6.

61 Kertzer, *ibid.*, p. 183.

Appendix 1
A chronology of reform in the Lords 1998–2004

April 1998	Changes to the Introduction Ceremony introduced
November 1998	House approves Lord Chancellor's plans to replace his breeches, tights and buckles with trousers and plain shoes
January 1999	Government publishes white paper and bill on reform of the House of Lords
February 1999	House of Lords Bill second reading takes place in the House of Commons
February 1999	White paper on reform of the House of Lords debated for two days
February 1999	Royal Commission on House of Lords Reform set up
March 1999	House of Lords Bill second reading takes place in the House of Lords
May 1999	Weatherill Amendment – retaining ninety-two hereditary peers – passed
November 1999	Results of the main hereditary peers election
November 1999	Royal Assent given to the House of Lords Bill
January 2000	Royal Commission on House of Lords Reform reports: 'A House for the Future'
April 2001	Appointments Commission proposes fifteen new Cross-bench peers
July 2001	House of Lords adopts a compulsory register of interests
December 2001	Government white paper on House of Lords reform
July 2002	Government introduces reform to House of Lords' working practices, including pre-legislative scrutiny of some bills
June 2003	Prime Minister tries to abolish post of Lord Chancellor during a cabinet reshuffle
February 2003	House of Commons rejects all options for reform of the House of Lords
November 2003	Government announces in the Queen's Speech plans to abolish remaining ninety-two hereditary peers and set up a separate court of appeal

| March 2004 | Bill to establish supreme court, abolish Lord Chancellor and set up a judicial appointments commission is referred to a committee by the House of Lords |
| May 2004 | Appointments Commission proposes seven new Cross-bench peers |

Appendix 2
Research methodology

Social anthropological theory and method

It is the methods and theoretical approach of anthropology that distinguish it from other disciplines. Since the founding father of modern social anthropology, Bronislaw Malinowski, carried out 'fieldwork' in the 1920s and 30s, anthropologists have been immersing themselves in societies and organisations. The point is to build up a detailed understanding of how different parts of a society relate to each other. In the case of the House of Lords, for instance, the voting behaviour of peers can only be understood if you find out about the:

- usual channels and their whips;
- the moral character of the relationship between political parties;
- the social background of peers and how they got there;
- peers' prospects and aspirations.

Whereas some researchers might rely on peers' opinions gleaned through interviews or focus groups, anthropologists take statements as the beginning and not the end of the story. Informants tend to take much for granted when explaining what they do, and to portray themselves as more heroic, or at least more consistent, than they are in practice, and they often say what they think you want to hear.

Anthropologists observe what people do and how they relate to each other, so that they can contrast opinion with behaviour. They work out when and why the rules of society are broken, and how the relationships between people are structured. They probe the ideologies within a society, the meaning of its rituals and symbols, and how people use them to make sense of the past, present and future. Finally, they explore the relationships between all aspects of this material and hope that meaningful patterns and explanations emerge.

Political anthropology emerged as a branch of anthropology only in earnest in the 1940s with *African Political Systems*, edited by Meyer Fortes and E. E. Evans-Pritchard. This divided African societies into those with primitive states and those with no centralized authority but rather with a political system based on kinship (see Chapter 8 for details). Numerous publications on African political taxonomy followed, until Edmund Leach wrote *Political Systems of Highland Burma* in 1954. To explain the three political systems in the Kachin Hills of Burma, he looked to ritual and symbolism. Max Gluckman, in the 1950s and 60s, also claimed that it was through rituals (in this case of rebellion against African kings) that equilibrium in a system is achieved. It was Clifford Geertz who then resuscitated the idea of ritual as the process of politics itself, rather than a servant to it, in his work on Bali (see Chapter 12). For the most comprehensive overview of anthropological perspective on political ritual, see Kertzer's book (below).

For more information about anthropology and political anthropology, its methods and theories, see:

Barnard, A. and J. Spencer, 1996, *Encyclopedia of Social and Cultural Anthropology*, Routledge, London.
Ellen, R. F., 1984, *Ethnographic Research*, Academic Press, San Diego and London.
Eriksen, T. H., 2001, *Small Places, Large Issues: An Introduction to Social and Cultural Anthropology*, 2nd edition, Pluto, London.
Geertz, C., 1973, *The Interpretation of Cultures*, Basic Books, New York.
Kertzer, D., 1988, *Ritual, Politics and Power*, Yale University Press, New Haven and London.
Lewellen, T. C., 2003, *Political Anthropology, An Introduction*, Praeger, Westport CT and London.
Peacock, J., 1986, *The Anthropological Lens*, Cambridge University Press, Cambridge.

Secondary and primary sources on the House of Lords

My main reference books about the House of Lords were:

Bromhead, P. A., 1958, *The House of Lords and Contemporary Politics 1911–1957*, Routledge and Kegan Paul, London.
Morgan, J. P., 1975, *The House of Lords and the Labour Government 1964–1970*, Oxford University Press, Oxford.
Shell, D., 1992, *The House of Lords*, Harvester Wheatsheaf, London.
Silk, P., and R. Walters, 1998, *How Parliament Works*, 4th edition, Longman, London (and the latest edition, R. Rogers and R. Walters, 2004, Pearson Education, Harlow).
Smith, E. A., 1992, *The House of Lords in British Politics and Society 1815–1911*, Longman, London.

During the research the official report of proceedings (Hansard), committee reports, minutes and evidence, annual reports, information leaflets, party briefings, newspaper articles and other documents were regularly consulted. The Registry (the House of Lords' clerks' collection of documents relating to procedure) was a useful source for procedural matters. The House of Lords Librarian, David L. Jones, kindly produced a bibliography of references relevant to the project.

Lord Stanley of Alderley generously gave access to his journal of thirty years of work at the House of Lords, and his extensive archive of letters, notes, party memos, speeches, and official reports.

A research assistant, Julia Kruger, was employed to input information about peers' party affiliation, type of peerage, gender, qualifications and experience from *Dod's Parliamentary Companion* (2002) to enable analysis of the range of peers' expertise.

Interviews

Unstructured

Unstructured interviews (30 minutes to 4 hours) were carried out with 119 peers, 63 House of Lords staff, and 26 others (advisers, former staff, secretaries, police officers, postal workers, academics, peers' spouses/relatives, journalists, Commons staff, non-governmental organisation staff). Most of the informants were interviewed once but some gave up to ten interviews. Care was taken to ensure that that the sample included roughly representative proportions of regularly attending members from each party/Cross-bench group (see Tables A.1 and A.2), life and hereditary peers, former MPs, ministers, women/men, older/younger, black/Asian/white peers and procedural experts.

Interviews were held mainly with regularly attending peers, rather than those visiting occasionally, although informal conversations were held with irregulars to find out why they stayed away. Meetings usually took place in a corridor, the peers' guest room or the Royal Gallery, where tape recording is not permitted. The main protagonists in the House of Lords Bill were taped (in their offices), on the condition that the recordings remained confidential.

Structured

Two questionnaires were carried out. The first sought to find out from peers: their kinship relation to other peers; why they attended the House; how they viewed the institution, self-regulation, staff/peer relationships; who they socialised with; their religion; their views on traditions and procedures; in what ways the House had changed; and what they would like reformed or preserved. The response was surprisingly good, and fairly representative of the whole sample of peers at that time, and replies were illuminating (177/1000 of attending peers replied – see Table A.3).

Table A.1　Party and peerage of all peers (August 1998)

Party	Life	Hereditary 1st creation	Hereditary by succession	Bishops	Total
Cross-bench	118	4	199		321
Conservative	171	4	296		471
Labour	147	1	17		165
Lib Dem	41		24		65
Other	25		87	26	138
Total	502	9	623	26	1160

Male: female peers = 1056:104

Lords without Writs of Summons = 67

Peers on leave of absence from the house = 68

Table A.2　Party and peerage of peers in the formal interview sample (Mar 1998–Jan 2001)

Party	Life	Excluded hereditary	Elected hered.	Life + hered.	Hered. office-holder	Total
Cross-bench	11	8	17	0	1	37
Conservative	14	6	9	3	1	33
Labour	27	2	2	2	0	33
Lib Dem	10	2	2	1	0	15
Green	1	0	0	0	0	1
Total	62	18	30	6	2	119

Male: female peers = 96:23

Table A.3　Party and peerage of peers in the questionnaire sample (Oct/Nov 1999)

Party	Life	Excluded hereditary	Elected hereditary	Total
Conservative	29	35	14	78
Labour	39	1	2	42
Cross-bench	16	18	6	40
Lib Dem	10	1	3	14
Green	1	0	0	1
Total	95	55	25	175

Male: female peers = 154:21

2 anonymous

The questionnaire on culture in the House of Lords, distributed in October 1999 and returned the following month, was as follows:

> This questionnaire is being sent to all peers who attended the House of Lords during the 1987/98 and 1998/99 sessions. It is part of a research project funded by the Economic and Social Research Council and approved by the Leaders of the Parties, the Cross-Bench Convenor and the Administration and Works Sub-Committee. Your answers will be seen only by the researcher and **anonymity** of informants when reporting or publishing the findings is guaranteed.

1. Name (and address if appropriate):

2. Names of any kinsmen, kinswomen and connections by marriage you have among peers, officers and staff and their relationship to you.

3. How long have you been an active member of the House of Lords?

4. Why do you attend the House of Lords? (If infrequently, please give reasons).

5. How is the atmosphere of the House of Lords different from other institutions or places you have: (a) worked in and (b) socialised in?

6. How does the absence of a Speaker on the model of the House of Commons influence the House of Lords and the relationship between peers?

7. Could you please describe the relationship between peers and staff (differentiating between different types of staff if appropriate) in the House of the Lords.

8. Which types of peers tend to be in your closer social circle (e.g., Conservative/ Labour/ Liberal Democrat/Cross-Bench, life/hereditary, front-bench/back-bench, former MPs/other professions, older/younger, men/women...)?

9. Have you a religious faith? If yes, which one, are you practising, and how does this influence your participation in the House of Lords?

10. Which traditions, ceremonies, procedures and customs of the House are particularly important and why?

11. What are the main ways in which the House of Lords has changed since you arrived?

12. What would you like to see preserved and/or changed in the House of Lords in the future?'

The second questionnaire was distributed to staff and received a lower response rate (48/349 staff). Those who did respond, however, did so candidly and in useful detail.

Participant-observation

Due to the informal working style of the Lords, and the support given to the research by the Clerk of the Parliaments, I was able to take part actively in House of Lords working life.

- I was given a staff pass, attended a staff induction course, and observed the induction process for peers.
- The Cross-bench peers permitted me to use one of their offices, allowing daily informal conversations with peers.
- Unplanned conversations with peers, staff (especially clerks and doorkeepers) and visitors were a substantial feature of every visit to the Palace.
- I worked for: (a) Black Rod's department, selling pictures to peers (1998), (b) the clerks on the hereditary peers' elections team (1999); (c) a Cross-bench peer investigating the current legal status of depression (1999); (d) the Cross-bench Convenor as a personal assistant (1999–2000).
- I spent many hours each week in the Chamber, where I observed policy debates, legislation (including passage of the entire House of Lords Bill, debates on procedure, working practices and homosexuality, and many 'parliamentary occasions'), motions, judgments by the law lords (including the Pinochet case).
- I attended meetings of committees, all-party groups, whips, ministers, back-benchers and every Cross-bench meeting during fieldwork.
- I observed commissions/committees taking evidence and a civil service final selection board for recruiting Lords' clerks.
- I shadowed members of staff and observed the Staff Adviser's (Inspector) interviews with staff.
- I watched parliamentary ceremonies (including State Opening from several points of view, the Introduction Ceremonies, prorogation, the appointment of the Common's Speaker, various Royal Commissions, Royal Assent) as well as others held in the Palace (such as the Loving Cup, the Judges' procession at the start of their year).
- I attended social functions (including parties, charity functions, Cross-bench get-togethers, the tug of war, electioneering parties by hereditary peers).
- I joined official guided tours of the Houses of Parliament and the Lord Chancellor's residence.
- I made visits to the homes of three peers (in Wales, Scotland and England) and to the Hellenic and Israeli parliaments.

Documentation and analysis

Unstructured interviews were recorded electronically in individual files. Observations on each event were written up in separate files. Responses to two questionnaire forms were held on hard copy. They were written up into detailed reports, a brief version of which was circulated to informants. In addition to the files on individuals and events, a diary was written throughout the period of fieldwork. In total the computerised fieldwork data alone amounts to 332 files containing 9 MB of information. While the fieldwork and documentation continued intensively from November 1998 to the end of 2000, some interviews were held and events observed during 1998 and between 2000–04. Material that could not be used, at the request of informants, and the identity of all informants are recorded in fieldnotes and will be deposited at the UK Data Archive, with a thirty-year embargo, by 2010.

Appendix 3

Glossary of places, words and phrases

The sources for much of this information are: House of Lords, 2000, *Companion to the Standing Orders and Guide to the Proceedings of the House of Lords*, The Stationary Office, London, and P. Silk and R. Walters, 1998, *How Parliament Works*, Addison Wesley Longman, Harlow.

Act	legislation once it has received assent and has become law
all-party groups	groups of peers and MPs who hold meetings about a particular subject or country
amendment	a change proposed to a bill by a member of the House
another place or house	House of Commons
baby clerks	new junior clerks
back-bench	members of the House with no official position in their party
backwoodsmen	peers who vote only when summoned by their whips but make no other contribution
bar of the House	railing at the peers' lobby end of the Chamber behind which peers enter and guests sit to watch proceedings. MPs and younger sons of peers may stand behind the bar to watch proceedings
baron	fifth-ranking peer, after duke, marquess, earl, viscount
baroness	woman peer, equivalent in rank to baron
Barry Room	one of the dining rooms for peers and officers
below bar	area reserved for peers' guests to watch proceedings
bill	draft of a law before it has received the approval of the two Houses of Parliament and Royal Assent
bishops	'spiritual' peers who sit in the House of Lords, usually twenty-four bishops and two archbishops
Bishops' Bar	bar for peers and officers ("the poshest pub in town")
Black Rod	the senior member of staff responsible for security, facilities and services for peers

Captain of Gentlemen at Arms	head of the Gentlemen at Arms, a ceremonial position held by the Government Chief Whip
career clerks	college of senior staff who advise on procedural matters and manage the administration of the House
chief whip	the head whip in each political party
Chairman of Committees	a salaried member of the House who chairs House committees and the whole House when in committee
Chamber	the hall where peers deliberate, hold debates and give judgments
Clerk of the Parliaments	top clerk and head of the permanent staff of the House of Lords
clerkly	behaving like a proper clerk; pedantic, precise, well-mannered
Cloth of Estate	a velvet canopy, once suspended above the Throne in the Lords Chamber, that symbolises the presence of the monarch
Committee Corridor	first-floor corridor where most of the committee meetings are held
committee stage	consideration of amendments to the bill
Cross-bench Convenor	a member of the Cross-benchers elected to act on behalf of Cross-bench peers, e.g., to call their Thursday meetings, attend other meetings on their behalf, and provide information
countess	a woman peer, equivalent in rank to earl, or the wife of an earl
Cranborne deal	the arrangement whereby ninety-two hereditary peers remained in Parliament after the House of Lords Act 1999. Also known as the Weatherill Amendment
Cross-bencher	peer belonging to no political party
delegated legislation	instruments or orders made pursuant to an Act of Parliament. Also called 'secondary' legislation
despatch box	box from which front-benchers speak, on the Table in the Chamber
Deputy Serjeant-at-Arms	assists the Serjeant-at-Arms, a post that has merged with the Yeoman Usher of the Black Rod
Deputy Speaker	a member of the house who stands in for the Lord Speaker (Lord Chancellor) and sits on the Woolsack presiding over proceedings
division	the vote
division lobbies	the corridors where peers go to vote, one for assent and one for dissent
domestic committees	those dealing with the administration of the House
doorkeepers	staff working for the Keeper of the Doors (Black Rod) and responsible for order, seating and security in the Chamber
down the corridor	House of Commons
duke	highest ranking non-royal peer

duchess	wife of a duke
earl	third ranking peer, after duke and marquess
Earl Marshal	Queen's representative, who manages the ceremonies of state; a hereditary post held by the Dukes of Norfolk
elected hereditary peers	ninety hereditary peers, elected by others to remain in the House after the House of Lords Act 1999 excluded the majority of hereditary peers
'execution'	peers' expression for the abolition of the hereditary peers
filibuster	intentionally wasting parliamentary time
first reading	introduction of a new bill
front-benches	the lowest benches in the centre of the Chamber on which senior party members sit, with the government to the right of the Throne and the opposition to the left
front-bencher	a minister or whip in one of the political parties who sits on one of the lowest benches in the Chamber
Garter King of Arms	advises on new titles, sells coats of arms, and participates in the Introduction Ceremony and the State Opening of Parliament
Gentleman Usher of the Black Rod	'Black Rod' acts as a messenger of the Sovereign when the Commons are summoned and is responsible for facilities, services and security
grace and favour residences	living accommodation provided within the Palace for officers of the House
Great Seal	the seal used for the authentication of documents of the highest importance, including Acts of Parliament, issued in the name of the Sovereign and in the custody of the Lord Chancellor
Hansard	Official Report, record of speeches made in the House
hereditary peer	peer who received a hereditary peerage or inherited it from a relative
hereditary peers of first creation	the first of a line, peers who have received a hereditary peerage rather than inherited it from a relative
House of Commons	primary or lower chamber of Parliament
House of Lords	second or upper chamber of Parliament
House of Lords Act 1999	the law that removed the right of most hereditary peers to sit and vote in the House of Lords
house rising	when proceedings in the Chamber come to an end
house sitting	when the lords are deliberating in the Chamber
Home Room	a restaurant grill for peers and officers
hybrid bill	public bills that affect specific private interests in a manner different from those of people or bodies of the same 'class'
joint committee	members of the three main political parties from both Houses who meet in committee to perform a task
lady	woman peer, equivalent to baron, or wife of a baron

lady peer	woman peer
law lords	judges, ennobled to become Lords of Appeal in Ordinary, who listen to appeals in the highest court, and sit as the Appellate and Appeal Committees in the House of Lords
Leader of the House	leader in the House of the party in government
Leader of the Opposition	leader of the largest party in opposition
Leaders	leaders of the three main parties
life peer	peers appointed for life
lobby	entrance-hall to the Chamber. Peers' Lobby at one end allows guests and strangers, Prince's Chamber at the other is reserved for peers, officers and doorkeepers only
lobbying	advising, persuading or pressuring peers (or MPs), and especially government, to exert influence in favour of particular interests
lord	peer or bishop
Lord Chancellor	Speaker of the House of Lords, presiding over the deliberations of the House, except when it is in committee; head of the Judiciary; Secretary of State for Constitutional Affairs
Lord Great Chamberlain	monarch's representative who has custody over those parts of the Palace not assigned to the two Houses (including Queen's Robing Room and Royal Gallery)
Lord Privy Seal	ceremonial role performed by a cabinet minister, often the Leader of the House of Lords
Lords' Bar	bar for all House of Lords staff and members
Lords' Staff Restaurant	canteen for staff, officers and peers
Mace	a gold and jewelled sceptre, symbol of the authority of the Sovereign in Parliament
maiden speaker	peer speaking in the Chamber for the first time
manifesto	a document outlining proposals, including new legislation, published by each political party before a general election
marshalled list	list of amendments numbered in the order that they will be considered
marquess	second-ranking peer, after duke
marchioness	wife of a marquess
measures	acts passed by the Church of England through the Ecclesiastical Committee
minute	minutes of proceedings recording the decisions of the House with future business attached
Moses Room	a large committee room off peers' lobby
O Group	officials and party representatives who worked out the details of the Weatherill amendment or Cranborne deal
off the floor	deliberations outside the Chamber

officers of the House	senior members of staff awarded that status
Official Report	see Hansard
on the floor	in the chamber
opposition	political parties in Parliament that oppose the party in government
other house	House of Commons
Palace of Westminster	the royal palace housing Parliament
Parliament	the building, the institution, or the life of a government
Parliament Act	the law defining the powers of the Houses of Parliament
peer	equal; person with noble rank: duke, marquess, earl, countess, viscount, baron or baroness
peeress	female spouse of a peer
Peers' Dining Room	restaurant for peers, officers and their guests, with a small area behind a curtain exclusively for peers and officers
Peers' Guest Room	coffee room and bar for peers, officers and guests
Peers' Lobby	entrance hall to the Chamber for peers, staff and guests
prayers	meeting between senior officials
primary legislation	public and private bills that are or have been debated and approved by Parliament. After receiving Royal Assent they become Acts of Parliament
Principal Floor	the first floor of the Houses of Parliament, with the two debating chambers and offices for principal ministers, officers and office-holders
private bill	bill that has a particular or local application only
private members bill	bill promoted by a backbench peer
Privileges Committee	Lords committee that deals with the privileges of the House and claims of peerage and precedence
Privy Counsellor	the private counsellors to the Sovereign: a coveted distinction bestowed on senior ministers, or former ministers,
Procedure Committee	Lords committee that considers proposals to amend the procedures of the House
procedures	rules governing deliberations in the Chamber or committee
private notice question	an opportunity to raise urgent matters on any sitting day, if the Leader of the House agrees
prorogation	ceremony that brings a parliamentary session to an end
public bill	draft legislation that would apply generally in Scotland, and/or England and Wales, or Britain or the UK
Question Time	thirty to forty minutes reserved at the start of business each sitting day for peers to ask the government for information

recess	holiday
regulars	peers who attend the House on more than 100 sitting days in one session (year)
report stage	third major stage of debate on bills with further discussion of amendments
retreads	clerks who have had a former career in the civil service
Royal Assent	once the monarch has given her consent bills become acts
Salisbury convention	in recognition of the right of the elected government to get its legislation through Parliament, the Lords do not reject at second reading any legislation that was in the government party's manifesto. (Also called Salisbury doctrine or Salisbury-Addison agreement)
second reading	discussion of the general principles of a bill
secondary legislation	see delegated legislation
self-regulation	the process whereby the preservation of order and maintenance of the rules of debate are the responsibility of all peers, rather than a chair or speaker
session	a year of Parliament
speakers' list	list of peers, arranged by the Government Chief Whip's office in consultation with the usual channels, who have put their names down to speak in a debate or second reading
Speaker	chair presiding during debate in each House of Parliament: in the Lords the Speaker only intervenes to call amendments and divisions; in the Commons their role is far larger and includes the maintenance of order, calling MPs competing to speak or ask questions and preventing time-wasting
Standing Orders	the most formal list of rules of the House
State Opening	ceremony opening Parliament at the start of each session
statutory instruments	see delegated legislation
Table	the table at which the clerks, and Chairman of Committees when the House is in committee, sit
Table clerks	clerks senior enough to sit at the Table and advise on procedure
Teller	member of the House appointed to count the votes during divisions and report to the clerk at the Table
terrace	uncovered area of the Palace by the River Thames used by peers, officers and guests for functions, recreation, and meetings
third reading and passing	formal motion that the bill be read a third time and, once any new amendments have been dealt with, followed by another that "the bill do now pass"
to move	to propose a motion or amendment to the House
Tory	Conservative

undesirable	out of order, against the rules
usual channels	party managers, and sometimes the Cross-bench Convenor, who exchange information and make agreements informally
Victoria Tower	tower at the other end of the Palace of Westminster from Big Ben, housing offices and the Parliamentary Archives
viscount	fourth-ranking peer, after duke, marquess, and earl
viscountess	wife of a viscount
Weatherill Amendment	an amendment to the House of Lords Act 1999 that made provision to retain two hereditary office-bearers and elect ninety hereditary peers to remain in the House. See Cranborne deal
whip	a statement of forthcoming business sent to peers and telling them when and how to vote; also a party official who is responsible for encourage peers to follow the whip
woman peer	peer in her own right (rather than spouse of a peer)
Woolsack	the seat, containing wool from different Commonwealth countries, on which the Lord Chancellor (or his/her deputies) sit
writ	writ of summons sent to peers by the Lord Chancellor from the office of the Clerk of the Crown in Chancery before the meeting of each Parliament
Yeoman Usher of the Black Rod	Black Rod's deputy

Index